Conducting Small-sca.
Educational Managem

This reader is one part of an Open University integrated teaching system and the selection is therefore related to other material available to students. It is designed to evoke the critical understanding of students. Opinions expressed in it are not necessarily those of the course team or of the University.

Conducting Small-scale Investigations in Educational Management

Edited by

Judith Bell, Tony Bush, Alan Fox, Jane Goodey
and Sandy Goulding

at the Open University

Harper & Row, Publishers
London

Cambridge San Francisco
Mexico City   São Paulo
New York   Singapore
Philadelphia   Sydney

in association with
The Open University

Selection and editorial material
copyright © The Open University 1984

First published 1984
Reprinted 1986, 1987

Harper & Row Ltd
28 Tavistock Street
London WC2E 7PN

British Library Cataloguing in Publication Data

Conducting small-scale investigations in
  educational management.
  1. School management and organization
  2. Universities and colleges—Administration
  I. Bell, Judith
  371.2   LB2805

ISBN 0–06–318293–9

Typeset by Inforum Ltd, Portsmouth
Printed and bound by Butler & Tanner Ltd, Frome and London

CONTENTS

INTRODUCTION

This book is intended for individual researchers in educational management who may have no statistical knowledge, no access to a computer, little or no funding and who have to plan, carry out and write up their investigations in a limited time – possibly as little as two or three months of part-time work. It is provided as one of two readers for the Open University course *Applied Studies in Educational Management* (EP851) but should also be of interest to anyone who wishes to investigate some aspect of school or college management but does not know how to begin.

Demand for courses in educational management is at present greater than ever before. It is not difficult to see why this surge of interest has come about at this time. The 1960s and 1970s saw rapid growth in education provision, but financial cutbacks, falling rolls, and demand for greater flexibility from teaching staff have forced education managers to rethink priorities and to make the best possible use of resources. Management skills of the highest quality are needed to cope with this changed perspective. Courses in education management are now provided in universities, polytechnics and colleges in many parts of the country. *Management and the School* (E323) and *Management in Post-compulsory Education* (E324) are two of the most popular courses in the Open University's School of Education. Many local education authorities provide in-service courses for their senior staff and the Further Education Staff College at Coombe Lodge continues to provide management training for staff in further and higher education.

A major difficulty for teachers and students alike has for some years been the shortage of suitable materials for education management training. Much of the theory has originated in the USA and has generally been based on industrial practice. However, the view of the course team responsible for this book and the Open University course it serves is that educational institutions differ sharply from industrial plants and cannot be managed in the same way as factories. Educational management studies require a context to which the professional staff engaged in the education service can relate and an approach which takes account of the special nature of educational institutions and the students and staff who work in them.

In this book and in the associated volume, *Case Studies in Educational Management,* practice and theory are firmly based in an educational context. Management is a practical activity and it is our view that practitioner-researchers can often play a significant role in investigating aspects of school or college life, provided they know how to go about it. There is certainly a need for large-scale research projects conducted by professional research workers but there is also a need for small-scale problem-orientated projects. This volume is designed to provide the 'tools of the trade' which will enable practitioners to undertake investigations, mainly in their own institutions.

Chapters have been contributed by experienced researchers, many of whom have been responsible for major projects. Nevertheless, all recognize the importance (and the difficulties) of small-scale studies. They provide helpful guidance about 'how to do it', give warnings about dangers of claiming too much for results, of overstepping the ethical boundaries and of taking on too much.

This is not a comprehensive volume covering all aspects of educational research. It provides a selection of articles which the editors consider will be of direct relevance to students and practitioners who wish to undertake small-scale investigations in the field of educational management. For example, we have excluded any reference to classroom observation, on the grounds that this activity may not form part of many projects on educational management, and have limited the discussion of quantitative techniques, on the grounds that practitioner-researchers are unlikely to have the time or the money to conduct large-scale surveys – and because it takes more than one or two chapters in a book to provide the statistical skills necessary to conduct and analyse complex surveys. Keeping within the limits imposed by time and expertise is one of the themes of this book and of the Open University course it serves.

Proof that worthwhile investigations can be planned, carried out and written up in a limited period of time is evidenced in the fact that the companion volume, *Case Studies in Educational Management* (Goulding, S., Bell, J.M., Bush, T., Fox, A. and Goodey, J. (eds.) (1984)), contains examples of projects conducted by individual researchers, which investigate issues and problems in educational management in settings as diverse as an infant school and a polytechnic. The two volumes complement each other. *Conducting Small-Scale Investigations in Educational Management* deals with techniques and approaches: *Case Studies in Educational Management* provides examples of projects successfully completed.

The best way to learn how to conduct a piece of research is to do it, but we hope the guidance provided in this book will help you to avoid some of the more time-wasting pitfalls, to establish good research habits at an early stage and to devise well-planned, well-conducted and well-reported projects.

CHAPTER 1

PLANNING SMALL-SCALE RESEARCH

Daphne Johnson

Daphne Johnson has had many years of experience, both as the leader of a team of professional researchers and as an adviser to students conducting small-scale investigations for higher degrees. In this chapter she takes us step-by-step through the stages of activity which are necessary to carry out and complete an investigation, from establishing the focus of the study to writing up and disseminating the findings. She stresses the need to plan, to select techniques of data collection that suit the topic, to tailor the scope and duration of the investigation to the resources available and to consider the sensitivities of those people who give their time to collaborate in a study.

The need to plan social research

Are you a planner by nature? Or do you prefer to take life as it comes? Whatever your temperament, when undertaking research of any type or scale, planning is a vital preliminary.

When embarking on *social* research, a category which, of course, includes educational research, investigators cannot assume that because a particular form of social life – perhaps school life – is going on all around them, they are in a position to 'research' it. However qualitative or flexible the research is intended to be, some structure must be imposed on everyday social experience. Even that indefatigable chronicler of social intercourse and activity, James Boswell, took pains so to order his social life, travels and correspondence that he met and spent time with the great literary men who were so important to his view of the world and made sure to be present to observe the events which he wanted to record. As a result, he has left us, in his writings[1], a sparkling and apparently unpremeditated account of eighteenth-century life, but one in which the careful reader can discern the hallmarks of skilled social research – the negotiation of access, the recording of data, their analysis, and the effective writing up and dissemination of what has been learned. On a smaller scale – perhaps a *much* smaller scale – the present-day social researcher must impose a structure on social experience, and give thought to planning the research which can feasibly be carried out.

What is meant by research planning

The fundamental principle of planning effective research is to match the research design to the resources available for its completion, and to the particular characteristics of the topic under consideration. Silvey (1975) considers that a research plan is at best a compromise between the aims of the research, the resources available and the feasibility of the area of study. His definition is realistic rather than pessimistic. Research is unlikely to be successful if the design is drawn from a text book on research methods, but takes no account of the time available for its execution, the amount of help which can be recruited, and the special requirements of those whose activities are being studied – for example, the frequent requirement that the researcher protect the anonymity of those who are the subject of the research.

Later in this paper consideration will be given to the selection of a research method from among the established range of quantitative or qualitative approaches. But this is only one aspect of research planning. It must be decided in the context of the whole projected investigation.

The stages of carrying out an investigation

The inexperienced investigator, faced with the need to 'do some research' as part of a course of study or to give a wider perspective to personal experience, may welcome the security of a list by which to order the research activity. The following has been found useful in classifying the stages of activity which must be worked through in carrying out and completing an investigation.

(1) Establishing the focus of the study.
(2) Identifying the specific objectives of the study.
(3) Selecting the research method.
(4) Arranging research access.

(5) Developing the research instrument.
(6) Collecting the data.
(7) Pulling out of the investigative phase.
(8) Ordering of the data.
(9) Analysing the data.
(10) Writing up.
(11) Enabling dissemination.

Each stage will be discussed in turn, bearing in mind that the investigation in question is likely to be small scale. Most of the examples used will be drawn from educational research, and the assumption will be made that the investigation is being undertaken as a means to a particular end (of academic qualification or occupational advancement) rather than as part of a continuing and professional research career.

(1) *Establishing the focus of the study*

When students are questioned about a preferred subject for a mini-project or research-based dissertation, they may say 'I'd like to do something about Saturday schools', or 'I've always been interested in pastoral care'. They are half way towards deciding on the general area for their study, but have many more questions to ask themselves before they have established its focus. Are they interested in examining Saturday schools as institutions for the perpetuation and promotion of particular cultures (in which case they might want to look at Polish schools and Hebrew schools, as well as the more recently established Saturday schools for Asian or West Indian children)? Or are they interested to establish the part played by parents in the setting up and resourcing of a Saturday school? In this case examples of recently established schools would give better access to memory and documentation than would a long-running school, the contributions of whose founding fathers and mothers have been overlaid by the sediment of rules and traditions. Does the student interested in pastoral care want to investigate it in terms of its implications for the career patterns of teachers? Or perhaps as an example of the cross-fertilization of ideas between the independent and maintained schools? Or in terms of the use of a pastoral care system to identify and help withdrawn pupils? All of these ideas, and many more, may be in the background of a student's 'interest' in a topic, but they cannot all form the subject of the same investigation.

It is true that, when set down in words, the focused subject of an investigation may sound as dry as dust. This is probably why so many dissertations, theses and projects have sub-titles, explaining the scope of the study, but preceded by a more eye-catching and evocative main title. For example:

SCHOOL CLOSURE – A Study of Changes in Governing Body Membership and Activity During a Programme of Secondary School Closures in One Local Authority.

The sub-title makes it plain what the investigator has set out to do, and what kind of information the reader can expect to be given. The overall title reassures them both that the investigation contributes to understanding of an important social phenomenon, and that this wider context is not forgotten in the account given of the investigation.

It is not until the investigator has so concentrated the subject of the study that it can be expressed in one sentence, that he or she can be said to have established the focus of the investigation and be ready to move to the next stage.

(2) *Identifying the specific objectives of the study*

The cynical investigator's approach to the setting of specific objectives is to 'wait until you have finished, see what you've managed to achieve, then say this was your objective'. Whilst it is to be hoped that this practice is rarely followed in any wholesale way, some minor *post hoc* modification of objectives probably contributes to the cut-and-dried tidiness of many a research account.

But the attempt to define specific objectives in advance should not be abandoned for fear they will not, in the event, be met. Identifying particular objectives helps the investigator along the road to choosing the research method and deciding on the forms of access needed, and may contribute to the selection and development of a suitable research instrument.

The background reading, or review of the literature, which is an essential contextual element of any piece of research, will ideally take place at this stage, so that it can influence the formation of research objectives. In practice, literature relevant to the subject of investigation may prove to be scanty, or may only be identified later in the research.

If the investigator has a particular personal interest in, and commitment to, the subject of study, one way to identify specific objectives is to ask 'What will I be disappointed not to have learned (or had experience of) when the study is over?' For example, in a study of home-school relations the researchers were particularly eager to learn how secondary schools were viewed from the point of view of the home, to complement the many accounts of home-school relations given from the point of view of the school.[2] One of the specific objectives of the study was, therefore, to recruit parental opinion, and to do this away from the milieu of the school. In fieldwork terms, this meant devoting nearly all the resources of the project to setting up and carrying out home interviews with parents. But meeting this particular objective of recruiting parental opinion also satisfied the researchers that they had not missed the opportunity to explore an aspect of home-school relations which they held to be neglected in other accounts (Johnson and Ransom, 1983).

If the researcher's approach to the subject of study is a more detached one, with little sense of personal involvement or commitment (as is probably most frequently the case with the kind of 'means-to-an-end' investigation discussed in this paper) the identification of specific objectives may seem more arbitrary. But it will still help towards later stages of the study by highlighting particular fieldwork needs. For example, the investigator planning to make the study of school closure in terms of its implications for the relevant school governing bodies, might set the specific objective of including pupil governors in the range of members interviewed. Or, in a study of the role of head teachers of comprehensive schools, an investigator might set the objective of including an equal number of head-mistresses and headmasters in the enquiry. (Such an objective would have implications for the geographical scope of the investigation, since head-mistresses are more thinly spread across the secondary school system than are headmasters.)

(3) Selecting the research method

This is the next stage in planning the study. Ideally the research method should not be decided until the focus and objectives of the investigation are clear. In practice, professional researchers tend to prefer those methods of investigation in which they have a cumulative expertise, and will tailor the subject of study to make possible the use of their well-tried research techniques. Inexperienced or self-supporting researchers may also feel tempted to decide on a research method before giving detailed consider-ation to the subject of their investigation. The requirements of their course of study, or the sparsity of research resources may, in fact, rule out the use of certain methods such as, for example, some of the 'unobtrusive measures' discussed by Webb et al. (1966) which have to be recorded over a lengthy period. Nevertheless, the selection of the research method is a crucial element in the planning of an investigation. A range of possible methods and some guidelines for choosing between them are discussed in a later section of this paper.

(4)   *Arranging research access*

If an entirely quantitative method is to be used, such as the issue of a postal questionnaire, the notion of arranging research access may seem super-fluous. People cannot prevent the post being delivered to their home or place of work. Nevertheless, even in such a case the investigator must give thought to what can be done to improve the receptivity of the addressee to the questionnaire, and hence increase the likelihood that he or she will complete and return it.[3] In one way or another the envelope, covering letter and questionnaire itself must perform the tasks which the investigator might otherwise carry out in person, when arranging research access. These tasks can be summarized as:

(a) imparting the conviction that the investigation is a worthwhile piece of work and the investigator a competent person to carry it out;
(b) explaining why the investigation seeks the cooperation of the person or institutions being approached;
(c) indicating the use to be made of the eventual research material.

In the case of educational research the negotiation of research access is unlikely to be a once-and-for-all event. The investigator must be prepared to reiterate, to a succession of audiences, the purposes, style, scope and utility of the proposed research, and these explanations may have to be communicated in a number of different ways. For example, to make a study of secondary school responses to the behaviour of disaffected pupils (Bird et al., 1981), getting research access entailed formal correspondence with selected chief education officers, meetings at local authority offices with particular head teachers, debate (and defence) of the proposed research in the staff rooms of their schools, and face-to-face assurances regarding the scope and confidentiality of the research to individual teachers and pupils who were asked to take part. This was a sizeable piece of research involving four researchers, and on a sensitive topic. However, the investigator whose chosen sphere is education is likely to find that almost any topic is deemed 'sensitive' by some of those asked to take part.

In setting up a single-handed study within the confines of one's own school or college, as many teacher-investigators are likely to do, there will still be a need to get the formal agreement of the head teacher and relevant heads of departments, and the active cooperation of any teachers, ancillary staff or pupils whose help is required. Depending on the subject of study, the head teacher may consider that the approval of parents must also be sought, and it is to be hoped that he or she will agree to obtain this by telephone or letter, on behalf of the investigator.

If documentary research is being undertaken, and the access required is to files and papers rather than individuals or situations, then it is with the keepers of the archives in question that access must be arranged.

Whatever the research method being used, the investigator will find that agreement to research access must be kept in good repair throughout the enquiry. Even if agreement has been given, the careless or offhand investigator may become *persona non grata* during the course of the research, and be unable to complete it. If files are left in disarray, papers borrowed and not returned, or respondents subjected to too lengthy or frequent interviews, at inconvenient times, the researcher's welcome will be worn out. All social researchers are to some extent mendicants, since they are seeking a free gift of time or information from those who are the subject of study. But researchers who bear this fact in mind, and who, without becoming the captive of their respondents, can contrive to make the research experience a helpful and profitable one, will almost certainly be gratified by the generosity with which people will give their time and knowledge.

(5) *Developing the research instrument*

The research instrument may be an interview schedule or a postal questionnaire. Or it may be a set of guidelines for an unstructured interview, or a pro forma for the classification of information selected from records. In some cases, the research instrument may be the trained capacity of an individual to make notes about the circumstances and content of a meeting. (A tape recorder, it should be stressed is *not* a research instrument. It is simply a means of enabling the reiteration of audible material in a place and at a time other than when it was recorded. The researcher's essential task of selection from and analysis of that material still remains to be done.)

The important point about research instruments is that they require development – they do not spring to hand in a perfect form, fully adapted to the particular investigative task. All formal texts on research methods mention the desirability of a 'pilot study', and this is one way in which a research instrument can be honed to its particular task. Trying out an interview schedule on a sample of respondents with similar characteristics to those of the intended survey population, for example, may quickly reveal gaps in the logical sequence of questions, or the incomprehensibility to the respondent of the wording used. 'I had no idea a Rising Five was a *child*', said one school governor. 'I thought it was something to do with fishing tackle.'

The luxury of a genuine pilot study, which tries out in miniature the viability of an envisaged investigation, is unlikely to be available to the student planning a small-scale short-term piece of research. But at least some attempt at 'trying it on the dog' should be made. Questionnaires and interview schedules in particular must be tried out on *someone* – friends, relations, neighbours. The investigator will get valuable feedback, for example, on whether 'closed' questions can readily be answered in the terms of the suggested range of replies.

Experience will be gained of how long it will take a respondent to fill in the questionnaire, or for an interview schedule to be worked through – important information for the overall planning of the investigation. Such *ad hoc* trials will confirm the need for any questionnaire or schedule to go through several draft stages, the number of which will depend on the time available.

In the case of a pro forma for recording information extracted from files, for example pupil records, the design of such a tool may have had to take place without prior knowledge of the range of information likely to be available. Teachers researching in their own institution will be more fortunate here, as they will have some notion of what is usually recorded. But if access is negotiated to the pupil records of *another* school, the range of information available may be different again, and the pro forma has to be rapidly adapted. Complete redesign may be needed in some cases, and it is to be hoped that the files can be studied on more than one occasion.

It can be seen that development of the research instrument may take place either before or during its use. Where the instrument is the researcher's own capacity to observe and record, this will certainly develop in the course of research experience. However, short-term small-scale investigations may provide only brief opportunities for 'learning on the job'. The investigator should do everything possible to prepare for the event to be observed. For example, in the case of a meeting the observer should try to sort out the names and roles of those present before the meeting starts or, if this is impossible, at least note some identifying physical characteristic of each person, and where they are sitting in relation to others. After the event, whether it be a case conference or a governing body meeting, a helpful informant may then be prepared to help the observer discover the identity and contribution of each person.[4]

One factor influencing the eventual form of any research instrument must be the form of analysis which is to be applied to the data after they have been collected. For example, the tables it is intended to draw up using collated information from questionnaires or schedules, should be decided on and listed at the time the research instrument is designed. If these decisions are left until after the fieldwork has been done, the investigator may find that a question vital to the analysis has not been asked. And although qualitative forms of investigation may be seen as exploratory, with the intention that any analytic theory shall be grounded in the research material which comes to hand during the fieldwork, interviewers or observers should still, at this 'research instrument' stage, provide themselves with guidelines which ensure the coverage of what are likely to be the eventual analytic themes of the research account.

(6) *Collecting the data*

Developing the research instrument may, as we have seen, lap over into data collection, but for many research designs the fieldwork period is a distinct and discrete phase of the investigation. Its clear demarcation may, in fact, be essential to the successful completion of the whole enquiry. This is the period during which the researcher is likely to be investing most in the study, by way of time and personal involvement. Marking out a definite period during which the fieldwork is to be pursued helps concentration and commitment to the task in hand, for the fieldwork period is one when other customary social or work activities may well have to be set aside, reduced or postponed.

What the fieldwork actually consists of will depend upon the research design. It may be interviewing, documentary study or observation – all are forms of data collection which, in a small-scale study, are likely to entail the personal involvement of the investigator. Only in the case of a postal questionnaire will there be a 'breather' for the researcher while the research instrument is in the field. In this particular case the pre- and post-fieldwork periods are likely to be the busiest, when the questionnaire is being designed and developed before its issue, and when the completed questionnaires are being studied after they are returned.

One problem for the researcher whose fieldwork takes the form of interviewing or observation is that the period set aside for fieldwork may, fortuitously, prove not to be a good time for the study of the social phenomenon he or she has set out to investigate. In social research there is rarely an opportunity for the use of a controlled experimental model. Social life is untidy and episodic, and although investigators may, like Boswell, contrive to insert themselves into the milieux in which they are interested, during a given period there may be few opportunities to acquire data by the method planned. A Master's student investigating the education provided to adolescents in hospital for short-term treatment had as one objective the interviewing of such patients, as well as the study of the organizational infrastructure of hospital schooling (Smith, 1981). From the point of view of the investigator it was a disappointment that during the period allocated for fieldwork only a few patients within the eligible group were, in fact, admitted to the hospital under study. The student had to make the most of her small available sample – but also had to resist the temptation to extend the fieldwork period, in the hope that more patients would be admitted.

For not only must the researcher decide when to *start* the fieldwork, but a decision must also be made when to end it. This is the essence of the next stage to be discussed.

(7) Pulling out of the investigative phase

Under this heading we can also discuss the whole question of 'getting away with the data', for the novice researcher may find it is just as difficult to pull out of a single interview as to say 'finis' to the fieldwork period as a whole.

To deal first with this problem of ending an interview, it is always the responsibility of the interviewer to do this, rather than waiting for the respondent to call a halt, however unstructured and relaxed the interview situation may be. It may have been difficult to negotiate access and to get in in the first place, but the interviewer who, once in, stays until he is thrown out, is working in the style of investigative journalism rather than social research.[5] Face-to-face interviewing evokes the conventions of normal polite social intercourse, and it is unethical and unfair to push the respondent into the position of breaking those conventions by saying he has had enough, when an interviewer outstays his welcome or his allotted time. The interviewer whose respondent says he can spare an hour should not outstay that period however much both parties may settle in to enjoying and profiting from the occasion, without formally raising the question of whether an extended discussion, or a second interview, would be desirable and feasible. If an interview takes two or three times as long as the interviewer said it would, the respondent, whose other work or social activities have been accordingly delayed, will be irritated in retrospect, however enjoyable the experience may have been at the time. This sort of practice breaks one of the ethics of professional social research, which is that the field should not be left more difficult for subsequent investigators to explore by disenchanting respondents with the whole notion of research participation.

There are other questions of more personal ethics to be borne in mind, when private interviews are being conducted. Respondents become vulnerable during the course of extended sympathetic interviewing, and if the interview is unduly prolonged may begin to say things they will subsequently regret[6] or talk themselves into a despondent frame of mind, if the interview has focused on problems. The interviewer may feel increasingly unable to terminate the interview and leave the depressed respondent alone, and is in danger of losing professional control of the situation by stepping out of the role of social enquirer to become the confidant of the person being interviewed. The writer makes it a rule, for example when conducting home interviews with parents, not to leave respondents in a worse state than that in which she found them. This can mean keeping an eye on how time is passing and devoting part of the available period to winding-down conversation which diverts the respondent from problems discussed to more positive aspects of their life experience.

Difficulties of this kind may perhaps be unlikely to crop up in small-scale research in which fieldwork may well be confined to interaction with known colleagues. Nevertheless, the novice researcher should be alert to the possibilities that such difficulties may occur, and may perhaps be precipitated by overlong research contact with one individual. A problem which all will encounter, however, is the wider one of calling a halt to the investigative period as a whole.

Can the researcher be flexible about how long to wait for questionnaires to come back? Can use be made of those which come trailing in long after the rest? If a meeting which it was hoped to observe is postponed, should efforts be made to attend it when it is reconvened? If the target population proves thin on the ground during the period set aside for interview, can that period be extended? In the case of small-scale research, the answer to any of these questions must usually be 'No'. The fault from which many amateur investigations – and some professional ones – suffer is that of an open-ended period of data collection. Almost all social enquiries produce more data than can subsequently be made use of, however short the fieldwork period. And if this is endlessly extended, perhaps because the researcher has become fascinated with the phenomenon under study, there is a danger that none of the material may be adequately taken through the outstanding stages of the investigation. Research which is not completed is no research at all; a point we shall return to later in this paper.

(8)   Ordering of the data

All research material, however collected, should be set in order and stored in a form in which it would be comprehensible to others, were they to be given access to it. Some kind of research archive or data bank must be established. However slender the data their sole repository must not be between the ears of the investigator, or a fundamental tenet of research – that the material must be testable and contestable by others – is not being met. Questionnaires and interview schedules must be collated and classified, field notes must be written up, and a reckoning should be kept of the timing and incidence of the fieldwork. Researchers must be prepared to be accountable for the investigations they have undertaken, even if they are never called to render that account.

A further reason for putting the data together in an orderly form is applicable both to large- and small-scale research. The disorganized investigator is in danger of making disproportionate use of the more striking or memorable research material and neglecting to balance this with other more humdrum data. When moving to the tasks of analysis the totality of the acquired data needs to be surveyed.

(9)   Analysing the data

The main general point to be made about this stage is that it must exist and be allowed for in the overall research programme.[7] An investigator should not move directly from data collection to writing up, however small-scale the study. A weakness of many dissertations or theses is that, although considerable pains may have been taken to set up and carry out an effective piece of fieldwork, little use is made of the data collected in the eventual discussion of the thesis topic. Instead, discussion appears to be chiefly based on the investigator's background reading and/or preconceived ideas about the subject of study. In such cases it is likely that the student has not allowed sufficient time to muse on and learn from the research material.

The broad analytic themes of the study will, as we have already indicated, have had to be identified before embarking on the fieldwork. But the data collected must be drawn on to illuminate those themes, and may well call into question the researcher's implicit assumptions about the topic.

(10)   *Writing up*

This is perhaps the most difficult, but potentially the most satisfying, phase of the research. By putting words on paper about his research the investigator makes it available to other scholars and, in the classic phrase, pushes back the frontiers of knowledge, however minutely.

Technical advice on the format of research accounts is fairly readily available[8] and cannot be included here. Important features are that the text shall be understandable and unambiguous, the referencing punctilious and accurate, and the overall conclusions or 'message' of the research be summarized in an assimilable and memorable form.

Writing up research can never be simply an exercise in handing on the data to the reader for his or her consideration. In a quantitative study tables may be compiled which, to the investigator, may seem self-explanatory, but some discussion of them must appear in the eventual text. In a qualitative study, quotations may be selected from the research material for inclusion in the research account, but these do not render superfluous a clear summative statement by the researcher of the beliefs or sentiments which the quotations serve to illustrate. The essence of an effective research account is that it conveys to the reader something of a researcher's empirical experience, together with his reflections on it.

(11)   *Enabling dissemination*

Although the active and continuing dissemination of research findings may not be a feasible part of a small-scale investigation, the investigator has a duty to make dissemination possible. Writing an account of the research may be all the investigator can do, but some thought should be given to the number and durability of copies of that account, and the formal and informal circulation of them which can be arranged or permitted.

Various methods exist by which the dissemination of research material can be agreed with those who participated in the enquiry. The nonconfidentiality of the materials may have been clearly accepted by participants from the outset, in which case no further negotiation is strictly necessary regarding the open circulation of the eventual research report. Nevertheless, it is courteous to supply a draft copy for comment to the principal 'gate keeper' who allowed the research to go forward.

It has already been pointed out that almost all educational research is felt to be sensitive by some of those taking part. If individuals or institutions are to be named in the research account, explicit 'clearance' of the document by those concerned is desirable and advisable.[9] Where anonymity has been required as a condition of the investigation, this should be scrupulously preserved by the use of pseudonyms and the editing of descriptive material in such a way as to make identification of individuals or institutions at least difficult, if not impossible.[10] This professional practice should not be regarded by the student investigator as unnecessary for a research account which 'no one will see'. The whole point of a research account is that someone other than the writer shall see it, and it may well prove of interest to a select or extended circle of researchers and/or educationalists.

By taking the trouble to meet the requirements of the research participants with regard to clearance or confidentiality, the investigator has made possible the wider dissemination of the research findings and given some protection to informants in the event of the account being circulated or reproduced without the researcher's permission. (Such practices, whilst undesirable, are not unknown.)

Verbal dissemination of research findings (supplementing, but never replacing, a written research account) may prove useful, and is perhaps especially desirable in the case of small-scale means-to-an-end research which does not lead to published work. Whilst it cannot be regarded as an essential stage of the research enquiry, the teacher-investigator may find it worthwhile to prepare a short list of key issues arising from his research which can form the basis of formal or informal discussion with colleagues or, where appropriate, pupils. Any other feasible form of dissemination should also be considered since, in addition to meeting the academic requirements of an enquiry, dissemination to some extent redresses the balance of researcher-participant indebtedness. By doing all he can to increase and disseminate understanding of the topic under study, the social enquirer is paying back something of what he has received by way of information and cooperation from his research participants.

Complete research

The many stages of a research inquiry which we have worked through may seem daunting to a novice investigator. For our purposes, the chief usefulness of such a list of stages is as a basis for research planning. The list underlines the necessity, already pointed out, of tailoring the enquiry to the resources available for its completion. If the research is *not* completed it would be preferable that it had not been begun. Aborted research wastes time and dissipates goodwill.

It is not only small-scale, 'amateur', investigations which stand in danger of not being completed. Many well-funded professionally staffed research projects have foundered because the investigative task has not been realistically appraised in the light of the time available for its completion, and the temperament and capacity of those intended to carry it out.[11] The means-to-an-end investigator, such as we are considering here, who undertakes research as part of a course of study or to give a wider perspective to personal experience, is likely to be well motivated to press through with the task, and if single handed will not need to adjust to the differing work pace and methods of personal organization of colleagues. But the need to plan out one's own use of the resource of time cannot be overstated. If there is a deadline by which, to be acceptable or usable, the research must be completed, that is all the time there is for *all the stages of the research* – including the writing up. Novice planners will be well advised to identify sub-deadlines for each stage – for establishing the focus of study, access negotiation, development of research instruments and so on – since the inevitable need to be flexible about one or more of those deadlines will keep them alert to the passage of time and the continuing drain on this major resource. Arranging access, for example, may well take longer than anticipated, and perhaps the only way to adjust to this is by reducing the time to be spent on developing the research instrument, or by reducing the scope of the proposed fieldwork. The sub-deadline to be preserved at all costs, however, is the one which marks the end of the investigative phase. In the concluding stages of a research enquiry, one more interview, or one more meeting attended, does not equal the value of an hour or two's reflective analysis and writing.

Single-handed research

The need to make measured use of the resource of time has been stressed because failure to do this is so common, and has disastrous consequences for the effective completion of research, whether large or small scale. Novice investigators who know they will be pressed for time and will also be 'single handed' in their research inquiry, may feel the required research task is well-nigh impossible. Some words of encouragement can, however, be offered which will aid positive thinking about the actual resources at their disposal.

The man or woman power resources available for the research task should not be appraised solely on a quantified basis, as the term 'single handed' research appears to do. Researchers should consider what particular strengths or attributes they have which will contribute to the research. Examples may be a network of personal or professional contacts which will help them gain entry to a particular field of enquiry; seniority or standing in an institution which will add persuasive power to requests for information; experience in meeting the public or in the analysis of documents which will be of use in the empirical stage of an investigation. 'Sponsors', if prestigious, may also lend strength to the single-handed researcher's arm.

Professional researchers frequently make sure that their sponsors, such as a research council or a charitable foundation, are mentioned in any account they give of a proposed research enquiry. Student researchers may not have sponsors of this kind, but could perhaps truthfully claim that they have been seconded by the local authority to undertake the work in hand, or mention that their enquiry has the approval of a senior colleague.[12]

In summary, single-handed investigators should carefully appraise what personal and political resources they have which are relevant for the research. For the means-to-an-end investigator it is sensible to design the research, perhaps even select its topic, so as to make maximum use of those resources.

Considerations of method

In this section we briefly consider a range of research methods, and discuss some criteria for choosing between them. More detailed discussion of particular modes of research will be found elsewhere in this book.

We have seen that research design has to take account of the aims of the study, the resources available and the general feasibility of the study area. But before embarking on the compromise which, this paper has stressed, is a characteristic of effective research design, it is as well to remind ourselves of the main forms of research method, in their basic form.

Research methods can be broadly divided into *quantitative* methods, taking a *positivist* approach, and *qualitative* methods which are *relativist* in their perspective. Researchers in the positivist tradition (Durkheim, 1895) take the view that social facts exist and can be ascertained. They may hypothesize that these facts occur together in certain patterns and are subject to particular causes. Their research purpose will be to measure the occurrence of these phenomena in such a way as to test their hypotheses.

Relativist researchers, on the other hand, are less confident of the existence of social facts. Their own view of the world, they believe, has developed cumulatively, contributed to by their particular life experience. They postulate that the world may look different to other people, and in their research they set out to understand more about the view of the world which some other people (or 'actors') (Silverman, 1970) have. Their purpose is not to obtain a set of facts, but to gain insight into a perspective.

As we have said, quantitative methods are usually associated with positivist research, and qualitative methods with relativist research. However, this is not always so. For example, while participant observation is held to be a qualitative research method, some early occupational and industrial sociology which used participant observation was undoubtedly positivist in its form of analysis (Roy, 1963). Equally, and almost quintessentially, the survey method is defined as quantitative. But some small-scale survey work is so detailed, exploratory, and sensitive that it illuminates a perspective on the world rather than providing a set of facts. Nevertheless, for the most part it can be asserted that surveys, using structured interviewing or postal questionnaire, come up with quantifiable facts, while participant observation in all its forms (Denzin, 1978) and exploratory interviewing, provide a qualitative perspective.

Most professional researchers pursue a career in either the positivist or relativist 'school', and are unlikely to switch between them. Means-to-an-end researchers may feel temperamentally attracted to one or the other school but should consider, as dispassionately as possible, which frame of reference is most appropriate and feasible in their case. Some broad guidelines can be offered.

In a *qualitative* study researchers should try to make sure they do not cramp their own style before they start. They know what group of people they are interested in (for example, disaffected pupils), (Bird et al., 1981) but do not want to make up their mind in advance who belongs to it, or what the important aspects of their life are. They will be deciding and refining that, in the light of experience, all the time they are in the field. So, for them, the research task is to get where the action is, to get access, one way or another, to the group and the activities that they want to explore. They should not commit themselves, in advance, to the study of an arbitrarily arrived at *number* of people, or *number* of settings. The work is intended to be intensive and illuminative, and will not lay claim to being representative and generalizable. In summary, the main requirement in qualitative research design is to give oneself the chance to be enlightened, and to avoid a research situation which rules out exploration and open-mindedness.

In a *quantitative* study, the researcher is setting out to make a statement, often in a numerical form, about the outcomes of broadly comparable experiences (for example, 15 000 hours of schooling) (Rutter et al., 1979) or the behaviour and aspirations of broadly comparable members of a social collectivity (for example, housewives with young children) (Gavron, 1966). Findings of the research may be descriptive or (if a hypothesis is being tested) interpretive. In both cases the researcher's intention is, using the laws of probability, to generalize from the research sample to a wider population. Because of this, an attempt should be made to guard against picking out 'exceptions to the rule', and to incorporate some measure of randomness into the selection of the research sample. And the sample should be drawn from a sampling frame that does not of itself introduce a bias relevant to the subject of enquiry.[13]

Moreover, since the quantitative study hopes to collect comparable information, this has implications for the type of information the researcher sets out to obtain, and the way in which it is collected. For example, a differently worded questionnaire would not be sent to each person in the sample, and if the research instrument is one of face-to-face interview, the research encounter should be as standardized as possible. In summary, the main requirement in quantitative research design is to provide a fair chance of being proved wrong, and to avoid the incorporation of bias which would tend to confirm the researcher's a priori hypotheses.

Which of these two broad types of research – qualitative or quantitative – is the most suitable form of research to inform a dissertation, or piece of required course work? Both have their attractions and their disadvantages.

The intensive but flexible mode of qualitative research has obvious attractions for the slenderly resourced single-handed investigator. But qualitative methods are slow, and may be anxiety creating because of the lack of structure or even an end goal, in the research design. Moreover, since the research question is being developed and refined during, rather than prior to, the research, it is more difficult to plan the research programme as a whole and get some parts of it (for example, establishing the framework of analysis) out of the way early on. Nevertheless, as this whole paper has attempted to make clear, the requirement to plan and allocate resources of time and effort cannot be set aside, however flexible the research approach.

Quantitative methods also have their attractions. For the novice investigator they appear more clear cut, with more obvious boundaries around the fieldwork phase. Researchers undertaking a quantitative study may find that it temporarily occupies their waking hours, but it is less likely to invade their way of life than, for example, the more participative and reflexive style of qualitative work (Whyte, 1955). But, to meet the requirements of its underlying positivist philosophy, quantitative research must be scientifically 'respectable', a requirement which entails rigorous design, administrative control and clerical accuracy. Moreover, it must be moderately large scale, in order to justify collation of the comparable material and enable some subtlety of analysis. At the least, there should be *some* respondents in each of the cells of a simple table (which might, for example, seek to sub-divide a pupil population by sex and reading age).

A few points should be made about *documentary research*, as this does not fall neatly into either the quantitative or the qualitative group of methods. Much depends on the type of document and the use made of it. It may provide a statistical, quantified input to back up or supplement a quantified study. (Here the researcher should bear in mind that the statistics being drawn on may not have been collected for the same purpose as the researcher's own data and may not therefore be entirely comparable.) Alternatively, documentary material may be used to provide another perspective on an area of qualitative study. For example, Gill (1977) used police records to give another angle on the activities of some young people, activities in which he had been a semiparticipant observer.

Files and records are frequently an untapped source of data which have never been used for anything other than administrative purposes, but which would repay analysis for a number of research purposes. Almost all social populations are in danger of being overresearched, so the small-scale investigator should never rush out to do yet another survey without considering whether a survey has in fact already been done, and the material be lying uncollated in the file of an institution to which he has access. For example, a Master's student worked extremely hard at carrying out and following up a questionnaire survey of 'drop out' students from the evening institute with which he was connected. When he came to compare his small and hard-won sample findings with records from previous years, it became evident that the records already contained the raw data for a much fuller analysis of student drop-out, which had never been undertaken by the institute in question (Delahunt, 1979). Any novice investigator who has full access, through work or voluntary activities, to records, all the weaknesses and strengths of which are already familiar, should think carefully whether they are potentially a body of data for survey analysis.[14]

The rewards of small-scale research

Many of the difficulties inherent in social research, especially for the slenderly resourced novice investigator, have been stressed in this paper. The imperative need to work to a research plan, and to tailor the scope and duration of the investigation to the resources available, has been repeatedly emphasized. What are the rewards of undertaking an activity so fraught with problems? Are those rewards worthwhile?

In the case of small-scale investigations, carried out for a dissertation or piece of course work, it is more likely that the rewards of the work accrue to the investigator rather than to the investigated. Nevertheless, most people find it of some interest to take part in a survey whose purpose they understand. In the case of face-to-face enquiries of an exploratory kind, it is not unusual for the person interviewed to comment that they have found it helpful to their own thinking to be required to focus on a particular aspect of their life experience and discuss it with someone less closely involved than themselves.

So far as novice investigators themselves are concerned, the experience of carrying out a piece of social research may benefit them by uncovering certain skills they did not know they had – these skills may be analytic, literary or administrative, or they may be skills in social relations. But the chief benefit – and the reason why so many courses of study require the student to carry out some sort of social enquiry – is that to do so fosters the enquiring attitude which is a prerequisite for successful academic work of any kind. The whole exercise of planning and carrying out a piece of social research forces the recognition, and usually the questioning, of the investigator's own assumptions about social life.

Notes

1. See, for example, Boswell, J. (1791) *The Life of Samuel Johnson*, Dilley, London; also Harris, M. (ed.) (1982) *The Heart of Boswell*, McGraw-Hill (a distillation of the first six volumes of the Yale edition of the private papers of James Boswell).
2. See, for example, McGeeney, P. (1967) *Parents are Welcome*, Longman; Lynch, J., and Pimlott, J. (1976) *Parents and Teachers*, Macmillan; Harris, R. (1980)

Parent teacher contacts: a case study, in Craft, M. et al. (eds.) *Linking Home and School*, 3rd edition, Harper & Row.

3. A classic source on this subject is Scott, C. (1961) Research on mail surveys, in *Journal of the Royal Statistical Society*, A.124, pp. 143–205.
4. For a more detailed discussion of observation of meetings, see Chapter 13 of this book.
5. Bernstein, in Bernstein, C., and Woodward, B. (1975) *All the President's Men*, Warner Books, p. 65, gives a vivid account of how an interview with a key informant was prolonged by the request or acceptance of numerous cups of coffee.
6. There is always a need to protect research respondents from the consequences of verbal indiscretions not relevant to the research. See Johnson, D. (1975) Enlisting the participation of teachers in educational research, in *Research Intelligence*, Vol. II.
7. Useful technical advice on the analysis of quantitative data is contained in Silvey (1975) Chapters 1 and 2 (see References).
8. See, for example, Chapter 15 of this book.
9. For a description of methods of 'clearance' see Packwood, T., (1984) The introduction of staff responsibilities for subject development in a junior school, in *Case Studies in Educational Management (EP851)*, Open University; also Johnson, D., Ransom, E., Packwood, T., Bowden, K., and Kogan, M. (1980) *Secondary Schools and the Welfare Network*, Allen & Unwin, Methods Appendix.
10. 'Informed guesses' as to the identity of anonymized schools or local education authorities participating in research may always be made by educational *cognoscenti*, but the use of pseudonyms will prevent unequivocal identification.
11. Platt, J. (1976) *The Realities of Social Research: An Empirical Study of British Sociologists*, Sussex University Press, gives a fascinating and salutory account of university research projects which failed to be completed. Team research seemed especially susceptible to problems of noncompletion.
12. However, in a classic paper, Deming points out that knowledge of the 'auspices' or sponsors of a piece of research may bias response. Deming, W.E. (1944) On errors in surveys, in *American Sociological Review*, Vol. 9, pp. 359–369.
13. The sample used by Gavron (see References) was criticized because the Housewives' Register (of women dissatisfied with a purely domestic role) was used as one sampling frame.
14. Questions of confidentiality and anonymity must, of course, be fully considered if existing records are used in this way.

References

Bird, C., Chessum, R., Furlong, J., and Johnson, D. (ed.) (1981) *Disaffected Pupils*. Brunel University.

Delahunt, D. (1979) *Continuing Education for Adults: Investigating One Local Authority Adult Centre*, unpublished dissertation, MA in Public and Social Administration. Department of Government, Brunel University.

Denzin, N.K. (1978) *The Research Act: A Theoretical Introduction to Research Methods*. McGraw-Hill, Chapter 7.

Durkheim, E. (1895) *The Rules of Sociological Method*, English translation edited by Catlin, G.E.C. (1950). Free Press of Glencoe.

Gavron, H. (1966) *The Captive Wife: Conflicts of Housebound Mothers*. Routledge & Kegan Paul.

Gill, O. (1977) *Luke Street: Housing Policy, Conflict and the Creation of the Delinquent Area*. Macmillan.

Johnson, D., and Ransom, E. (1983) *Family and School*. Croom Helm.

Roy, D. Efficiency and the 'fix' – informal intergroup relations in a piecework machine shop, in Litterer, J.A. (1963) *Organisations: Structure and Behaviour*. Wiley.

Rutter, M., Maugham, B., Mortimore, P., and Ouston, J. (1979) *Fifteen Thousand Hours*. Open Books.

Silverman, D. (1970) *The Theory of Organisations: A Sociological Framework*. Heinemann.

Silvey, J. (1975) *Deciphering Data*. Longman.

Smith, Jill (1981) *An Exploration of the Schooling of Pupils Aged 13 to 16 Who Have to Spend A Short Time in Their Local General Hospital*, unpublished dissertation, MA in Public and Social Administration. Department of Government, Brunel University.

Webb, E.J., Campbell, D.T., Schwartz, R.D., and Sechrest, L. (1966) *Unobtrusive Measures: Non-Reactive Research in the Social Sciences*. Rand McNally.

Whyte, W.F. (1955) *Street Corner Society: The Social Structure of an Italian Slum* 2nd edition. University of Chicago Press.

Daphne Johnson (commissioned for this volume). Department of Government, Brunel University.

Daphne Johnson is Senior Research Fellow, Department of Government, Brunel University.

CHAPTER 2

STYLES OF RESEARCH

M.J. Wilson

One of the problems of reading about research methods is the terminology. Researchers make use of terms and occasionally jargon which may be incomprehensible to the lay person. It is the same in any field, where a specialized language develops to ease communication amongst professionals. In this chapter some of the terms used in social and educational research are explained and discussed. It is taken from Open University course *Research Methods in Education and the Social Sciences* (DE304) and gives a simple account of three styles of research, namely ethnographic, survey and experimental. The author discusses the advantages and disadvantages of each style and provides a working idea of the basic methods of each. These are not the only ways of labelling approaches to educational enquiry. They can be classified according to discipline, according to methods of gathering evidence and in fact in any way that provides readers with a clear understanding of the nature of the approach. All styles will make use of many different techniques. It is the nature of the research, rather than the methods normally used, which give it its character.

1 The ethnographic style of research

1.1 The first style originated in the methods of social and cultural anthropologists of the early twentieth century who studied at first hand the culture (the beliefs, customs and folkways) of simple societies mainly in Africa, the Pacific and the Americas. These simple cultures (simple in the technological sense) were invariably small in population, preliterate and relatively homogeneous in comparison to European societies.

1.2 Accordingly a method of investigation – *fieldwork* – developed which was one of observation of the culture in its natural habitat. This involved learning the language of the people (because few would know a European language well), observing the rituals and everyday life of the people, and talking at length to a variety of informants in a natural conversation. Of course, the anthropologist was a distinctive type of alien in such societies. He or she would be white, have access to a high-technology culture, and would always be an outsider. By careful preparation and by being willing to spend months or even years in the field it was hoped that the disturbing effects of an outsider could be overcome, and that the complete culture of a small and simple society could be understood and written down for a European audience.

1.3   Research based on the method of observation of 'natural' social processes is no longer confined to anthropology and the study of simple societies. The methods and principles of ethnographic research are used by social scientists in modern Western societies. Examples of this style of research include a study of street gangs in a poor quarter of Boston, USA (Whyte, 1955), a study of machine operators in an American factory (Roy, 1952, 1955), and a recent study of bread round salesmen in England (Ditton, 1977). [. . .]

1.4   The term *ethnography* is an historical one and originally meant the description (-graphy) of the institutions and customs of peoples (ethnos – Greek for people or race). The original use of the word fitted the simple societies studied by classical ethnographers which were small and well-defined communities where everyone seemed to share the same beliefs and where the differences in social positions were few and clearly known. Thus, because these societies were not complex or large, an ethnographer could hope in time to understand that society's structure and culture. Modern societies are large and complex, and an account of British society with its many institutions (economic, political, familial) and its elaborate differentiation (into social classes, occupational groups, regional groups) would tax any social science method but particularly the ethnographic one. What the ethnographic method can be and is used for is the detailed examination of small groups within a complex society. Groups which involve face-to-face social interaction, which means that they must be relatively small, and where the number of social positions is few, are the settings for modern ethnographic research.

1.5   [. . .] A well-known problem in the sociology of work and in management theory is how factory workers respond to systems of payment. Piece-work payment, where a worker's pay is bigger the more he produces, appears to be rational, on the assumption that workers wish to maximize their earnings. However, experience shows that workers in the same job produce less than management expects and a group of workers have outputs which are very close to one another. Normally one would expect a group of workers to show considerable differences between individuals in the quantity of work each produced, according to their different skills or their need to earn less or more money. Roy (1952) became an operator in an American machine shop in order to find out how and why workers control the output of their group. His role as a researcher was unknown to both management and workers and, to all appearances, he was simply another shopfloor employee.

1.6 Roy's method is what is called *participant observation* because he shared the experience and work of the group he joined as a full, ordinary member, although not all participant observers need to keep their role secret. Every day he kept a diary of the conversations he had with fellow workers. Some jobs had piece-rates which workers thought to be poor and the rule here was to underproduce so as to force the rate-fixers into retiming the task. Other jobs had very easy piece-work norms and were 'protected' by the workers by producing a comfortable amount, but not too much! The belief was shared by the work group that easy rates would be retimed by management if the fact became known. Roy noted how new recruits were guided by their fellow workers on how to perform, and failure by a new worker to understand the oblique remarks or hints and suggestions of the old hands led to harassment and even ostracism. Eventually nearly all the workers conformed to the group's own rules of factory life.

1.7 Now the behaviour of a work group such as the one Roy studied is full of subtleties and is very dependent on context. If you or I were to take work as a machine operator, and so full of enthusiasm in our first week that we managed 150 percent of a piece rate norm, then we might well hear the remark 'don't rupture yourself'. But what would it mean? It could be a sardonic but *casual* greeting from a fellow toiler, or the first instance of group pressure to obey the hidden rules of limiting output. The correct interpretation of the remark depends on our sharing a common set of meanings with our fellows. These meanings must be learnt and may only be learnable by long-term participation rather than a short interview. Few of us placed in a British factory would be in doubt for long as to the implicit significance of the words and actions of others, precisely because we share the culture of which factory workers are a part.

1.8 The ethnographic style of research has as its strength that it is *naturalistic*. As a method it studies groups and individuals in their natural settings, and with regard to how behaviour and meanings depend on interaction with others and how statements taken from their contexts can be distorted and lead to bias. It is a good method for investigating covert behaviour and meanings but is not limited to these. Any social group is full of spontaneous activity which reflects a structure and set of beliefs which are difficult, if not impossible, to capture by a formal method of questioning. The behaviour of members in the group is what defines social positions and shared beliefs and to interrogate a respondent in isolation can easily miss the group nature of social behaviour. If we add to this that individuals are inarticulate usually when asked to *reflect* on the full meaning of their acts, then an observer inferring meanings by understanding the context (through participating in the group's life) is in a better position to get an account of the group's collective purpose than is a social scientist who is limited to 'artificial' interviews or the use of questionnaires.

1.9   So far, in giving a simplified picture of the ethnographic method, I have emphasized the advantages of a naturalistic method for the investigation of social phenomena. Such methods have been used in modern societies to study the interaction between teacher and pupils, to study the conversion to a shared set of beliefs of medical students in medical school, as well as the hidden prescriptions of a work group in Roy's example. But the method has disadvantages as well, so that alternative traditions in social science methods are current, each with its own balance of advantages and disadvantages.

1.10   The most obvious disadvantages of the ethnographic method are that it is laborious and time-consuming. To do the job effectively requires acceptance of the researcher by the individuals or group being studied. If the investigator needs to keep his research role secret for fear of biasing the results, then he or she must also play a normal role besides that of being the researcher. Studies of school pupils in the classroom have often been done by researchers who were also teachers, as did Lacey (1970) in *Hightown Grammar* [. . .]. Even if the need to do two jobs (researcher and employee) is not demanded by the nature of the research, there still remains another disadvantage. A naturalistic method of study means that a group (whether a tribe or a work group) has to be followed for the whole of its natural cycle. The ethnographer is observing and recording as things happen. He or she cannot easily short-circuit natural processes but must follow them in real time. Roy, for instance, had he investigated his problem by asking individual members of the group 'why do you limit output?' or 'how do you get new workers to toe the line on how much they produce?', would perhaps have been met by suspicion (because he would have revealed his true position) or by incomprehension because group members do not normally think of the significance of their behaviour in abstracted terms. Group rules are not written constitutions; they are embedded in concrete behaviour and must be inferred from what people *do* rather than what they say that they do. Although the group under study may be a simple one, even so it may need several months to follow through behaviour in the group before repetition of behaviour is found.

1.11   *Summary*. Ethnographic methods are usually both laborious (need for the researcher to combine two roles) and time-consuming (need for the researcher to remain for the life-cycle of the group).

1.12   There are other problems involved in using ethnographic methods. [. . .] One problem is that of *typicality* (or *representativeness*). If resources and time limit observers to only one group, as is often the case, how do we know that such a group is typical of the many such groups in a modern, complex society? How do we know, for example, that all or even most work groups in modern factories behave like the single one which Roy studied? Without many such studies repeating Roy's methods and investigations, we cannot be sure.

1.13   Another difficulty arises *if influences from several sources have an effect on the behaviour under study*. If Roy, again, suspected that family patterns also affected workers' output he would have had to investigate the family life of his group of machine operators. Investigating each source of influence is like entering another group as an observer with the same need to gain acceptance and to follow the natural life-cycle of the new group.

1.14   The last difficulty or disadvantage of the ethnographic method has to do with the *reliability of the observer's analysis*. The notes which an observer makes in the field (Roy's diary, for example) refer only to a small part of a day's activities and information gained. Selection of significant actions or comments has to be made by the researcher and thus what is seen as unimportant will not be recorded. Reliability in science lies in the requirement that another observer, using the same methods on the same group, will obtain the same results. But ethnography is not a method in the sense of fixed rules of procedure which can be written down and followed exactly by another observer. It is much more elastic and flexible than the above rule of reliability allows. The observer is necessarily unique in his own behaviour (and how it affects his respondents), in what he chooses to record as important, and in the interpretation of his findings. The *replication* of an ethnographic study in order to check the author's findings is thus very difficult. There are principles of good ethnographic method [. . .] but they are not as precise and hence open to inspection as perhaps those of other methods are.

1.15 *Summary.* The style of research which we shall call ethnographic has the advantage of naturalism and the disadvantages of being time-consuming, often difficult for the researcher to practise, questionable as to the representativeness of the group under study, and less reliable than other methods. Some of these disadvantages can be overcome in practice, but the choice of research style always rests on the balance of losses and gains in a particular case. [. . .]

2   The survey style of research

2.1   In 1801 the government of the day was authorized by Parliament to carry out a census of all the inhabitants of England and Wales. This step was not taken lightly. Regular censuses were suggested as far back as 1690 and a Bill to institute them was presented to Parliament in 1753 and rejected as 'totally subversive of the last remains of English liberty'. However, 1801 saw the first of the continuing series of ten-year censuses. The first four censuses were very simple affairs by modern standards. The Overseer of the Poor in each parish visited every house in his area and questioned each householder. His enquiries furnished the following information for each parish: the number of houses inhabited, the number of families occupying them, and the number of uninhabited houses; the number of persons and their sex; the number of persons engaged in agriculture, trade, manufacturing or handicrafts, and other persons.

2.2   Although it is called a *census* (in fact, The Census) it is an example, and in 1801 a simple example, of a *social survey*. An *interviewer* (the Overseer of the Poor) questions *respondents* (the householders) according to a fixed schedule (a questionnaire). The questions would not have been printed with separate copies for each household as is done in modern censuses, but the principle of using a standard set of questions for each interview was there in 1801, and so we may call it a schedule.

2.3   The questions in the first census were simple ones but even so the Overseer of the Poor would have had to be ready to supplement the questions about occupations (for example) or to prompt his respondent for more detail so as to *code* his reply in one of the four required categories ('agriculture', etc.). An important rule in surveys is that a question (which will be asked of all respondents) has the same meaning for each respondent. This is not as easy as may first appear. The modern census asks the respondent to list all members of his or her household but the word 'household' may mean different things to different respondents (D291, Open University, 1975). The census uses a definition of household so as to ensure (it is hoped) that replies are comparable. Printed on the first page of the 1971 Census Form is the definition: 'A household comprises either one person living alone or a group of persons (who may or may not be related) living at the same address with common housekeeping'. Persons staying temporarily with the household are included. *Comparability of responses* is the principle underlying the rule that a question should have the same meaning to each respondent.

2.4　In 1801 the majority of the population were illiterate. Printed forms for each head of household to fill in would have been pointless and, of course, expensive. Overseers of the Poor were ready-made interviewers who had a good knowledge of the inhabitants of their parishes and of local trades and handicrafts. In this sense the Overseers of the Poor were reasonably skilled interviewers for their time, although the skills required of modern interviewers are much wider in the light of the biases which we now know interviewing can produce if care is not taken [. . .]. In 1841 the ten-year census began to use *self-completion questionnaires* for each head of household. The census enumerators had still to deliver and collect the forms and, in many cases, to assist in their completion where the respondent was wholly or partially illiterate. The census was still restricted to a few basic questions and the change from *interviewer-administered questionnaires* to self-completion ones is thought to have made little difference to the accuracy of the census.

2.5　Contemporary surveys will usually use interviewers if the subject matter of the survey is sensitive or difficult or if the respondents are ill at ease with form-filling. Other things being equal, an interviewer-administered survey is to be preferred on the grounds of accuracy and because the proportion of respondents who eventually complete the questionnaire is higher than with self-completion ones. Self-completion questionnaires are much cheaper (no interviewer costs) and so are often used if no especially strong reasons are present for needing an interviewer-administered survey. The modern census form had eight pages in 1971 with 36 separate questions and was a self-completion form for the head of household. Though elaborate by the standards of the nineteenth century, the 1971 census is simple in comparison to academic surveys. Even so, the respondent is advised 'If you need help, do not hesitate to ask the enumerator' and enumerators often used the census form as an interviewer-administered one and completed the entries for the illiterate, the old, and those with poor English.

2.6   The census is intended to be a complete *enumeration* of the entire population of Great Britain. It tries to be complete by contacting every household in the country. There are errors and omissions, naturally. In 1801 vagabonds and highwaymen would tend to be missed out; nowadays those of no fixed abode, squatters and some immigrant groups will tend to be underrecorded. The census is the chief example of a 100 percent *sample survey*. This is a pompous way of saying that most surveys are conducted only on a fraction or sample of the target population where a census (the generic word) is a survey of the whole of a target population. Why use a *sample* of the population? Because if certain conditions are observed, the results from a sample can be used to describe the whole of the population from which the sample was taken. This is a very much cheaper way of obtaining information and sample surveys of populations are the norm. The conditions under which a sample may stand for a population are summed up in the word *representativeness*. In simple terms, if the population is known to contain 50 percent males, then the sample must also have 50 percent males in it, and so on for any characteristic of the population which is relevant to the study. There are statistical methods of drawing representative samples. [. . .] You should remember only that a representative sample may be used to stand for the whole of the population from which it is drawn.

2.7   *Population* requires definition as a social science term. In the everyday meaning of the word it means all the inhabitants of a country, or a region, or even of the world. The population covered by the census is the inhabitants of Great Britain. In surveys in general, the population means the category of people for whom the survey results are meant to stand. Populations in this more exact sense include as examples in surveys: *voters* (citizens of the UK who are 18 years or more and who are not lunatics, peers, or prisoners) as in political opinion polls; *OU graduates* (those students registered with the OU as undergraduates who have graduated since the OU was founded and before the month in which the questionnaires were sent out) as in the survey of OU graduates conducted in 1977 by the Survey Research Department of the OU; *primary school children* (all pupils in primary schools in England in 1964/1965) as in the National Survey of Primary School Children conducted for the Plowden Committee. The population at which the sample survey is aimed requires careful definition so as to be sure who is included in it and who not. When the population is defined, ways of obtaining a representative sample of it may be dealt with.

2.8 To summarize the characteristics of the survey method:

(a) The survey method requires a sample of respondents to reply to a number of fixed questions under comparable conditions.

(b) The survey may be administered by an interviewer who completes a form for each respondent by asking him or her the survey questions, or a form on which the questions are printed is sent to each respondent for self-completion.

(c) The respondents in the survey represent a defined population. If all the members of a population are interviewed or fill in a self-completion form then a census (or 100 percent sample survey) has been taken. If only a fraction of the population is covered, then a sample survey has been conducted.

(d) A survey sample should be representative of its population. If it is, then we can generalize results from the sample to the population.

(e) By using the same questions for a sample of respondents comparisons of individuals within the sample may be made.

2.9 The survey method has its own advantages and disadvantages, as does each of the other two styles of research in social science. Let us look at the major strengths and weaknesses of the survey method. An interviewer (or a well-designed self-completion questionnaire) can elicit information from a respondent which covers a long period of activity yet can be summarized in answer to a question in a few minutes. The National Survey of Primary School Children, for example, wanted to know if parents took responsibility and initiative for their child's schooling (the survey wished to assess the extent to which parental attitudes to schooling affected a pupil's attainment at school). One way in which this source of influence on pupils was measured was a question which asked 'Does your child talk to you much about the work he/she does in school, or show you the sort of things he/she does?' The interviewers coded or categorized the replies into one of two boxes: (a) Yes, often (b) No, only occasionally, or hardly ever. This question, taking only a short while to ask and answer, is a way of abstracting an important aspect of the interaction between child and parent. An alternative method of collecting such data could be the sustained observation of the child at home, where the observer carefully notes family discussion of school work both for frequency and for content. To use this method would mean that the observer would have to become virtually a family member over a long period! With a sample of 3349 pupils and parents in the study the cost and time of observing family interaction puts such a method out of the question.

2.10   The chief advantage of the survey method is its ability to collect a lot of *information* (many respondents and many replies) in a relatively short period. Its costs, in terms of the information gained for each pound spent, is low compared to the ethnographic method. With comparable information for a number of respondents in a sample the social scientist can move beyond the description of social phenomena to looking for patterns in the *data* – to relating, for example, poor achievers amongst pupils to the sort of parental encouragement which this group in the sample received. In this way social science begins to explain *why* social patterns are as they are, as a first step to remedying social defects.

2.11   The survey method has defects to go with its strengths. Firstly, the respondent may have exaggerated how often she discussed school work with her child (in the Plowden survey the mother was normally interviewed) because she wished to show a good face to the interviewer. No interview is ever neutral: the subject matter of the questionnaire and the personal characteristics of the interviewer may alter the responses, as research has shown [. . .]. An awareness of how a 'good mother' should encourage her child may well be present in an interview devoted to children and their schooling. Secondly, the question and the answers allowed do not touch upon the quality or intensity of the mother's concern for her child's progress at school. There is no measure of how significant her talks with the child were, only of how often she recalls them taking place.

2.12   The attempt to produce comparable information by the survey method can lead to an obscuring of the subtler differences in behaviour, which may be discovered by an observational method in a context which is more natural than the formal interview. The use of standard measures over a large sample in order to find regularities and patterns in the characteristics of the respondents still remains a strength of the survey method but the price of simplification of the replies may have to be paid.

2.13   The simplification of replies may be lessened by testing questions on a small part of the sample beforehand, using a looser, more conversational, method of interview in which replies are probed more deeply than is possible in the full-scale survey on the main sample. If, in the Plowden example, a clear difference emerges in the question-testing phase between those who review their child's progress frequently and carefully on the one hand, and those who seldom talk to the child about school work at all, and then only casually, the twofold categorization of replies may not be as inaccurate as it appears to be. Well-conducted surveys have a number of '*pilot*' *interviews* before the main questionnaire is arrived at.

2.14 *Summary.* The survey style of research allows information from large samples to be collected quickly and relatively cheaply, allows comparisons between individuals because answers to questions are comparable, but may be superficial in measuring sensitive or difficult aspects of behaviour.

3 The experimental style of research

3.1 A simple *experiment* could be organized to test the effect of fluoridated toothpaste on the rate at which dental caries occurs in children's teeth. Two groups of people are selected randomly from the population of children aged three years to twelve years, the age group in which caries occurs at the maximum rate. The groups are not too small (at least 30 children in each is desirable) and correct procedures of *random selection* are used [. . .]. The two groups may be assumed to be equal in all respects *as groups*. This means that the characteristics of the groups are matched: average height, average income of family, ratio of boys to girls, average social status of family, etc. Any characteristic of one group will be the same as that of the other group (with a small chance of a difference between the two groups which can be known and allowed for by probability theory [. . .]. Note that 'equal groups' does not mean that individuals within a group are equal nor that an individual of one group has an exactly corresponding opposite number in the other group. If one group contains a Cabinet Minister's son, his family income is sure to be higher than that of a fireman's son in the other group. The Cabinet Minister's salary is submerged in the group's average income and so will the fireman's salary be included in the other group's average income. It is the average income of the two groups which will be equal [. . .].

3.2 One group is taken as the *experimental group* and the other as the *control group*. It does not matter how the choice is made – the toss of a coin could decide – since both groups are equal in every respect. Both groups are given individual dental examinations to establish the level of caries for each child. This examination is the *pre-test* one.

3.3 Now the *experimental treatment* begins. The experimental group of children are supplied with fluoridated toothpaste and instructed (and their mothers are brought onto the scene by learning the instructions for their children) to use only the special toothpaste until further notice. The control group are given similar instructions, but supplied with nonfluoridated toothpaste.

3.4   One year later, all children are given dental inspections to establish their new levels of caries. This is the *post-test*. The difference between the pre-test and post-test levels of caries can then be calculated for each child and the *average* change in caries levels may be found for the experimental group and for the control group.

3.5   If the rate of tooth decay on average is much higher for the control group than for the experimental group what can be concluded? We may draw the conclusion from this experiment that the use of fluoridated toothpaste is the cause of fewer decayed teeth. [. . .]

3.6   The steps in the experiment can be summarized as:

(a) Two identical groups.
(b) Pre-test to establish baseline for caries.
(c) Experimental treatment applied to one group but withheld from control group.
(d) Post-test.
(e) Difference between two groups after experimental treatment is calculated by subtracting the pre-test caries from the post-test caries and comparing the scores for the two groups.
(f) *Therefore*, we argue, a difference between the groups after the experimental treatment can only be *because* of the experimental treatment, since the two groups were identical before the treatment began.

3.7   The conclusion in (f) above shows the main advantage of the experimental method – *a well-designed experiment makes it easier to connect a cause with its effect.* In the survey style of research deciding what is cause and what effect is nearly always difficult and sometimes impossible. If you had data to show that a high proportion of children of above average attainment had parents who strongly encouraged their school work, what would you conclude? That parental encouragement is a cause of good pupil attainment? It is tempting to draw this conclusion but another conclusion could be drawn equally easily from the data. It could be that parents of children who performed well at school took a greater interest because of it and so gave more encouragement to their child. Ambiguities such as this concerning causes and their effects are avoidable in the experimental style of research. But experiments are difficult to carry out in social science, and this problem is one major disadvantage of the experimental method. [. . .]

3.8   The essence of an experiment is to be in a position to treat one group differently to another similar group and to compare the results. But planned, deliberate, social changes for selected groups are frequently impossible and sometimes unethical. Could we investigate whether (and by how much) differences between the social classes in the ways in which they bring up their children cause differences in the average IQ of the social classes? Only if a child was not brought up by its natural parents but allocated by experimenters to parents of another social class could we hope to be able to run such an experiment. Such a requirement is politically and socially impossible and ethically indefensible. *Treatments or assumed causes cannot always be assigned to individuals or to groups as an experimenter thinks fit. This limits the use of experimental methods in the social sciences.*

3.9   Another limitation of the experiment in the social sciences is that social causes do not work singly. An effect such as low school attainment or high IQ is the product of multiple causes. To isolate each cause requires a new experimental group each time and the length and difficulty of the experiment increases rapidly. It is possible to run an experiment in which several treatments are put into practice simultaneously but many groups must be made available rather than just two. To get large numbers of people to agree to take part for a long period is difficult and many will drop out before the experiment is finished, so perhaps biasing the results. *The causes of social phenomena are usually multiple ones and an experiment to study them requires large numbers of people often for lengthy periods. This requirement limits the usefulness of the experimental method.* The survey which can obtain information from a respondent in a short period of time and over many questions is superior to the experiment in this respect but, of course, surveys make it difficult to draw conclusions about causes and effects.

3.10   Where experiments can be done on problems which are not politically or socially sensitive (which education is) and which may take only a short period to run they are feasible. This is one of the reasons why psychology uses the experimental method as its predominant research style to study such phenomena as, for example, perception, learning and memory where the treatments are usually in the form of innocuous tasks which are completed in a few hours at the most.

3.11   *Summary.* The experimental style of research allows strong conclusions to be drawn about cause and effect. Its application in social science is limited by the need to run lengthy and large-scale experiments because social causes are usually multiple ones. There are also strong practical and ethical limitations to the manipulation of individuals which experiments require if they are to work.

4   Conclusion

4.1   Many social scientists work within one research style because of their training and because of the accepted practices of their discipline. Styles of research are, for some social scientists, *traditions*, a word which implies a tendency on the part of the scientists not to reflect sufficiently on whether methods from other styles may not also be used to study a problem. It is believed by some [. . .] that research would gain by the use of more than one method to investigate a problem because of the way in which the strengths of one method may offset the weaknesses of others. [. . .]

References

Ditton, J. (1977) *Part-time Crime*. London, Macmillan.

Lacey, C. (1970) *Hightown Grammar*. Manchester, Manchester University Press.

Open University (1975) *D291 Statistical Sources*, Unit 3, *Population*, pp. 7–13, 'The population census'. Milton Keynes, The Open University Press.

Roy, D. (1952) Quota restriction and goldbricking in a machine shop, *American Journal of Sociology*, Vol. 57, pp. 427–442.

Roy, D. (1955) Efficiency and 'the fix': informal intergroup relations in a piecework machine shop, *American Journal of Sociology*, Vol. 60, pp. 255–266.

Whyte, W.F. (1955) *Street Corner Society*. Chicago, University of Chicago Press.

M.J. Wilson for the course team. Open University course DE304: *Research Methods in Education and the Social Sciences*. Block 1 'Variety in Social Science Research' Part 1, pp. 9–25. Copyright © 1979 The Open University.

Michael Wilson is a senior lecturer in Social Sciences at the Open University

CHAPTER 3

ACTION RESEARCH

Louis Cohen & Lawrence Manion

Action research investigates problems identified by practitioners, and is essentially directed towards greater understanding and improvement of practice over a period of time. In this chapter, Louis Cohen and Lawrence Manion describe the main features of action research and offer a flexible framework to illustrate procedures for setting up a project. They propose eight stages in the process which could in practice serve as an outline for any research project – action research or not. This approach has some appeal for practitioners because it is firmly based in practice, is directed towards problem solving, and when a project is 'complete', participants continue to review, evaluate and improve practice in their own institution.

Introduction

Action research has received rather more publicity over the years than most other methods in the social sciences. This may indeed stem from the implied tension in its name, *action research*, for *action* and *research* as separate activities in whatever context each have their own ideology and *modus operandi* and when conjoined in this way, lie as uneasy bedfellows. To give a comprehensive definition of the term at this stage is difficult because usage varies with time, place and setting. None the less, we may offer a conventional definition and use this as a starting point: *action research is small-scale intervention in the functioning of the real world and a close examination of the effects of such intervention* (Halsey, 1972). By looking at a few examples of the use of the method in the research literature, we may further identify other tangible features: action research is *situational* – it is concerned with diagnosing a problem in a specific context and attempting to solve it in that context; it is usually (though not inevitably) *collaborative* – teams of researchers and practitioners work together on a project; it is *participatory* – team members themselves take part directly or indirectly in implementing the research; and it is *self-evaluative* – modifications are continuously evaluated within the ongoing situation, the ultimate objective being to improve practice in some way or other. According to Blum (*Association for Supervision and Curriculum Development*, 1959), the use of action research in the social sciences can be resolved into two stages: a *diagnostic stage* in which the problems are analysed and the hypotheses developed; and a *therapeutic stage* in which the hypotheses are tested by a consciously directed change experiment, preferably in a social life situation.

The scope of action research as a method is impressive. Its usage may range at one extreme from a teacher trying out a novel way of teaching social studies with his class to, at another, a sophisticated study of organizational change in industry using a large research team and backed by government sponsors. Whatever the situation, however, the method's evaluative frame of reference remains the same, namely, to add to the practitioner's *functional knowledge* of the phenomena he deals with. This type of research is therefore usually considered in conjunction with social or educational aims (Corey, 1953).

It will be useful here if we distinguish *action research* from *applied research*, for although they are similar in some ways, there are important differences between them which need to be made explicit, for confusion between the two does sometimes arise. Both utilize the scientific method. Since applied research is concerned mainly with establishing relationships and testing theories, it is quite rigorous in its application of the conditions of this method. To this end, therefore, it insists on: studying a large number of cases; establishing as much control as possible over variables; precise sampling techniques; and a serious concern to generalize its findings to comparable situations. It does not claim to contribute directly to the solution of problems. Action research, by contrast, interprets the scientific method much more loosely, chiefly because its focus is a specific problem in a specific setting. The emphasis is not so much on obtaining generalizable scientific knowledge as on precise knowledge for a particular situation and purpose. The conditions imposed on applied research, therefore, are normally relaxed with action research. Of course, as action research projects become more extensive in their coverage, the boundary between the two methods becomes less easy to define. A curriculum project involving 100 schools, say, or a community action programme embracing a number of major conurbations, will tend to yield rather more generalizable knowledge and information than purely localized undertakings.

Having drawn this distinction between action research and applied research, we are now free to concentrate on the former and ask ourselves the question: what kinds of intervention programme are featured in action research? The following examples, while by no means exhaustive, give some idea of the contexts in which the method may be used. They are not mutually exclusive so there may be considerable overlap between some of them. There is the kind: (1) which acts as *a spur to action*, its objective being to get something done more expeditiously than would be the case with alternative means; (2) which addresses itself to *personal functioning, human relations and morale* and is thus concerned with people's job efficiency, their motivations, relationships and general well-being; (3) which focuses on *job analysis* and aims at improving professional functioning and efficiency; (4) which is concerned with *organizational change* in so far as it results in improved functioning in business or industry; (5) which is concerned with *planning and policy making*, generally in the field of social administration; (6) which is concerned with *innovation and change* and the ways in which these may be implemented in ongoing systems; (7) which concentrates on *problem solving* virtually in any context in which a specific problem needs solving; and (8) which provides the opportunity to develop *theoretical knowledge*, the emphasis here being more on the research element of the method.

Equally diverse are the situations in which these different kinds of intervention may be used – almost any setting, in fact, where a problem involving people, tasks and procedures cries out for solution, or where some change of feature results in a more desirable outcome. Notable instances of the use of action research may be found in such starkly contrasting worlds as insurance, prisons, social administration, ships, hospitals, community projects, education, industry, coal-mining and business management. Examination of the work of the Tavistock Institute of Human Relations which has done so much to develop action research as a methodology will illustrate how the method may be applied in these diverse areas (Brown, 1967). For our own purposes, however, we shall now restrict our discussion chiefly to the use of action research in the field of education.

Although the action research movement in education was initiated in the United States in the 1940s, the scene for its appearance began to be set in that country in the 1920s with the application of the scientific method to the study of educational problems, growing interest in group interaction and group processes, and the emerging progressive movement. Indeed, the latter is seen by some as the principal causal agent for subsequent developments in action research. One writer (Hodgkinson, 1957) says: 'Action research . . . is a direct and logical outcome of the progressive position. After showing children how to work together to solve their problems, the next step was for teachers to adopt the methods they had been teaching their children, and learn to solve their own problems cooperatively.' Reaching its peak in the 1960s, the movement had multifarious aims of a decidedly practical nature which were often embellished with ideological, even political, counterpoints. Some, for instance, saw it as a necessary corrective to the failure of official bodies to implement traditional research findings; others, as a means of improving the quality of life. Action research in Britain has enjoyed something of a revival since the establishment of the Schools Council in 1964 under whose aegis it has been used to implement curriculum research and development. The purposes of action research in school and classroom fall broadly into five categories: (1) it is a means of remedying problems diagnosed in specific situations, or of improving in some way a given set of circumstances; (2) it is a means of in-service training, thereby equipping the teacher with new skills and methods, sharpening his analytical powers and heightening his self-awareness; (3) it is a means of injecting additional or innovatory approaches to teaching and learning into an ongoing system which normally inhibits innovation and change; (4) it is a means of improving the normally poor communications between the practising teacher and the academic researcher, and of remedying the failure of traditional research to give clear prescriptions; and (5) although lacking the rigour of true scientific research, it is a means of providing a preferable alternative to the more subjective, impressionistic approach to problem solving in the classroom.

[. . .] Who actually undertakes action research in schools? Three possibilities present themselves. First, there is the single teacher operating on his own with his class. He will feel the need for some kind of change or improvement in teaching, learning or organization, for example, and will be in a position to translate his ideas into action in his own classroom. He is, as it were, both practitioner and researcher in one and will integrate the practical and theoretical orientations within himself. Second, action research may be pursued by a group of teachers working cooperatively within one school, though of necessity functioning against a bigger backdrop than the teacher working solo. They may or may not be advised by an outside researcher. And third, there is the occasion – perhaps the most characteristic in recent years – where a team of teachers work alongside a team of researchers in a sustained relationship, possibly with other interest-

Box 1

Humanities Curriculum Project – aim and premisses

Aim:
To develop an understanding of social situations and human acts and of the
controversial value issues which they raise.

Premisses:
1. That controversial issues should be handled in the classroom.
2. That the teacher should accept the need to submit his teaching in controversial areas to the criterion of neutrality at this stage of education, that
   is, that he should regard it as part of his responsibility not to promote his
   own view.
3. That the mode of enquiry in controversial areas should have discussion,
   rather than instruction, as its core.
4. That the discussion should protect divergence of view among participants,
   rather than attempt to achieve consensus.
5. That the teacher as chairman of the discussion should have responsibility
   for quality and standards of learning.

Source: Butcher and Pont (1973)

ed parties, like advisers, university departments and sponsors, on the
periphery. This third possibility, though potentially the most promising,
may also be the most problematic, at least initially, because of rival
characterizations of action and research by the teachers and researchers
respectively. We shall return to this point at the end of the chapter.
Advocates of action research believe that little can be achieved if only one
person is involved in changing his ideas and practices. For this reason,
cooperative research tends to be emphasized and encouraged. One com-
mentator (Hill and Kerber, 1967) notes:

> Action research functions best when it is co-operative action research. This
> method of research incorporates the ideas and expectations of all persons
> involved in the situation. Co-operative action research has the concomitants of
> beneficial effects for workers, and the improvement of the services, con-
> ditions, and functions of the situation. In education this activity translates into
> more practice in research and problem-solving by teachers, administrators,
> pupils, and certain community personnel, while the quality of teaching and
> learning is in the process of being improved.

Characteristics

The principal characteristics of action research which we hereupon describe are more or less present in all instances of its usage (those having an experimental slant need to be considered in a somewhat different category). We have already referred to its prime feature – that it is essentially an on-the-spot procedure designed to deal with a concrete problem located in an immediate situation. This means that the step-by-step process is constantly monitored (ideally, that is) over varying periods of time and by a variety of mechanisms (questionnaires, diaries, interviews and case studies, for example) so that the ensuing feedback may be translated into modifications, adjustments, directional changes, redefinitions, as necessary, so as to bring about lasting benefit to the ongoing process itself rather than to some future occasion, as is the purpose of more traditionally oriented research. Unlike other methods, no attempt is made to identify one particular factor and study it in isolation, divorced from the context giving it meaning. That the findings are applied immediately, then, or in the short term is another important characteristic, although having made this point we need to qualify it to the extent that members of research teams – especially in curriculum projects – frequently have a more long-term perspective. The following extract from Stenhouse's account of the Humanities Curriculum Project illustrates how some of the points we have just made appear 'in the field':

> During the session 1968–9 the schools worked on collections on war, education, and the family. Feedback on materials was by questionnaire supported by interviews with the schools officer or other team members when they visited schools. Information was sought on coverage of the collection, accessibility of the material to the students (readability and sophistication of ideas), and the extent to which materials provoked or supported discussion. Most schools used only a small proportion of materials (as was intended) so that feedback on any one piece was not extensive. It was also frequently contradictory, particularly as to readability. Collections were radically re-edited as a result of experience in schools; often only half the trial pack survived.

The principal justification for the use of action research in the context of the school is improvement of practice. This can be achieved only if teachers are able to change their attitudes and behaviour. One of the best means of bringing about these kind of changes is pressure from the group with which one works. As we have seen, because the problems of teachers are often shared with other teachers in the same school, action research has tended to become cooperative involving many or all of the teachers in the school. Group interaction is frequently another characteristic, therefore.

A feature which makes action research a very suitable procedure for work in classrooms and schools (as well as other field settings) is its flexibility and adaptability. These qualities are revealed in the changes that may take place during its implementation and in the course of on-the-spot experimentation and innovation characterizing the approach. They come out particularly strongly when set against the usual background of constraints in schools – those to do with organization, resources, timetabling, staff deployment and teachers' attitudes, for example, as well as pressures from other agencies involved and from competing interests.

Action research relies chiefly on observation and behavioural data. That it is therefore empirical is another distinguishing feature of the method. This implies that over the period of a project information is collected, shared, discussed, recorded in some way, evaluated and acted upon; and that from time to time, this sequence of events forms the basis of reviews of progress. In this one respect at least it is superior to the more usual subjective, impressionistic methods we have already alluded to. Where an experimental note is introduced into a project, it is generally achieved through the use of control groups with a view to testing specific hypotheses and arriving at more generalizable knowledge.

In our earlier comparison with applied research, we said that action research took a much more relaxed view of the scientific method. We return to this point here because it is a characteristic which forms the basis of persistent criticisms of the method by its opponents. Travers, for example, in reviewing a number of action research projects writes:

> The writer's evaluation of the last fifty studies which have been undertaken which compare the outcomes of one teaching methodology with another is that they have contributed almost nothing to our knowledge of the factors that influence the learning process in the classroom. Many of them do not even identify what the experimentally controlled variables are and indicate only that the study compares the outcomes of educational practices in the community where the study originates with educational practices elsewhere.

That the method should be lacking in scientific rigour, however, is not surprising since the very factors which make it distinctively what it is – and therefore of value in certain contexts – are the antithesis of true experimental research. The points usually made are: that its objective is situational and specific (unlike the scientific method which goes beyond the solution of practical problems); its sample is restricted and unrepresentative; it has little or no control over independent variables; and its findings are not generalizable but generally restricted to the environment in which the research is carried out. While these criticisms hold in most cases, it is

Box 2

The ideal teacher for an Integrated Studies Project

The ideal teacher for an Integrated Studies Project would be one willing to maintain his subject discipline within a team and to engage in planning integrated work through discussions with other specialist colleagues. This teacher would be an active producer of new materials, teaching methods and ideas for integrated subject work. He would keep accounts of his innovatory work, fill in the questionnaires sent him by the project team and feed his experience back to them. He would organize his work so that children would not only come to see and use the concepts within separate subject disciplines, but would learn the skills of those subjects through enquiry-based programmes.

Source: Adapted from Shipman (1974).

important that we refer again to the qualification made earlier: that as action research programmes become more extensive and use more schools, that is, become more standardized, less personalized and more 'open', some of these strictures at least will become less valid.

Occasions when action research as a method is appropriate

We come now to a brief consideration of the occasions when the use of action research is fitting and appropriate. The answer in short is this: that action research is appropriate whenever specific knowledge is required for a specific problem in a specific situation; or when a new approach is to be grafted on to an existing system. More than this, however, suitable mechanisms must be available for monitoring progress and for translating feedback into the ongoing system. This means that, other things being equal, the action research method may be applied to any classroom or school situation where these conditions apply. We have already referred to the suitability of the approach to curriculum research and development. Let us now take this further by identifying other areas in school life where action research could be used and illustrating each area with a concrete example: (1) *teaching methods* – perhaps replacing a traditional method by a discovery method; (2) *learning strategies* – adopting an integrated approach to learning in preference to a single subject style of teaching and learning; (3) *evaluative procedures* – improving one's methods of continuous assessment, say; (4) the realm of *attitudes and values* – possibly encouraging more positive attitudes to work, for instance, or modifying pupils' value systems with regard to some aspect of life; (5) the personal *in-service development* of teachers – improving teaching skills, developing new methods of learning, increasing powers of analysis, or heightening self-awareness, for example; (6) *management and control* – the gradual introduction of the techniques of behaviour modification; and (7) *administration* – increasing the efficiency of some aspect of the administrative side of school life.

Of course, it would be naive of us simply to select a problem area *in vacuo*, so to speak. We have also to consider the context in which the project is to be undertaken. More specifically this means bearing in mind factors that will directly affect the outcomes. One of these concerns the teachers themselves and the extent to which they are favourably disposed towards the project, particularly when they are part of a collectivity working with outside agencies for, as we shall see in our final section, this very factor on its own can be a source of intense friction. It is important, therefore, that the teachers taking part in the project are truly involved, that they know what the objectives are, what these imply, and that they are adequately motivated – or at least sufficiently open-minded for motivation to be induced. Another important factor concerns the organizational aspect of the school so that there is a reasonable amount of congruence between the setting and the programme to be initiated. This can be achieved without too much discord when a programme is internally organized by the school itself. When outside parties are involved, however, who themselves are working

Box 3

Metaphors reflecting teachers' perceptions of a curriculum project

1. *The exchange of gifts:* The project as reciprocal obligation.
2. *The other drummer:* The project as unselected affinity.
3. *Troubled waters:* The project as agitation or distress.
4. *The gift of grace:* The project as salvation.
5. *New props for identity:* The project as theatre.
6. *Free sample:* The project as commercialism.
7. *Ground bait:* The project as exploitation.
8. *Taking issue:* The project as management consultancy.
9. *Cargo cult:* The project as overwhelming technology.

Source: Shipman (1974)

concurrently in other schools, difficulties may arise over such matters as implementing a new style of teaching, for example, or use of project materials, and so on. One further factor concerns resources: are there enough sufficiently competent researchers at hand? And has the school got reasonable access to college and university libraries to consult appropriate professional and research journals should this need arise? Some or all of these factors need to be reviewed as part of the planning stage of an action research programme.

Some issues

We have already seen that the participants in a change situation may be either a teacher, a group of teachers working internally, or else teachers and researchers working on a collaborative basis. It is this latter category, where action research brings together two professional bodies each with its own objectives and values, that we shall consider further at this point because of its inherent problematic nature. Both parties share the same interest in an educational problem, yet their respective orientations to it differ. It has been observed (Halsey, 1972), for instance, that research values *precision, control, replication* and attempts to generalize from specific events. Teaching, on the other hand, is concerned with *action*, with *doing things*, and translates generalizations into specific acts. The incompatibility between action and research in these respects, therefore, can be a source of problems. Marris and Rein (1967), for example, on reviewing the relationship between the two in a number of American community action programmes concluded that the principles of *action* and *experienced research* are so different and so often mutually exclusive that attempts to link them into a single process are likely to produce internal conflict and the subordination of one element to another. They express it thus:

> Research requires a clear and constant purpose, which both defines and precedes the choice of means; that the means be exactly and consistently followed; and that no revision takes place until the sequence of steps is completed. Action is tentative, non-commital and adaptive. It concentrates upon the next step, breaking the sequence into discrete, manageable decisions. It casts events in a fundamentally different perspective, evolving the future out of present opportunities, where research perceives the present in the context of the final outcomes. Research cannot interpret the present until it knows the answers to its ultimate questions. Action cannot foresee what questions to ask until it has interpreted the present. Action attempts to comprehend all the factors relevant to an immediate problem whose nature continually changes as events proceed, where research abstracts one or two

factors for attention, and holds to a constant definition of the problem
the experiment is concluded.

Those who are not quite as pessimistic about the viability of the action/
research coupling would question whether the characterization of *action* and
research as put forward by Marris and Rein necessarily holds in all contexts.
They would advocate a more flexible approach to the relationship. Some
researchers (Halsey, 1972), for instance, suggest that projects could vary
along a number of dimensions such as the degree of control exercised by
the action and research components, the amount of knowledge about the
means of achieving the desired outcomes, and the level of cooperation
between action and research. Such a classification could be linked to
different kinds of action research (see p. 42) and suggest what combinations
of action and research were most appropriate for particular conditions. In
short, what seems to be needed is a clear and unambiguous statement of the
project's objectives such that all participants understand them and their
implications; and a careful analysis of the context(s) in which the programme is to be mounted to determine the precise, but flexible, relationship
between the two components. This would help to ensure that the positive
contributions of both are maximized and that the constraints of each on the
other are kept to a minimum.

Procedures

We now trace the possible stages and procedures that may be followed in an
action research programme, or from which a suitable selection may be
made. As we have already seen, projects may vary along a number of
dimensions – whether they are to be conducted by teachers only, or by
teachers in collaboration with researchers, whether small or large samples of
schools are involved, whether they tackle specific problems or more diffuse
ones, for example. Given the particular set of circumstances, an appropriate
model may be selected to guide procedures, one that will be tailor-made to
meet the needs of the change situation in question. As we are here concerned with a review of procedures in general terms, however, and not with a
specific instance, we offer a basic, flexible framework by way of illustration:
it will need to be interpreted or adjusted in the light of the particular
undertaking.

The *first stage* will involve the identification, evaluation and formulation
of the problem perceived as critical in an everyday teaching situation.
'Problem' should be interpreted loosely here so that it could refer to the

need to introduce innovation into some aspect of a school's established programme. The *second stage* involves preliminary discussion and negotiations among the interested parties – teachers, researchers, advisers, sponsors, possibly – which may culminate in a draft proposal. This may include a statement of the questions to be answered (e.g. Under what conditions can curriculum change be best effected? What are the limiting factors in bringing about effective curriculum change? What strong points of action research can be employed to bring about curriculum change?). The researchers in their capacity as consultants (or sometimes as programme initiators) may draw upon their expertise to bring the problem more into focus, possibly determining causal factors or recommending alternative lines of approach to established ones. This is often the crucial stage for the venture as it is at this point that the seeds of success or failure are planted, for unless the objectives, purposes and assumptions are made perfectly clear to all concerned, and unless the role of key concepts is stressed (e.g. feedback), the enterprise can easily miscarry. The *third stage* may in some circumstances involve a review of the research literature to find out what can be learned from comparable studies, their objectives, procedures and problems encountered. The *fourth stage* may involve a modification or redefinition of the initial statement of the problem at stage one. It may now emerge in the form of a testable hypothesis; or as a set of guiding objectives. In Box 1 we give an example of an aim and accompanying premisses which were used in this connection in the Humanities Curriculum Project. Sometimes change agents deliberately decide against the use of objectives on the grounds that they have a constraining effect on the process itself. It is also at this stage that assumptions underlying the project are made explicit (e.g. in order to effect curriculum changes, the attitudes, values, skills and objectives of the teachers involved must be changed). The *fifth stage* may be concerned with the selection of research procedures – sampling, administration, choice of materials, methods of teaching and learning, allocation of resources and tasks, deployment of staff and so on.

The *sixth stage* will be concerned with the choice of the evaluation procedures to be used and will need to take into consideration that evaluation in this context will be continuous. Box 4 provides a set of evaluation objectives from the Humanities Project by way of example. The *seventh stage* embraces the implementation of the project itself (over varying periods of time). It will include the conditions and methods of data collection (e.g. bi-weekly meetings, the keeping of records, interim reports, final reports, the submission of self-evaluation and group-evaluation reports, etc.); the

Box 4

The objectives of the Evaluation Unit in the Humanities Curriculum Project

1. To ascertain the effects of the project, document the circumstances in which they occur, and present this information in a form which will help educational decision makers to evaluate the likely consequences of adopting the programme.
2. To describe the present situation and operations of the schools we study so that decision makers can understand more fully what it is they are trying to change.
3. To describe the work of the project team in terms which will help the sponsors and planners of such a venture to weigh the value of this form of investment, and to determine more precisely the framework of support, guidance and control which is appropriate.
4. To make a contribution to evaluation theory by articulating our problems clearly, recording our experiences, and perhaps most importantly, by publicising our errors.
5. To contribute to the understanding of the problems of curriculum innovation generally.

Source: Butcher and Pont (1973)

monitoring of tasks and the transmission of feedback to the research team; and the classification and analysis of data. The *eighth and final stage* will involve the interpretation of the data; inferences to be drawn; and overall evaluation of the project. Discussions on the findings will take place in the light of previously agreed evaluative criteria. Errors, mistakes and problems will be considered. A general summing up may follow this in which the outcomes of the project are reviewed, recommendations made, and arrangements for dissemination of results to interested parties decided.

As we stressed, this is a basic framework: much activity of an incidental and possibly *ad hoc* nature will take place in and around it. This may comprise discussions among teachers, researchers and pupils; regular meetings among teachers or schools to discuss progress and problems, and to exchange information; possibly regional conferences; and related activities, all enhanced by the range of current hardware – tapes, video-recordings and transcripts.

Conclusion: examples of action research in the field of curriculum development

So far in our review of action research as a method, we have touched upon its principal characteristics, occasions when it may be used, conceptual issues and the stages of its implementation. Another important feature which we have only mentioned in passing concerns the problems and difficulties encountered in mounting this kind of project, especially when on a fairly ambitious scale. It is these problems and difficulties which help to give this particular methodology its special flavour. Often unforeseen, and therefore not prepared for, they are as valuable for what can be learned from them as are the planned aspects of a project. We conclude this chapter, then, with a problem-oriented look at two action-research-based projects of some magnitude which have been undertaken in the field of curriculum research and development in recent years – the Humanities Curriculum Project and the Keele Integrated Studies Project.

The first of these, the Humanities Curriculum Project, was set up in 1967 under the joint sponsorship of the Schools Council and the Nuffield Foundation. Its aim and premises we have listed in Box 1. The overall task of the project was to discover a teaching strategy which would implement these premises in the classroom, to report this strategy, and to support teachers who wished to develop it with training and if necessary with materials.

The problems and difficulties in mounting this project appear to have stemmed in the main from mistaken or incongruent attitudes and expectations on the part of the teachers in the experimental schools. Thus, their initial outlook tended to be coloured by earlier, more traditional approaches to the curriculum based on single-subject specialisms with the emphasis on improving teaching methods in these fields. They failed to appreciate that the venture had a social science basis and that they would need to adopt a suitably detached stance in keeping with its experimental nature. Having this kind of basis, the project was seen by the researchers as a means of testing hypotheses; many of the teachers, however, in awe of the presumed authority of the Schools Council, its sponsors, felt that they themselves were on trial. As a result, some of the experimental feedback was distorted. Misunderstandings with respect to the researchers' time perspective were another source of difficulty. The research team was concerned with long-term development; yet they were often perceived as attempting an instant and easy solution to problems. Finally, the teachers in the experimental schools tended to harbour feelings that the project would in some way help to solve problems of discipline and control. As it was, 'It made them more acute [and] opened them up instead of containing them' (Stenhouse).

The second example of the use of action research is that of the Keele Integrated Studies Project initiated in 1969. Notwithstanding the success of the project and the value of the accrued experience in implementing it, we here again restrict ourselves to some of the more problematic aspects. Difficulties arose once more from the way the project was perceived or misperceived by the teachers in the experimental schools, as well as from the ambiguous relationship they had with it (we refer you to Box 3, which lists the metaphors selected by one of the parties involved to describe the teachers' perceptions of the project). We will, however, focus our remarks on the problem of communication between teachers and researchers which seemed to persist throughout the undertaking.

Efforts on the part of the research team to inform the schools at the outset of the project's objectives by means of meetings, conferences and circulars met with sustained complaints from the teachers about jargon and the lack of specific advice. The latter at this stage were indifferent to the researchers' attempts to explain the principles of integration and theories of curriculum development. This bears out the point we made earlier about rival characterizations of teaching and research. Subsequently, however, after having experienced the practical difficulties of implementing integrated studies, the teachers reversed their complaint, demanding explanation and theoretical reasoning for what they were doing. The discrepancy between what they requested and what they were prepared to do resulted in a lasting tension. As Shipman (1974) points out, they wanted 'both academic rigour and easy-bake recipes from the same source'.

A further serious problem, yet another aspect of the communication gap, arose from the low priority given by the teachers to feedback. To this may be added their general reluctance to seek advice. In spite of the provision made by the researchers, only two out of the thirty-eight schools involved provided regular feedback to the research team. As Shipman again observes, this omission may be traced to the fact that the definitions of the project team and of the teachers were at different levels: 'The teachers were involved with their own problems and defined the project out of their own experience in their own classrooms. As a consequence the basic principles behind the project were usually misunderstood and often unconsidered.'

We see from all this that what is involved is group process and that this is not easy to handle. Favourable conditions for action research include the following: a willingness on the part of the teachers to admit limitations and to make themselves familiar with the basic techniques of research; the provision of opportunities to invent; the encouragement of new ideas; the provision of time for experimentation; a mutual trust of those involved; and a knowledge on the part of the participants of the fundamentals of group processes. Additionally, it must be realized that many minds working on the same problem will increase the number of ways of looking at it. There will be more suggested solutions and more effective criticisms of each proposed solution. It must also be recognized that action research involves a reeducation of teachers; that their attitudes and values will need to change; that the longer they have been in the job, the more difficult this will be; and that in all probability, it will be more difficult for secondary teachers (as opposed to primary teachers) because they are less used to working together.

In conclusion it might be added that in a representative sample of action research studies conducted in the United States, it was found (Hodgkinson, 1957) that the teachers taking part were generally enthusiastic. They seemed to feel that the staff worked more as a unit than before the research, that staff members were drawn closer together with the knowledge that they shared problems and goals, and that respect for individuals, both teachers and pupils, had increased.

References

Association for Supervision and Curriculum Development (1959) *Learning about Learning from Action Research*. National Educational Association of the United States, Washinton, DC.

Brown, R.K. (1967) Research and consultancy in industrial enterprises: a review of the contribution of the Tavistock Institute of Human Relations to the development of Industrial Sociology, *Sociology*, 1, 1 pp. 33–60.

Butcher, H.J. and Pont, H.B. (eds.) (1973) *Educational Research in Britain 3*. London, University of London Press.

Corey, S.M. (1953) *Action Research to Improve School Practices*. New York, Bureau of Publications, Teachers College, Columbia University.

Halsey, A.H. (ed.) (1972) *Educational Priority: Volume 1: E.P.A. Problems and Policies*. London, HMSO.

Hill, J.E. and Kerber, A., (1967) *Models, Methods, and Analytical Procedures in Educational Research*. Detroit, Wayne State University Press.

Hodgkinson, H.L. (1957) Action research – a critique, *J. Educ. Sociol.*, 31,4 pp. 137–153.

Marris, P. and Rein, M. (1967) *Dilemmas of Social Reform: Poverty and Community Action in the United States*. London, Routledge & Kegan Paul.

Shipman, M.D. (1974) *Inside a Curriculum Project*. London, Methuen.

Stenhouse, L., The humanities curriculum project, in Butcher and Pont, *Educational Research in Britain 3*. (op. cit.).

Travers, R.M.W., extract quoted in Halsey (ed.) *Educational Priority* (op. cit.).

Louis Cohen and Lawrence Manion (1980) in *Research Methods in Education*. Croom Helm, pp. 174–189.

Louis Cohen is Professor of Education at Loughborough University. At the time this material was written, Lawrence Manion was Head of Music at Manchester Polytechnic.

CHAPTER 4

IMPLEMENTING SCHOOL-BASED ACTION RESEARCH: SOME HYPOTHESES

John Elliott

In this chapter John Elliott describes how a DES Regional Course, planned in three phases over the 1977/1978 school year, helped teachers to carry out action research into the problems faced by schools in the area of mixed-ability teaching. Phase I identified, clarified and shared possible problems for investigation and explored the kinds of research methods which would be appropriate and feasible for teachers to use in collecting data in their schools. Phase II provided seminars and readings on methods of field research in school and support for the action research teams from LEA advisers acting as Area Leaders. At this stage, research reports in the form of case studies were produced. These formed the basis for discussion and analysis at the Phase III conference, held in April 1978.

About a third of the way through Phase II, it became clear from Area Leaders' verbal reports that many teams were having difficulty in getting themselves 'off the ground'. The hypotheses which follow were based largely on the data Area Leaders collected and reported to John Elliott. To test the extent to which they genuinely articulated the views of the teachers involved, a first draft of this document was discussed in small groups at the Phase III conference. The groups were given the task of testing the hypotheses against the experience of their members by citing supporting and counter-evidence. They were also asked to formulate any additional hypotheses they could generate from personal experience. This chapter incorporates the material contained in the small group reports, provides helpful guidance on likely problems in action research, and ways of avoiding or minimizing them.
[. . .]

Hypotheses

1. *Head teachers tend to be anxious about staff expertise at conducting action research in problem areas which are 'sensitive' within their schools.*

'The head felt that she had to be certain that the staff involved had sufficient expertise to carry out the research in a way that would make the results acceptable to the rest of the staff.'

It seems that the anxiety here is not so much about purely technical competence in the area of 'research methods', but about ethical competence when it comes to dealing with staff anxieties about the uses of the data collected by teacher-researchers. The following comment from another Area Leader's report would tend to support this view:

'Head teachers may fear that the procedures to be adopted will cause embarrassment for them or their schools. Frank discussion – within the school – should dispel this if the head teacher and the researcher are joined by someone such as an adviser, who will not only oversee the work when it begins, but also act as a link between the school and the course director, detailing the nature of the proposed exercise and giving an official reassurance about potentially confidential matters.'

Group 5 commented on this hypothesis at Phase III:

'Just as course members overestimated the amount and scope of work involved in this project, so heads and senior staff tended to overreact in terms of the implications they foresaw arising from action research.'

2. *When staff are not involved in or consulted at the planning stage they may react negatively when their cooperation in securing the teacher-researcher's access to data is required later.*

'The head felt it necessary to keep knowledge of the project to the science department in order not to cause parents to become disturbed. He did, in fact, have worried phone calls from them about it and the researcher was told by one teacher that he would have refused to allow any child of his to take part as he did not approve of children being used as guinea pigs. The question, therefore, of access to information in the project needs discussion before the start.'

Group 1 commented on this hypothesis at Phase III:

'The lack of response from faculty staff to a report about this course, and the failure to implement any action research, could be attributed to a lack of consultation with all the faculty staff prior to the course.'

3. *If the teacher-researcher's normal workload is reduced in ways which increase the workload of other teachers a 'boomerang' effect will occur when it comes to securing their cooperation in getting access to data.*

'. . . some extra time was given to the teacher-researcher at the expense of some staff, and part of his workload was shed onto other members of the department. The department obviously supported the project but there was a suggestion that not all members were keen . . .'

4. *(a) The emergence of 'a division of labour' between teachers who do research*

and those who don't is unlikely to foster staff cooperation in getting access to data; (b) The more research is viewed as a process to which all can contribute the more teachers will cooperate in giving each other access to data.

'Teacher-researchers may have difficulty in enlisting the cooperation and indulgence of their colleagues. Collaboration with them would be easier if they felt they too were part of the whole thing.'

Teachers in Group 1 cited some interesting evidence relevant to these hypotheses in their comments at Phase III:

'Giving staff specific tasks was successful in those situations where the staff felt that they were learning specific techniques as a result of doing the task, e.g. validation of objective tests.'

'Teachers were willing to cooperate with the researcher, but less willing to participate as researchers. Subsequently these teachers have all given permission for information gained by the research to be shared by others.'

'Staff were prepared to feed information to the researcher, but not to each other. Surprisingly, they then were willing to allow the researcher to pass their information to other staff.'

The first comment tends to support 4(a) inasmuch as it implies that staff cooperation in securing access to data is facilitated when staff are provided with opportunities to develop research skills.

The second and third comments appear to negate hypothesis 4(b) inasmuch as they suggest that the existence of a division of labour between teachers and teacher-researchers enables teachers to give each other access to data about their practices and views.

In my experience, outside researchers tend to serve the function of indirectly facilitating the sharing of data when teachers have been unable to share directly. I used to think this could be explained by the fact that 'outsiders' were not in a position to use the information against the teachers who give access. But the above comments suggest either that certain 'insiders' can also be perceived as not in a position to harm, or that they are perceived to be in a position to protect teachers against the harmful consequences of release, for example if they are sufficiently powerful in the hierarchy to exercise sanction against those who misuse information they receive.

Group 1 went on to generate a new hypothesis about the problems of securing staff cooperation for action research; namely,

The 'course syndrome' means that teachers who gain experience on courses can expect negative attitudes from the staffroom, which make it very difficult to implement action research in the school.

The following situations were cited in support:

'The reaction of departmental staff to a proposal for action research, arising out of the course, was felt by the researcher to have been provoked simply by attendance on the course.'

'Other members of the department initially reacted against new ideas for writing worksheets following my attendance of a short course. However, over a period of several months several new ideas were gradually incorporated into new worksheets being written. A time lapse seems to be part of the acceptance process.'

These examples are evidence of the tendency of teachers to treat ideas generated outside 'their situation' with suspicion and scepticism. Only when their origins are forgotten do they become accepted. This suggests that the effects of in-service courses based outside schools should be monitored in the long term as well as the short term. It is only now, over a year after the Phase I conference, that course members are beginning to claim that other staff are becoming involved in action research within their schools.

5. *'Undercurrents' among the staff may make it impossible for any individual or group within a school to initiate and sustain either (a) collaborative action research among staff; or (b) staff cooperation with the teacher-researchers in the school. In these circumstances the intervention of an external 'change agent' is necessary.*

'There is also some disappointment at the paucity of support eventually gained from members of the staffrooms of participating schools. The original hope, that conference members should be representative of a larger group within each school, was not realized, and in hindsight it is clear that Area Leaders should have taken a more active part in the initial dissemination of information and encouragement. The intention was a good one. There was clearly a psychological advantage if the motivation could spring from within the staffroom, but in at least one case the undercurrents were underrated.'

6. *Collaborative programmes of action research are unlikely to be sustained in schools when they are given low priority at the levels of either school or departmental policy.*

'Difficulties still encountered were explained as being due to lack of priority within individual schools and subject departments.'

7. *Teachers are unlikely to commit themselves to action research in their schools if commitment receives little recognition or reward from 'senior management'.*

'The prestige of the teacher within the school hierarchy is an important factor for success, and may need to be boosted from outside.'

The following example was provided in Group 1 as relevant to hypothesis 6.

'The head teacher spoke highly of the work to be done to governors, visitors, etc., but in confidence told the research team that due to staff shortage, heavy timetabling commitments and a full school programme the research was "low priority". This resulted in a reduction of the effectiveness of the project.'

Group 1 posed the following counter-hypothesis to No. 7 asserting 'benefits directly related to their teaching' as a greater motivational force than more extrinsic benefits derived from recognition by the hierarchy.

Teachers are likely to commit themselves to action research in their schools if commitment results in personal benefits directly related to their teaching.

'Although no apparent career gains are forthcoming from the action research personal benefits have made it well worthwhile.'

'Unexpected side benefits from action research, such as deeper awareness of my effectiveness as a teacher, interactions between teacher and students, and students and students, made the undertaking of research a worthwhile project in itself.'

The following example was offered in support of the new hypothesis:

'Interest in working parties within the school had lapsed, probably because recommendations were not being implemented. However, as part of his involvement in action research, the deputy head started an evaluation of the options system letting it be known that changes were to be considered seriously. This created interest among staff outside the original action research team and a series of well-attended meetings produced a radically new option scheme which has been adopted in the school.'

This example, however, doesn't unambiguously support the counter-hypothesis rather than No. 7. The motivation to participate in the research could have sprung as much from the fact that it was recognized as important by a member of 'senior management' as from the fact that it would lead to improvements in practice. At least one member of the group expressed some scepticism as to whether *all* teachers were motivated by 'benefits directly related to their teaching':

'When it became apparent that no rewards of recognition, that is "free time guarantees" could be made then only staff who were motivated by intrinsic rewards would participate.'

Group 2 collapsed hypotheses 6 and 7 into the following proposition:

Teachers are unwilling to commit themselves to, and sustain, action research in schools unless support is seen to come from senior management in the form of encouragement and forward planning.

'In planning our project issues arose that required senior management to create the necessary situations for action research to take place. From an early date no commitment was given to establish such situations and this naturally limited the aspirations of the researchers. Consequently, the only safe approach thought likely to produce an end product was research on an individual basis. However, without free time to carry out the suggested methods of research, the researcher neglected the more time-consuming elements of that research and produced material based on opinion, observation, or known staff evaluations of work collected over the researcher's teaching experience.

'Nevertheless, data collected in this manner was considered to be of value when drawing conclusions and suggesting modifications to existing programmes of work. Also staff in the school showed a willingness to participate in the project once it was clearly shown that the help sought would most likely lead to some improvement in the effectiveness of their own teaching.

'When we reported to a head of department meeting that the maths department would embark upon a programme of action research into problems in mixed ability teaching there was a nil response. Senior management did not show a willingness to commit themselves or the school to action research but were quite willing for the maths department to be committed. Within the department the time factor was a great influence – most staff have heavy teaching loads and extra responsibilities.'

Group 2 made the following recommendations with respect to institutional support of action research:

General recommendation:

It is essential that all staff be informed of the total commitment involved and the support available for any action research.

Specific recommendations:

(i) Heads join initial discussions.
(ii) All staff to be informed of the commitment by head/senior team member.
(iii) Timing of research to be realistic in terms of academic year and length of research.
(iv) Heads to indicate to staff the *now* formulated research requirements. This will be given once areas of investigation have been decided.
(v) If 'other' schools are involved in the research the liaison and meeting with staff be instigated by the head.

(vi) Careful selection of research and research members, high status of individual research. If team research then junior members would be accepted/desirable.

(vii) Workload to be reduced by interdepartmental reallocation or consideration given to timetable allocation at the beginning of academic year.

(viii) To ensure complete interdepartmental collaboration each department propose one of their members to liaise with research team to carry out 'sensitive area' investigations.

(ix) 'Pats on back' accompanied with 'you are doing a grand job'. Jealousy of other members of staff notwithstanding!

The comments on hypotheses 6 and 7 as a whole could be interpreted as indicating general support for No. 6 but some reservations about No. 7 with respect to action research conducted by individual teachers into their own perceived classroom problems (as opposed to collaborative investigations of 'departmental' or 'whole school' problems). Hence perceived benefits to their teaching, rather than hierarchically bestowed recognition and rewards, might be a more powerful factor in the motivation for research at the level of individual teachers' particular classrooms.

8. *Initial research aspirations remain unfulfilled when teachers receive no allocation of 'bounded time', in which they are free to set aside other commitments to give priority to action research.*

One Area Leader reported the following comments made by teachers:
'Time is an obvious factor but one which works in multitudinous ways. At risk of sounding like a union representative I have three lunchtimes a week taken out by duties and one break per week. I have two evening meetings of 1½ hours each per week as part of my necessary school role. (Neither meeting is strictly productive in terms of work in the classroom, but administrative.) My duty allocation is slightly less than for non-Heads of Department. Year group planning meetings are additional to this basic load. There is considerable resistance to additional new activities unless directly related to work in hand, assessment, moderation or mutual support in the context of here and now.

'It may be a purely personal factor but I find I need a long steady spell at working on research activities and mulling through new ideas. I tend not to make headway when interrupted by third-year English, break duty, requests for repair of equipment, sorting out the office's mistaken orders, seeing students in trouble, etc. Schools tend not to be the places where you can retreat never to be found by the Secretary.

'Much of what we already do is in a sense action research in that we break new ground continually for ourselves, both in resourcing courses from our own devices and in coping with new ability groupings. This continually has strong elements of assessment, discussion of tactics and organization. But of course it tends to lack form, and we work on the "suck it and see" basis. There may often be a fear of knowing only too well when one fails – having it rubbed in does not always help! Equally, we need to know more about why things go well. What we need is periodical time to stand back, in a more relaxed way, allow the daily tensions and flotsam to ebb away and see things in a clearer perspective – and this is probably the heart of the matter: one dons so many different hats in a day and has such continual change of activity that it is desperately hard to see any one thing long enough to think about it.'

In another Area two advisers summed up the feelings of many teachers:

'The time allocation for work of this nature needs to be carefully gauged, and its relationship to the normal patterns of the school year remains critical.'

A member of Group 1 described the effects of reductions in time allocation on the research conducted in his school:

'The project team had hoped to implement their planned research some of which was to take place during existing "free time". However, illness, staff shortage, etc., resulted in a significant and sustained loss of this existing free time and consequently the planned research was modified and shortened to compensate for this. This in fact meant that the research became quantitatively biased.'

9. *A common cause of failure by teachers to implement an action research plan is that it tends to be overambitious and unrealistic both with respect to scale and to the methods and techniques employed.*

'. . . despite clear and timely warning from the course director, most participants have underestimated the workload involved in research of this kind. When this has led to compromise solutions, or a curtailed version of the project, there is a mistaken yet understandable sense of failure.'

'Difficulties may arise if head teachers, advisers, heads of department, and the teacher-researchers themselves do not appreciate the implications of doing research in school. They should be made aware of the time, consultations, techniques, and active support that will be necessary so that the size of the task they commit themselves to is realistic.'

In Group 1, one school team argued that:

'Our projects were not overambitious in content but the period available for research was both too short and unsuitably aligned in relation to the major fixed events of the school year. A four-term span would have been more realistic in that it would have made it possible to incorporate data only available late in the spring term and a research project involving another school would have been more easily incorporated within a prepared scheme of work.'

Group 2 commented:

'This is only a viable statement where a clear objective for the research has been established with all of the likely participants before the research has commenced.'

Where long-term research is involved there are too many variables concerned in teaching that cannot be foreseen, measured or controlled and it is the effect of these variables that is the dominant cause of any apparent failure to complete the task within the desired time.

Where there has been a failure to complete an area of research based on the work of the course it has been brought about by (a) confusion in the beginning as to the purpose of the exercise; and (b) the uncontrollable limitation of the time factor by outside influences, for example staff and pupil changes, absence of staff-pupils, etc., and schools being subjected to massive reorganizations.

10. *Teacher-researchers in schools tend to opt for quantitative methods of data collection – questionnaires and objective tests – rather than qualitative methods – naturalistic observation and interview – because the latter involve 'personalised' situations in which the colleagues and pupils observed or interviewed find it difficult to mentally divorce a person's position and role as researcher from his/her other positions and roles within the school.*

The problem of teacher-researchers using qualitative methods has been well reported by Davidson, a teacher who was not a member of the mixed-ability research team in her school, but who found herself observing one of her colleagues who was. The colleague was 'standing in' for the class's normal teacher, whom Davidson had originally negotiated her observational study of the class with. But the presence of the 'stand in' teacher brought another observer in the class in the form of one of my full-time Advanced Diploma students who was helping her to collect data as part of the mixed-ability project. Davidson, who had taught the class she was observing and was Head of House in the school, writes:

'. . . the students were extremely curious about the presence of the observer who was known to them. Although the teacher could generally command the students' attention, there was noticeable distraction, as students turned around to observe the observer, and discussed amongst themselves whether the tape recorder was running or not.

'When the class began practical work a whole procession of children came to ask the observer, "why she was there?", "what was she doing?", "was the tape recorder recording them?", and the observer was placed in a quandary – to satisfy their curiosity would take too long, and disrupt the lesson further; not to reply would shroud the whole procedure in mystery and increase their curiosity.

'The observer was sitting at a side bench about half-way between the teacher and the back of the class. The outside observer was sitting at the side, but right at the back of the class.

'Interestingly no children appeared to approach him, although subsequently he reported that one or two had done so.

'Two other problems occurred when students, involved in practical work, were encountering problems, and because the class teacher was busy with another group, they approached the observer for help – naturally enough as she was known to them as a science teacher. The second involved the observer's normal reaction to misbehaviour in the classroom. When observing a group who were obviously just playing about, the temptation to become a "teacher" and intervene was extremely strong.

'It became apparent as the lesson progressed that the unexplained presence of another member of staff in the classroom was so disturbing that some explanation to the students would have to be made. As the lesson ended the observer followed the class to its next lesson and asked the teacher for a few minutes of time. Something of what the observer was trying to do was explained to the class, and they were asked that in future they would try to ignore the observer's presence as much as possible. They were also asked why their response to the two observers (one known to them, the other not) was so different. "You had a tape recorder", "We know you, we didn't know him", were the two main replies.'

Davidson found her presence not only disruptive with students initially but with the class's normal teacher as well. At one point during the lesson she felt her presence was so inhibiting the normal responses of the teacher to the kind of situation that had arisen, that she decided to leave.

'During the third visit the observer only remained in the room for the formal part of the lesson, when the teacher was working with the whole class. The decision to do this was partly due to pressure of time but also the unease felt by the observer in a practical situation; because the teacher seemed to exercise less control over the activities of the class than he would have done with the observer absent. That is, the observer gained the impression that her presence inhibited the response of the teacher to groups or individuals who were misbehaving.'

Two comments issued from members of Group 5 on this tenth hypothesis:

'In the light of current pressures and concerns over the use of more objective criteria for assessment should it not have been foreseen that course members would opt for quantitative methods of data collection in preference to more subjective alternatives, for example naturalistic observation and interview?'

As course director I was aware of these pressures and attempted to introduce qualitative approaches at the Phase I conference and then to further develop understanding in response to specific methodological problems as they arose during the research. I thought I had made it clear that I could be used as a consultant on research methods and that teachers on full-time secondment undergoing a course in qualitative methodology would be available to assist them in the collection of qualitative data. The other comment from a member of Group 5 indicates that at least one person felt that inadequate provision had been made for developing an understanding of, and skills in, quantitative methods.

'The use of quantitative methods of data collection, questionnaires and objective tests, introduces another level of expertise and understanding. If it was foreseen that course members might fall back on these rather than qualitative methods then some attempt might have been made to introduce them to these techniques.'

The view that teachers feel less competent and confident in using qualitative methods than they do with quantitative methods and require specialist training is echoed in Group 2's comments on this hypothesis:

'In general we agree with the hypothesis although if true this tends to run counter to the previous hypothesis (9) since it indicates that the researcher has been realistic by using methods with which he is familiar and feels competent to handle.

'The qualitative method is a valuable tool but it requires a degree of training which is not normally available to teachers. Interviewing techniques require a special discipline in the preparation and presentation of questions and in the interpretation of answers over and above that required for quantitative methods because of the personalized, face-to-face nature of the technique.

'We consider that it is true to say that even though interviewer and interviewee try to completeley divorce themselves from their normal roles as colleagues and holders of positions within the school hierarchy, this presents difficulties since even if they do attempt this it immediately brings a further artificiality into the situation.'

Guidelines for research conducted by teachers

Group 3's discussion of the hypotheses resulted in the production of suggestions for resolving the kinds of problems they refer to. The guidelines document they submitted reads as follows:

'Research can be conducted by teachers in their schools in a number of ways and for a variety of reasons.

'Given that a teacher wishes to undertake some research in his school, the first task is to decide on the appropriate people to consult. This is necessary both for organizational and ethical reasons. Diplomacy and sensitivity are prerequisites for any kind of successful work. It is impossible in these guidelines to be more precise about who to consult since this depends on the nature of the research, the position in the school of the teacher concerned and the general ethos of the school. One simple example will perhaps make these points clear. Let us suppose that a class teacher wishes to undertake some research purely for his own benefit. Let us suppose that the research, though taking place in school time, in no way affects the normal activities of that teacher's class. Let us suppose further, that the teacher requires no extra time and no special equipment or materials. In no way does the research intrude on or involve the activities of anyone else. *Even so* it would be a matter of courtesy for the teacher to inform his head of department, quite apart from the fact that the results of his research might well be of interest to other people.

'The next stage after initial consultation is for the teacher to issue a statement of intent. There is no point in doing this first of all since original ideas will probably have been modified during the consultation stage.

'Having established the necessary areas of agreement and cooperation and having decided on the nature of the research the teacher then needs to make a detailed plan. During the planning stage four major factors need to be considered. These are: (i) the time scale; (ii) the people involved; (iii) the methods used; (iv) the end result.

'The first detail about the time scale is that the total period of time involved should be specified. Next, the period of work should be tailored to fit the varying work load within any one school year. Even if the thinking-planning stage is fairly lengthy the aim for actively carrying out the research should be for a short period of fairly intense activity:

If it were done when 'tis done, then 'twere well it were done quickly.

(Macbeth I, i)

'The involvement of other people covers three main aspects, namely, protocol, logistics, and active participation. All three groups need to be consulted during the detailed planning stage.

'The active participants also need to be involved when deciding on the research methods to be used. When considering methods there is a temptation to aim for the collection of too much data. The aim should always be to collect the smallest usable quantity of data involving the simplest suitable methods. If the teacher is unable to decide which method to use then it would be sensible to plan for a brief trial run in which the various methods can be compared and one selected for the main body of the work. No details can be offered on specific methods – there are too many. But whichever method is used two big questions have to be satisfactorily answered.

'(i) Is the method suitable for the people involved – in other words can they do it and will they like it?

'(ii) Will this method provide the necessary information? (This is a truism, but unless teachers design their own research methods they could be tempted to use someone else's impressive technique without considering suitability. The frequent misuse of standardized tests is a classic example of this.)

'One final area that needs consideration during the detailed planning stage is that of confidentiality and dissemination of information. The details here need to be worked out very precisely indeed.

'And so to action. There is little that can be said about this stage except to offer one useful technique and to advise one necessary procedure. The technique is to keep a diary of events – the ground plan and what actually happens. The procedure is to regularly check progress in order to ensure that the right data are being collected in the easiest way. When analysing work in progress every effort should be made to avoid "arranging" the results. Too many issues in education are not properly resolved precisely because people start with an unproven assumption and carefully select data to "prove" it.

'Having undertaken the research we move to the final stage. There is a logical sequence of events in the final stage:

(i) Drawing conclusions. It is quite possible that the involvement of others here would be a good idea. The sheer mass of data might make it difficult for one person to cope. If the research is on a controversial subject then acceptance of the results is probably more likely if "less involved" people are brought in to help in the final assessment.

(ii) Presentation and dissemination are clearly important. Exactly how the results are presented depends of course on what "after-effects" are hoped for. Unless it is intended that others should use the raw data for their own conclusion making, then it is probably better to present that data in a clear condensed form. Anyone who doubts this last point should reread the Bullock Report. Data presentation deserves some thought and not simply about who to. The most effective time, manner and place ought to be considered carefully as well. A brief mention in a crowded agenda for Friday afternoon staff meeting is not likely to generate very much enthusiasm.

(iii) Implementation of the findings may well involve further negotiation. An essential part of any form of implementation should be continuous monitoring of progress.

(iv) Lastly, it is very probable that the initial research and its implementation will prompt further research – and so this process continues.'

John Elliott (1979) *Cambridge Journal of Education* Vol. 9, Part 1, pp. 55–71.
John Elliott is Tutor in Curriculum Studies at Cambridge Institute of Education.

CHAPTER 5

CASE STUDY

J. Nisbet & J. Watt

Open University students will be familiar with the case study as a method of studying an institution or process. A case study approach is particularly appropriate for an individual researcher, because it gives an opportunity for one aspect of a problem to be studied in depth within a limited timescale, though it must be said that some case studies have been conducted over a long period of time. John Nisbet and Joyce Watt in this chapter, and Clem Adelman, David Jenkins and Stephen Kemmis in Chapter 6 discuss the advantages and disadvantages of this approach, techniques that may be used and methods of recording evidence. They give guidance about analysis, draw attention to the importance of social skills in the conduct of a case study and stress the desirability of using plain language in reports wherever possible. Case studies are not easy to do, as is pointed out in Chapter 6, but the guidance provided in this and the following chapter will be invaluable for any investigator embarking on a case study for the first time.

1 Introduction

The experienced lecturer knows how effective it is when he uses a specific instance to illustrate a general principle. The interest of the audience is held when he talks about real people or an actual event instead of theoretical principles and abstract ideas. The journalist's technique is to start with a person or a story, and to move later to his general theme. Students in a course often remember the illustrative anecdote, even when they have difficulty in recalling the point which it illustrated.

But it is not just a matter of creating or maintaining interest. Often we understand an idea better if we have an example before us. The specific detail is something which we are familiar with, and the single instance helps us to see how the abstract principles fit together. Quoting cases to illustrate gives the picture a three-dimensional reality.

Researchers frequently use individual cases in this way in their reports, to back up the results of their analytic studies, and to help the reader to understand their conclusions. For example, a study of transition from primary to secondary school (or from school to university) may show the importance of giving pupils some preliminary introduction to the next stage of their education. A specific instance of a school which has done this, describing what was done, how it was arranged, the problems encountered and what the pupils said about it, helps to clarify what is implied by the more technical findings of the research study.

A case study is more than just an extended example or an anecdote interestingly narrated. It has the same virtues – interest, relevance, a sense of reality – but it goes beyond mere illustration. First it gathers evidence *systematically*, in a 'scientific' way, as will be explained. Second, it is concerned essentially with the *interaction* of factors and events. Sometimes it is only by taking a practical instance that we can obtain a full picture of this interaction. Statistical analysis can identify important determining factors in a problem area; but to establish how these factors relate to each other in the real situation, it may be necessary to examine a specific case systematically and in detail. Such a systematic investigation of a specific instance is *case study*. The instance may be an event or a person or a group, a school or an institution, or an innovation such as a new syllabus, a new method of teaching or a new method of organization.

Freud used cases in this way to develop his theories, and was criticized for basing conclusions on samples of one. Case study, however, can sometimes penetrate aspects which are not readily accessible by methods which rely on large numbers. Sometimes case study can be used complementary to large-scale inquiry, each method making its own distinctive contribution to understanding an overall problem.

In recent years, educational researchers have begun to use case study methods more extensively. There has been a growing acceptance of case study as a research methodology in its own right, and a recognition that it is possible to develop general procedural guidelines. As a research method, it is still developing, but already there is sufficient agreement among the researchers who use this method to allow us to set down rules of procedure and requirements to be met if a particular study is to be accepted as a valid contribution to knowledge.

2 Case study as research methodology

2.1 *What is a case study?*

The case study draws on the techniques of observational studies, and aims to give a portrayal of a specific situation in such a way as to illuminate some more general principle. The definition adopted in the 1976 Cambridge conference on the topic (Adelman et al., 1977, pp. 139–150) is that *'case study is an umbrella term for a family of research methods having in common the decision to focus an inquiry round an instance'*. As mentioned above, a shorter definition is suggested: *'a systematic investigation of a specific instance'*. The method attempts to give a fair and accurate account of a specific case in such a way as to allow the reader to penetrate the superficial record, and also to check the author's interpretations by examining an appropriate selection of the objective evidence from which the case study has been built.

This description obviously begs a number of questions. What is an 'appropriate selection'? What is 'objective evidence'? Can one give a 'fair and accurate account'? These issues are matters of keen debate among the researchers who are trying to develop this new style.

In case study, evidence is gathered by a variety of techniques. These include observation, interviews, examining documents or records or pupils' work. Several different sources of information are likely to be used in any one study. Sufficient should be presented to allow the reader to see how the conclusions are reached and also to allow him to develop alternative interpretations. Though interviews and observation, and even the selection of documents for study, are all likely to be influenced by subjective judgement or personal bias, it is possible to achieve a degree of objectivity by bringing bias out into the open. A basic principle in case study work is *cross-checking* findings from one interview with those of another, or checking interviews against documents and vice versa [. . .]. Other ways of ensuring that the report is fair and accurate are described in subsequent sections.

2.2 *Examples of case studies*

One of the most substantial studies of this kind was Elizabeth Richardson's report on Nailsea School. The report of her three-year study of this one school was published in the book, *The Teacher, The School and the Task Of Management* (Heinemann, 1973). Nailsea School was in the process of changing from a selective secondary school to a comprehensive school. Elizabeth Richardson's special concern was to study how the school administration adapted to this change. With the generous cooperation of the head and staff, she sat in on meetings, interviewed staff and collected a mass of information. As a detached observer, she attempted to interpret what she saw, and tested her interpretations in discussions with the staff. Her portrayal of the 'task of management' had a depth which would have been impossible if she had tried instead to cover a large number of schools using conventional survey techniques.

A rather different role, that of participant observer, was taken by David Hargreaves in his study of a secondary modern school (*Social Relations in a Secondary School*, Routledge & Kegan Paul, 1967). Participant observation is a special kind of technique, in which the researcher becomes a member of a group or institution and records what it is like to be actively involved in the events which he is studying. By describing 'from the inside', he has access to information which would probably be denied to an outsider. Obviously the role of participant, of being involved, is difficult to reconcile with the detached neutral role of the conventional researcher. [. . .]

Case studies are often limited to quite specific issues. As a final example, before we go on to set down guidelines for tackling a case study, here is a brief summary of David Hamilton's work on a specific curriculum innovation, 'Handling innovations in the classroom: two Scottish examples' (published as Chapter 5 in Reid and Walker, 1975).

Hamilton's purpose was to study a new science syllabus – the Scottish Integrated Science scheme, outlined in Curriculum Paper 7 of the Scottish Education Department (HMSO, 1969) – and in particular to see how the syllabus was implemented in the classroom. He observed the teaching of the syllabus in two comprehensive schools, which he called 'Simpson' and 'Maxwell'. He also conducted interviews with teachers, and gave six short questionnaires to pupils, during sixteen weeks of fieldwork in a period from October 1970 to March 1972. The results are very different for the two schools, and Hamilton was able to show how the unique conditions in each school influenced, modified and even distorted, the implementation of the syllabus.

The practical constraints of school organization, the attitudes of staff, and the availability of equipment, resources and accommodation proved to be important factors; and the description shows clearly the interaction of these factors in two contrasting settings.

There are many examples of this style of inquiry; for example, Marten Shipman's analysis of the Keele Integrated Science Project, *Inside a Curriculum Project: a case study in the process of curriculum change* (1974).

The evaluation of the Humanities Curriculum Project, *Towards Judgment* (Hamingson, 1973) makes effective use of the method, as does the Safari Project (Norris, 1977). Both of these projects were linked with the Centre for Applied Research in Education, University of East Anglia, which has done much of the pioneering work in refining the case study approach.

2.3   The strengths and weaknesses of the case study method

The *case study* looks at a single instance, and aims to identify the unique features of interaction within that instance. Its *strengths* are that the results are more easily understood by a wide readership beyond the professional research circle: they are immediately intelligible (if the report is well written) and have a three-dimensional reality, like a good documentary. Also the case study provides suggestions for intelligent interpretation of other similar cases. A particular important benefit is the possibility of a case study identifying a pattern of influences that is too infrequent to be discernible by the more traditional statistical analyses. It is a style of inquiry which is particularly suited to the individual researcher, in contrast to other styles which require a research team.

It has a number of *weaknesses*. The results are not easily generalizable, except by an intuitive judgement that 'this case' is similar to 'that case'. Again, the observer in a case study has to be selective but his selectivity is not normally open to the checks which can be applied in rigorously systematic inquiries such as large-scale surveys – it tends to be personal and subjective. It is, however, flexible, and thus it can pick up unanticipated effects; it can change to take account of a new insight. But we cannot tell how the observer's perception has affected the conclusions reached.

These strengths and weaknesses can be seen more clearly if we contrast the case study with the systematic techniques of the *survey*. The survey identifies the elements which are *common* to a number of persons or observations. Its strengths are that it leads to generalizable findings (though generalization is sometimes dubious), and its procedures (questionnaire, interview schedule, sampling) are well tested. It has two serious weaknesses. First, it may obliterate the unique features and patterns within small groups, or even within an institution or an individual (in the sense of an interacting constellation of factors) which may hold the key to the puzzle. Second, the researcher finds only what he seeks: if something is not covered in the survey instruments, it will be missed unless the respondent particularly wishes to supply extra information.

Both survey and case study involve formulation of *hypotheses*. Without hypotheses, both become merely a formless and uninformative rag-bag of observations. Hypotheses have to be specified at an earlier stage in a survey, and this makes it more rigorous, but also more limited. In case study, it is possible to preserve a more open approach until the researcher has really begun to 'get the feel' of the situation.

The two approaches can be used to complement each other: together, they represent the macro and micro approaches. A large-scale survey can be followed up by case studies, to test out conclusions by examining specific instances. Alternatively, for opening up a new problem where it is difficult to formulate hypotheses, the case study may precede a survey, to identify key issues.

2.4 The status of case study

Case study is a standard procedure in other fields such as law, medicine and business studies. In educational reports, it has long been the practice to include descriptive accounts of schools, classes, experiments and even individual children. In education, however, this kind of descriptive writing was not generally considered as 'research'; essentially, it was seen as an activity which required artistic or literary skills, in contrast to 'true research' which was sometimes thought to depend more on the skills of numeracy and statistical analysis.

Participant observation studies, from the 1950s proved that they could open up areas of investigation which were not accessible to conventional research techniques. Whyte's *Street Corner Society* (1955) in the USA, and the work of Hargreaves (1967) and Lacey (1970) in Britain are early examples. These studies began to develop specialized techniques to guard against impressionist journalistic writing. In sociology, as in other social sciences, there has been a reaction against exclusive reliance on precise experimental design, especially the kind which is accompanied by sophisticated (if sometimes unintelligible) statistical analysis. In education Glaser and Strauss (1967) argued that theory should not precede the design of a research study, but should be the product of it, being grounded on observation. In Britain, the work of Parlett and Hamilton (1972) on 'illuminative evaluation' was the corresponding 'trigger' for a swing away from conventional psychometrics in educational research. Generally, there is now a greater willingness to accept an 'open' style of research, at least as complementary to conventional styles.

The point is illustrated by a widely publicized address by Cronbach in 1975, who criticized the precise experimental design which characterized his own previous research; an approach which had won him an international reputation as an educational psychologist. He proposed instead a more open approach.

> Instead of making generalization the ruling consideration in our research, I suggest that we reverse our priorities. An observer collecting data in one particular situation is in a position to appraise a practice or proposition in that setting, observing effects in context. In trying to describe and account for what happened, he will give attention to whatever variables were controlled but he will give equally careful attention to uncontrolled variables.

The phrase 'observing effects in context', is important. It is the context which is often the key to understanding effects in education. The context performs an integrating function, and it cannot be ignored, because each context is unique. The empirical style of research which builds a theory by establishing experimentally tested findings and adding them together, has to be supplemented by the style of inquiry which looks at the whole scene in context. In this sense, the whole is more than the sum of its parts.

3   Design and development

One of the strengths which we have noted in the case study method is its capacity to take into account the uncontrolled variables, those aspects of a situation – often important ones – which you have not clearly foreseen at the time when you begin to gather your data. Consequently, a case study should start with an *open phase*, a general review without prejudgement. Then you must *focus* on those aspects which you identify as of crucial importance. The third stage involves putting on paper, in *draft* form your interpretation. Before you can put this into its final form, you must *check* your interpretations with your informants, to take account of (but not necessarily accept) their critical comments.

3.1   The open phase

Start with an initial open approach – read and observe, but resist the pressure to construct hypotheses or a conceptual framework, and put aside preconceptions. This is easier said than done. It is impossible to be absolutely open, for the choice of a case for study emerges from the belief that it is important, and this implies certain preconceived values. All observation implies some element of selection, by which you decide what to pay attention to. In an interview, the process of question and answer can seldom make much progress unless both you and the respondent share some common assumption on what kind of answer is expected. However, it is possible to frame your questions in an open style rather than in a closed format: 'What happened then?' rather than 'Was it a success?,' or 'Who was involved?' rather then 'did Mr X decide?' (see section 4.1 for a fuller account). In observation, or in scanning documents, try to get a general impression rather than look for evidence for or against some hypothesis. Ted Wragg says of this stage:

> There is something of a risk involved . . . The observer plays intelligent Martian and waits for areas of concern to invade his consciousness. 'What if none appear?' is the awful thought. Presumably the observer is then reduced to describe the apparently massive importance of every-day banalities, like a frantic ethnomethodologist in search of profundity.

Brian Jackson (1978) describes his method for this stage in a series of case studies of immigrant children starting school:

> My method was to have no method. A bit like the old Yorkshire advice: Hear all, see all, say nowt. Try it. It is, I find, extremely difficult . . . Instead of going for the measurable, I've gone for the texture of growing up; instead of asking, I've tried to listen and see.

How long this first stage should last is difficult to say. Much depends on how long you have for the whole study. It is often an anxious time for the researcher and you have to resist the temptation to resolve the anxiety by a premature decision (some of the difficulties and pressures are described in section 6). Even in the traditional hypotheticodeductive method of research, it is a mistake to formulate your hypotheses too soon; but in case study, you must be prepared for a rather longer period for the initial open phase.

3.2 Focus

Eventually, you must identify the central events or features in the case, or key individuals in an institution. You focus these selected aspects, and tentatively formulate your hypothesis to explain them. It is still necessary to keep an open mind and to be ready to revise or abandon these preliminary ideas. It is unlikely that you will get it right first time. But in the second phase, your collection of evidence becomes more systematic and thorough. Unless you introduce a focus in your inquiries, you will end up with a mass of unconnected detail.

3.3 *Draft*

It was suggested earlier (section 2.4) that case study is an art which requires literary skill as much as research expertise. Certainly, the expression in words of the evidence and its interpretation is a very important part of the whole process. This is discussed more fully in section 6. You have to find a way of recording your data concisely and yet lucidly and as impartially as possible.

So, at quite an early stage in the process, you must try to summarize the evidence you are gathering and to write down the interpretations which you are making. This is the third stage in a case study, and it too is a difficult stage.

All these stages overlap one with the other. At stage two, the points of focus emerge gradually from the open phase; and similarly this task of preparing a draft report gradually takes over from the gathering of evidence, although you will still find it necessary to continue with data collection while you are trying to express in writing what you have found so far. One way of doing this is to set aside time to write up groups of interviews, or summarize a document review, or record a sequence of events. These are preliminary drafts, which will be helpful when you have to bring all the material together in your final report. When you are using interviews, make a special note of statements which express attitudes clearly or vividly. These are particularly valuable in conveying an impression of what was said, if they are recorded in the actual words used. The reader senses the different vocabulary and manner of speech used by the person quoted and this is more persuasive than a version written in your own style. Another method is to keep a diary; you need to do this in order to have a record of work, but you can also use it to try out the formulation of your ideas in private.

3.4 *Check*

When you have provisional drafts of parts of your report, it is important to check what you have written with those persons who have given you the information. There are several reasons for this.

First, it is part of the contract which you make when you embark on a case study. When you interview someone, or are given permission to consult documents, you should give an undertaking that you will allow the person involved to see and comment on that section of your report before it is put into final form (see section 5) if they so wish. Some case study workers argue that the other person should be given a veto, that the final version should be 'negotiated'. Our own experience is that a prior agreement on these terms often leads to an impasse, or to a bland report in which one has to read between the lines to get beyond commonplaces. Our recommendation is to promise informants the right to see the section of the report and the records which refer to them (subject to confidentiality); to undertake to take full account of these and modify the original where possible; and if not agreed, to guarantee the right to have their comment, criticism or reply published alongside. When this is done, it is at least made clear whether the participants accept or reject the interpretations made.

Second, where a statement or viewpoint is attributed to an individual person, he must be given the opportunity to check whether he accepts it. Even if you know that he actually said what you have written, your evidence is immediately suspect if he subsequently denies this, or argues that it is misleading because it is out of context.

The most important reason for checking your draft with those who have supplied information is that they are often helpful in suggesting a better way of expressing the point, or they may add other evidence in support, or they may wish to qualify the statement. Certainly you should not see your task as wresting information from unwilling informants. If a relationship of mutual trust can be established from the start [. . .], you will be surprised at the help which people will give, and the interest they take in ensuring that the record is straight.

It is therefore important to leave time for this final stage of consultation. You may have to make quite a lot of changes, and so you should not be too possessive about your draft. The final report will usually be greatly improved as a result of these discussions, if they are skilfully and tactfully handled.

4 Suggestions on procedure

For each of the methods of gathering data for your case study – interviews, observation and study of documents – it is possible to give suggestions on procedure.

4.1 *Interviews*

In case studies of educational institutions, such as a school, a community centre, a social group or club, or an innovation or experiment, the interview is the basic research instrument. The case study interview has a style of its own. The interview method used in large scale surveys follows a carefully constructed interview schedule, so that the responses from each person can be aggregated, each question having been presented in a standardized form. The case study interview is much more loosely structured. It has to allow each person to respond in his own unique way. Consequently, you let the respondent set the pace and choose the direction of the interview. Provide minimal stimulus, enough to start him talking and to maintain the flow. Let him structure his response: don't impose your structure.

However, you cannot play a wholly passive role. You have to give some indication of the topics or the general area you want him to talk about. To be ready for this, you may need to do some previous study of documents or records of other interviews, so that you know which aspects are important for him and so that you can demonstrate your own understanding of his role and thereby show that you are a serious enquirer, competent, knowledge-able and intelligent. To strike the proper balance between openness and structure is difficult.

The solution to this dilemma is to alter the balance gradually as the interview proceeds. At the beginning, play a listening role. Use non-directive techniques: for example, make your comments neutral and brief; or, when he pauses, rephrase the respondent's last statement with an interrogative intonation, and this provides a neutral encouragement for him to continue developing the point he is making. If a judgement is implied anywhere, rephrase his statement and check that you have caught the correct implication. You do not need to believe all that you are told, but for most of the interview do not challenge or contradict. In the later stages of the interview, however, you may begin to take a more positive part in the questioning. You will have formed some interpretations: check these, either by referring back and rephrasing, as already suggested in this paragraph, or by deliberately presenting challenging statements. This last point is an example of a procedure which has to be applied intelligently: you must avoid any suggestion of threat. Usually, it is helpful to prepare in advance a *checklist* of the points which you wish to cover. You cannot work down the list systematically but you can tick off the points (preferably mentally) and use the later stages of the interview to take up aspects which seem to you to have been missed.

Finally, leave time to invite the person at the end to mention any further points which he feels have been missed. Some of the most important information is obtained in this way.

A crucial decision is of course the choice of who to interview. One strategy is to start with people on the fringe, who are more likely to have an overall view, even if not a detailed one. From their remarks, you can identify some at least of the key individuals, and their interviews will suggest others. When studying an institution such as a school or an administrative unit, it may be wise to leave the senior persons – those personally involved in decision making – until near the end, so that you can make the best use of your time with them. But be sure to interview individuals at all levels in the hierarchy, to obtain a variety of perspectives. Thus, in a study of a school, the views of pupils, caretakers, and perhaps of local residents as well as those of teachers may make an important contribution to your study.

One question often asked by students is whether they should use a tape recorder in interviews. Naturally this depends on the situation, since people will hesitate to make confidential statements if the conversation is being taped. Also you must ask permission to record, and declare whether you alone will hear the tape and whether it will be destroyed subsequently. To avoid all this fuss, it is tempting to dispense with the tape recorder. However, properly used it is a most valuable aid. The small battery-operated pocket recorder can be placed unobtrusively on the floor, so that it can be quickly forgotten by the person interviewed. Do not rely entirely on the recording; use it in conjunction with your own notes of the interview, so that particularly important points can be checked easily afterwards by referring to the statements made and recapturing the actual words used.

Do not transcribe interviews [. . .]. One hour of interviewing becomes ten hours' work when transcribed; and the mass of words and paper interferes with one of the main tasks, which is to identify key statements and graphic illustrations. This is best done from notes, supplemented by a recorder.

A useful hint is to make all your notes on standard-size paper, head each page (before the interview begins) with the name and date and page number, and use space lavishly, leaving room to fill out your rough notes. In arranging an interview programme, leave time between each interview to allow you to go over notes afterwards in this way, and also to prepare for the next interview by looking over whatever notes you have been able to prepare in advance, and to allow for overrunning. It is wise to leave an interval equal in time to the length of the interviews; if interviews last about one hour, leave an hour between each. Finally, since this work is tiring, don't do too many in one day.

4.2 *Observation*

There are other kinds of case study where interviews are less appropriate, and data must be gathered by observation or even from casual encounters and remarks. Classroom studies, or studies of informal groups, for example, usually have to be based on observation, for interviews would disrupt the natural interaction which you are studying, and would introduce a rather artificial element into the situation. This is not necessarily a weakness: quite the contrary, for direct observation may be more reliable than what people say. Interviews reveal how people perceive what happens, not what actually happens. Both the actual events and the perceptions are important data, and so usually you have to combine interview and observation.

Observing is a task which requires a category system. Decide what event or behaviour to look for, and note how frequently or in what situation or sequence this occurs. It isn't possible to observe and record everything which happens; and it is seldom helpful merely to write a descriptive account of your impressions on each occasion when you observe. You may have to use unstructured notes in the first 'open' phase: in the second phase, you have to focus on selected categories.

For classroom observation, there is a wide choice of published observation schedules (see Galton, 1978; Cohen, 1976). Flanders' Interaction Analysis Categories (FIAC) is one of the best known examples. Unfortunately, you will probably find that none of the published versions fits your requirements exactly, and you will be tempted to construct your own observation schedule. Do not decide this too hastily. The work involved is substantial, as pilot runs are essential to ensure that you have defined the categories correctly and that the schedule provides you with a usable discriminating record.

A rule which applies whichever method you use to gather data, is to keep a *diary*. This is essentially a day-to-day note of what you have done, but it is helpful to use it also to record impressions and ideas and methodological assumptions. Like many personal diary entries, you may end up burning it, or be amused later at your earlier naivety and optimism; but it may also help to clarify your thinking and keep alive those moments of insight which come only too rarely. [. . .]

4.3 *Documents*

Documents are an important source of information. The existence of some of the more obvious ones may be known to you already, but passing references may also be made to informal records and reports during interviews. These documents may be no less crucial and you should try to trace them. If you are trying to establish how or why a certain decision was made, minutes of committee meetings or situation papers are essential. The advantage of contemporary documents such as these is that they do not change with hindsight, as people's memories do. But sadly, they are often disappointing because they usually record only decisions, seldom the consideration which led to the decisions. Remember too that minutes are drafted by busy administrators, and vetted by the chairman. Consequently, even these factual records are selective, for they contain only what someone originally decided to include, and they may omit points which were difficult or inconvenient to include.

4.4   *Cross-checking*

In order to guard against being misled, either in interview or by documents, you must check one informant against another, and test what they say against any documents which exist. Similarly, observations in one context must be checked against others in comparable situations. This process is called *triangulation*. The basic principle in data collection for case study is to check your data across a variety of methods and a variety of sources.

4.5   *A conceptual framework*

When it comes to analysing your data, trying to fit all the varied information into a coherent story or picture, you will have to decide on a framework of concepts. Again, you have a difficult balance to maintain, avoiding the two extremes of forcing the data to fit your preconceptions (or omitting these awkward bits that do not fit) and presenting the information in such a disorganized form that it is impossible to make sense of it.

If you have held back from a premature dive into interpretations, your framework should emerge as the study proceeds. But it is optimistic to speak of it 'emerging' like this, for we can only make sense of information by imposing some kind of framework on it. The balance is secured by providing supporting evidence to explain the framework – and quoting the exceptions – so that the reader can at least see how the concepts have 'emerged', and possibly develop some alternative concepts of his own from the evidence.

By studying published case studies (see Appendix), you will find that almost all are unique, and use their own framework to provide an individual structure for the report. However, there are certain concepts in published reports which you may find helpful. For example, in case studies of innovation, Per Dalin (1976) has suggested ten categories by which to assess an innovation:

1. *Centrality:* the extent to which an innovation attempts to change the goals, norms, or patterns of behaviour that are central to the institution; the amount of displacement resulting from the innovation.

2. *Complexity:* the extent to which an innovation proposes complicated, far-reaching changes; the ripple effect, or the number of persons or groups affected.

3. *Consonance:* the degree of fit between the goals of the innovation and the accepted goals of the institution.

4. *Competition:* interference from other aspects of the institution's activities or status structure or rival innovations.

5. *Visibility:* the extent to which the innovation is observed or monitored by nonparticipants; the publicity, or 'public-ness' of success or failure.

6. *Feasibility:* the availability of the resources needed, and the practicability of implementing the innovation (related to, but different from 1).

7. *Support:* the backing given by those in authority both within the authority and by those in key positions in related institutions, in terms of financial and material support, and also in terms of interest, encouragement and sympathetic understanding (related to, but different from 6).

8. *Divisibility:* can the innovation be introduced in part?

9. *Compatibility:* can it be combined with established practice? (related to 1, 3, and 4).

10. *Adaptability:* can it be modified to suit individual circumstances?

Dalin's hypothesis is that innovation has greater chance of success where there is positive evidence on each of these ten counts. These concepts apply only to one particular category of case study but they are set out here to illustrate the kind of analysis which is needed to raise a case study above the descriptive level.

5   Relationships

5.1   *The importance of social relationships*

In case study you as a researcher have the luxury and dilemma of being your own 'chief instrument'. Ultimately the success or failure of your efforts will depend on your ability to develop good personal relationships. Inevitably you will be part of the 'living experience' you study, and your personal skills within that social environment will be crucial, both in allowing you access to the data you want and subsequently in giving validity to your findings.

There can be no specific rules in establishing relationships since they are dependent on individual personality, or intuition, and on particular context. It is important, however, that researchers should be aware of the anxiety which can be engendered by the case study approach and ensure from the outset that they have done everything in their power to establish relationships of mutual trust.

5.2   Freedom and dependency

In case study the relationship between 'researcher' and 'researched' is curiously ambivalent. It is one which demands a large element of freedom for you the researcher, but which also acknowledges a considerable degree of dependency on those who are an integral part of your research. You need the freedom to explore the nature of your 'case' and avoid premature conceptualization; you need the freedom of the detached outsider who takes neither the system nor its apparent problems for granted. On the other hand, you must understand the system and how it works and you will be at least in part dependent on those who operate it for the eventual conceptualization of the data you collect. To establish such a relationship successfully demands a high degree of mutual trust and it will depend largely on tactful, sensitive handling of the initial approach. In the last analysis, the 'researcher' is entirely dependent on the goodwill of the 'researched'. It is a practical as well as a moral necessity to ensure that the initial approach is well considered.

5.3   The approach

Before you make your initial contact, be clear in your own mind about the purposes of your research and about what you want. Ensure that you have given some consideration too to what you can offer in return. Some things must be left vague and tentative; it is in the nature of case study that in the initial stages you cannot see a clear path ahead. Be honest about that and explain the reasons for it; remember that what you see as valid flexibility may be interpreted as vague confused thinking if badly explained.

If you are to be working in a school, what kind of access do you want? Will it be regular or spasmodic? How much disruption are you likely to cause? How long will each interview take? What kind of methods will you use? What kind of data will you collect, what will happen to it? Be prepared for all these questions, and others. You won't have specific answers to them all, but show you have considered them – raise them yourself if appropriate. If you are also seen to be aware of their possible implications for the school, its pupils, parents and staff, you will have gone a considerable way in establishing a relationship of mutual understanding and trust. Without that, your research will be in constant danger.

Be ready to give without being asked. It may be appropriate to offer access to your research proposal, to your own previous work or to other relevant documents. You will certainly want to discuss ownership and use of the data you collect and the rights of participants to comment or to disagree publicly with your interpretation.

The relationship may well be a delicate one and it may be tested at many stages of the case study process. It is an ambivalent relationship of anxiety and trust in a situation where little can be predicted with confidence and nothing can be taken entirely for granted.

5.4   Coming to terms with the case study role

Relationships are no less important at the stage of fieldwork, particularly if you are using techniques of interviewing or of participant observation. Before you can make effective relationships with others, however, you must first come to terms with yourself in your case study role: Are you at ease with the open-ended nature of case study methodology? Do you live happily with the personal and professional risk involved? Are you open-minded, confident and flexible enough to change your approach as appropriate or as circumstances allow and to conceptualize the nature of the 'case' and its apparent problems?

Perhaps more subtly: Have you the skills of introspection and sensitivity which would allow you as appropriate either to present a neutral stance on a contentious issue or to reveal your own feelings? Could you analyse either how you yourself have affected a situation or have been affected by it?

Personal qualities and skills such as these are important in themselves and in promoting your own self-confidence but are also fundamental if you are to win the confidence of others on whom you will be dependent for data.

5.5   Some important social skills

Research workers in case study are often told they must be 'sensitive', 'perceptive', 'sympathetic', 'sceptical' in their fieldwork relationships. Such attributes and skills are more easily recognized than described, practised by intuition rather than as the result of self-conscious preparation. Nevertheless, as you pursue your fieldwork, interviewing, observing, participating, try being consciously *'sensitive'* (to emotions, to atmosphere, to timing), *'perceptive'* (of apparent irrelevancy, of subtle meaning) *'sympathetic'* (to differing viewpoints, to personal difficulty or inadequacy) *'sceptical'* (of personal grievances, of apparent prejudice, of tortuous arguments). [. . .]

To be realistic, none of us succeeds in every kind of social encounter, nor do we see ourselves objectively. Most often we cannot know whether we will succeed or fail; we become aware of our professional social strengths and weaknesses by trial and error. But sadly, *in case study research, we may well provoke damage which goes well beyond any done simply to ourselves. That is why it is important to be aware of what is involved, and by careful planning avoid as far as possible the obvious potential causes of frustration and tension.* There is risk all round in case study; everyone knows that and it heightens the feelings of anxiety, but for those who have or are willing to develop the relationship skills there are many rewards in a process which can bring its own personal as well as professional satisfaction.

This section has tried to argue that human relationships and social skills are fundamental to the success of the case study. The relationships which the researcher encounters and his handling of them ensure that he will not emerge from the case study experience unchanged (or unscathed!). As his own 'chief instrument' some modification is inevitable – perhaps it is desirable before he is ready to be relaunched and 'field-tested' again!

6 The product

6.1 *The aim*

The aim of a case study can be expressed as *portrayal*. The word is deliberately chosen to suggest that case study writing is, at least partly, an art. Anecdotes and detail need to be set in context, as indeed they are in other literary art forms, like the novel. But the case study is not just a work of art: it is also a form of scientific writing, and therefore the generalizations must be amply supported by evidence. The report must present a clear and realistic picture and, as has been argued in section 4.5, there must also be a deeper level of theoretical analysis.

6.2   *Evidence*

Inevitably the report of a case study is long; but it must not be tedious. One way to avoid the danger is to keep the conclusions separate from the evidence, so that the reader may see which is inference and which is fact. The use of appendices is often an effective way to achieve this: the reader can skip the detail if he does not wish to challenge the author's interpretation, but he can develop and check his own if he wishes. Such 'verifiability' is intrinsic to a good case study; but it is a demanding quality to achieve.

The essential evidence must be woven into the main text, and the case study writer has to be able to alternate generalization and illustration. He builds up towards his conclusions by a cumulation of evidence [. . .].

It is obviously impracticable to quote all the evidence, and thus the scientific status of the case study is disputed by some research workers. Why should you, the case study writer be believed, in preference to anyone else who has been in contact with the specific case? It is hardly an adequate criterion that you write persuasively, or that you have an established reputation as a researcher, or that, being uninvolved, you are assumed to be impartial. Somehow in your style of presentation, you must establish a credibility. How can you do this?

6.3   *Style*

The case study is comparable to the documentary in film or television. Allow the evidence to speak for itself, as far as you can, resisting the temptation to make judgements about what is good or bad. By withholding value judgements, or by making them explicit and showing how different standpoints give different interpretations, it is possible to demonstrate impartiality, and present an all-round portrayal of a situation. Like many other suggestions in this guide, this is easier said than done. But there is a fundamental difference between theoretical concepts which provide a framework for judgement and a biased presentation which takes away the act of judgement from the reader. The style to aim at is that of an anthropological study, which portrays what it is like 'to be there', what the alien culture is all about, but avoids explicit or implicit judgement on it.

A simpler but equally important principle of style is to use plain language wherever possible. Sometimes this can be achieved by using the actual words of the informants; but this is not a certain guide, for all of us at times take refuge in the use of jargon. Technical terms are necessary, and are important in explaining an analysis, but they should be used sparingly. When they are used they should be defined if the reader is likely not to understand the term.

6.4 Dangers to avoid

These points may be clearer if we state them negatively, as dangers to avoid in writing a case study. The most serious dangers are:

Journalism – picking out sensational aspects of the case, and distorting the account in order to emphasize these.

Selective reporting – choosing only the evidence which supports your conclusions.

Anecdotal style – letting the illustrations and the detail take over, so that the case study becomes a catalogue of trite and tedious trivialities.

Pomposity – striving to derive profound theories from banal events, by wrapping up the account in elaborate verbiage or jargon.

Blandness – uncritically accepting the informants' interpretations, presenting only those aspects where there is consensus, and consequently implying that there are no serious differences of opinion.

We hope that in our account of case study method, we ourselves have managed to avoid the worst of these faults.

References

Adelman, C., Jenkins, D. and Kemmis, S. (1977) Re-thinking case study: notes from the second Cambridge conference. *Cambridge Journal of Education*, 6, 139–150.

Cohen, L. (1976) *Educational Research in Classrooms and Schools: A Manual of Materials and Methods*. London, Harper & Row.

Cronbach, L.J. (1975) Beyond the two disciplines of scientific psychology. *American Psychologist*, 30, 2, 110–127.

Dalin, P. (1976) *Guidelines for Case Studies*. Oslo: IMTEC, University of Oslo. Mimeograph.

Galton, M. (1978) *British Mirrors: A Collection of Classroom Observation Systems*. Leicester, School of Education, University of Leicester.

Glaser, B.G. and Strauss, A. (1976) *The Discovery of Grounded Theory*. Chicago: Aldine Press.

Hamilton, D. (1975) See Reid and Walker (1975) below.

Hamilton, D., Jenkins, D., King, C., Macdonald, B., Parlett, M. (1977) *Beyond the Numbers Game*. London, Macmillan.

Hamingson, D., (ed.) (1973) *Towards Judgment*. London, Schools Council.

Hargreaves, D. (1967) *Social Relations in a Secondary School*. London, Routledge & Kegan Paul.

Jackson, B. (1978) *Beginning*. London, Croom Helm.

Lacey, C. (1970) *Hightown Grammar: the School as a Social System*. Manchester, Manchester U.P.

Norris, N. (1977) *Safari: Theory in Practice*. Norwich, University of East Anglia, Centre for Applied Research in Education.

Parlett, M. and Hamilton, D. (1972) Evaluation as illumination: a new approach to the study of innovatory programmes. Occasional Paper 9, Centre for Research in the Educational Sciences, University of Edinburgh. Reprinted in Hamilton et al. (1977) – see page 27.

Reid, W.A. and Walker, D.F. (1975) *Case Studies in Curriculum Change*. London, Routledge & Kegan Paul. Chapter 5 by D. Hamilton. Handling innovations in the classroom.

Richardson, E. (1973) *The Teacher, The School, and The Task of Management*. London, Heinemann.

Scottish Education Department (1969) *Science for General Education*. Curriculum Paper 7, Consultative Committee on the Curriculum. Edinburgh, HMSO.

Shipman, M. (1974) *Inside a Curriculum Project; A Case Study in the Process of Curriculum Change*. London, Methuen.

Whyte, W.F. (1955) *Street Corner Society*. Chicago, University of Chicago Press.

Wragg, T. (1976) Private communication.

Appendix

Some examples of case studies (in addition to those mentioned in the References)

Becker, H. (1961) *Boys in White*. Chicago, University of Chicago Press.

Dalin, P. (ed.) (1973) *Case Studies of Educational Innovation*. Paris, OECD.

Vol. 1　At the central level
　　2　At the regional level
　　3　At the school level
　　4　Strategies for innovation in education

Hamilton, D. (1977) *In Search of Structure*. London, Hodder & Stoughton.

Patrick, J. (1973) *A Glasgow Gang Observed*. London, Eyre Methuen.

Schools Council (1973) *Evaluation in Curriculum Development: Twelve Case Studies*. London, Macmillan.

Stake, R., (ed.) (1974) *Case Studies in the Evaluation of Educational Programmes*. Paris, OECD.

Whiteside, T. (1978) *The Sociology of Educational Innovation*. London, Methuen. Chapter 5, Case studies of change.

J. Nisbet and J. Watt, Rediguide 26: *Guides in Educational Research*, Nottingham University, School of Education. Series editor M.B. Youngman. ISBN 0 946069 06 9. Published by TRC–Rediguides. Copyright © TRC (Oxford) England.

John Nisbet is Professor of Education at the University of Aberdeen. Dr Joyce Watt is Senior Lecturer in Education at the University of Aberdeen.

CHAPTER 6

RETHINKING CASE STUDY

Glen Adelman, David Jenkins & Stephen Kemmis

Over the last ten years there has emerged a tradition of educational research and evaluation whose procedures, methods and styles of reporting have come to be collected under the general rubric of 'case study'. Although case studies have made a considerable contribution to the corpus of knowledge and practical wisdom about education, they are often regarded with suspicion and even hostility. Their general characteristics remain poorly understood and their potential underdeveloped.

In an attempt to explore the problems and possibilities of case study, an international conference sponsored by the Nuffield Foundation was held at Churchill College, Cambridge in December 1975, to consider *Methods of Case Study in Educational Research and Evaluation.*

At one level the conference discussion might be construed as an attempt to produce a general theory of case study; at another to produce a practitioner's guide based on the accumulated experience of those present. But case study itself is about moving between the general and the particular. Decisions about how case studies should be planned, conducted and reported are as much *practical* decisions as theoretical, governed by the exigencies of the situation, as well as by general views of educational research and evaluation.

In what follows we present a number of particular concerns which occupied much of the conference. Some of these reflect the underlying logic of the evolving case study paradigm, others the more immediate problems faced by the conference members *qua* practitioners.

What is a case study?

Case study is an umbrella term for a family of research methods having in common the decision to focus on enquiry around an instance. Not surprisingly the term 'case study' remains a slippery one. It may be easier to begin by clearing up some misunderstandings.

Case studies should not be equated with observational studies, participant or otherwise. Such a view would rule out historical case studies, not least because the past is not directly observable.

Case studies are not simply pre-experimental. Although case studies have often been used to sensitize researchers to significant variables subsequently manipulated or controlled in an experimental design, that is not their only role. The understandings generated by case study are significant in their own right. It is tempting to argue that the accumulation of case studies allows theory building via tentative hypotheses culled from single instances. But the generalizations produced in case study are no less legitimate when about the *instance*, rather than about the *class* from which the instance is drawn (i.e. generalizing *about* the case, rather than *from* it).

'Case study' is not the name for a standard methodological package. Research methodology is not *defining* in case studies but does determine the form of the particular study. In general, the techniques for collecting information for a case study are held in common with a wider tradition of sociological and anthropological fieldwork. Case study methodology is eclectic, although techniques and procedures in common use include observation (participant and nonparticipant), interview (conducted with varying degrees of structure), audio-visual recording, field note-taking, document collection, and the negotiation of products (e.g. discussing the accuracy of an account with those observed).

Case study research always involves 'the study of an instance in action'. Yet lying behind the concept 'instance' lurk problems concerning the relationship of the 'instance' to the 'class' from which it is drawn. Case study research may be initially set up in one of two ways:

1. An issue or hypothesis is given, and a bounded system (the case) is selected as an *instance drawn from a class*. For example, a group of researchers wishing to explore what happens in fringe religious groups prophesying the end of the world on a stated date when their prophetic utterances are disconfirmed will select any instance of such a group within the class.

2. A 'bounded system' (the case) is given, within which issues are indicated, discovered or studied so that a tolerably full understanding of the case is possible. The most straightforward examples of 'bounded systems' are those in which the boundaries have a common sense obviousness, for example an individual teacher, a single school, or perhaps an innovatory programme.

The first type of study will be predisposed towards making generalizations *about the class*. The instance may be chosen because it has a prima facie representativeness. However, during the conduct of the study the description of the case will increasingly emphasize its uniqueness. Loosely speaking this means that the study will reveal increasingly some apparently case-bound features of the instance *vis-a-vis* the class. More strictly speaking, the study will transcend the principle of selection (i.e. selecting the instance as representative of a given class) and become a study of a unique case. It does not follow that the researcher, by virtue of this shift, abandons the hope of generalization, though he may do so. Rather the basis of generalization itself has changed.

Thus we can see that the term 'generalization', as used in case study research and evaluation, may be equivocal. Three different kinds of generalizations are possible from case study. The first kind is from the instance studied to the class it purports to represent (e.g. a study of comprehensivization in one school may tell us about comprehensivization in other schools). The second kind is from case-bound features of the instance to a multiplicity of classes (e.g. Festinger et al. (1964) actually studied a religious group whose prophesy failed, and generated a range of insights outside the scope of their initial hypotheses about such diverse matters as leadership patterns in unstructured groups and the workings of the local press). Studies in which the case is selected as an instance of a class will be predisposed towards making these kinds of generalizations. Studies which do not begin by asserting the instance-class relation, however, will be inclined towards the third kind of generalization: generalizations about the case.

The second type of study will be predisposed towards making generalizations about the case. In its most significant form, generalization about the case promotes generalization from case to case. As in art, which teaches by example rather than precept, the second type of study begins from the internal coherence of the case. However, as the study progresses the boundaries of the system appear increasingly permeable. For example, it is not possible to treat an innovative programme as a bounded system isolated from its host institution. In short, the boundaries are no longer given: they have become problematic. We cannot answer questions about the effects of the innovation without reference to the history of the school, local authority politics, or the self-images and career aspirations of the teachers. Each case turns out to be profoundly embedded in its real world situation.

In practice these two 'types' refer more to *purposes* than to distinct approaches in case study. Sometimes the audience for the study will be more concerned with given systems, sometimes with the exploration of given issues. In both contexts, the case study worker must treat the boundaries of the system and the issues as problematic, and attempt to define the immanent organization of the case, that is its uniqueness. But he cannot take an indulgent view of the idiosyncrasy of the case; all cases are unique, and uniquely embedded in their real world situations. The extent to which the case is characterized as unique will be limited by the purposes of the study.

It has already been pointed out that case study is not simply pre-experimental. It might be asked whether the generalizations produced in case study are stronger or weaker than those of experimental research. Stronger or weaker, they tend to be different. At the risk of over-simplification it might be argued that case study and experimental research are based on different views of social science; case study might be seen in the context of an historical or interpretive tradition; experimental research in the context of a natural science tradition. In practice the two most important differences are in the way claims are made against truth and in the demands made upon the reader. Experimental research 'guarantees' the veracity of its generalizations by reference to formal theories and hands them on intact to the reader; case study research offers a surrogate experience and invites the reader to underwrite the account, by appealing to his *tacit* knowledge of human situations. The truths contained in a successful case study report, like those in literature, are 'guaranteed' by 'the shock of recognition'. The difference between the two kinds is expressed in Stake's (1975) distinction between 'naturalistic' and 'formalistic' generalizations.

Getting it together

Case studies are not easy to do. (Some of our best friends are presently trapped inside case studies, trying to get out. Almost none will escape unscathed.) In the conduct of a case study a whole range of problems will have been resolved, for better or for worse. In planning a case study considerations arise about the *circumstances of the case, the conduct of the study and the consequences of the research*. Since these considerations are fundamentally interrelated, choices in one domain will have implications for the others. If the case study worker is not to lose control of these implications he must 'get it all together', that is have a considered stance on the issues raised across the board.

1. The circumstances of the case

A case study might arise out of the case study worker's own interests, or might be sponsored by a funding agency with its own agenda. In evaluation research, the circumstances in which a case study is conducted will vary according to whether the evaluation is by mandate, invitation or negotiation, and whether the funding agency is 'outside' the institution to be studied. At its crudest this means that any particular case study will have been sought, bought or sponsored.

Case studies are carried out in 'real' situations in which the people studied have responsibilities and obligations with which the study may interfere. The case study worker too may accept obligations and create expectations which must be honoured. The expectations generated during initial contacts impose frameworks and constraints affecting the conduct of the entire study. Because case studies are often 'close up' accounts, it may be necessary to readjust the balance of power between the research community and those studied. One way of making salient the rights of those studied may be through a more explicit 'research contract'. Relevant questions include:

(a) The credentials of the research team. Can they show examples of their previous work? Do they supply references?
(b) The formal proposal. Is the written research proposal itself open to inspection and by whom? What are its goals, its personnel, its financial arrangements? What are its likely products and for whom are they intended?
(c) The extent of likely involvement. What access do the research team require? When, where, and to whom and what?
(d) The possibility of disruption. What is the likelihood of substantial disruption of the setting attributable to the research? How obtrusive is the study?
(e) The conventions or principles governing access to and use of

information. Will there be 'coownership' of data? That is, will informants have the right to place restrictions on information given or control
its subsequent release? Will the subjects of the research have the right to
comment/alter/suppress the draft or parts of it on the grounds of
accuracy/truth/discretion/protection/relevance/balance, etc.?

(f) The status of alternative viewpoints, particularly the interpretations
and analysis of events held by those observed *vis-a-vis* those put forward by the researchers. How will any disagreements over interpretation be handled?

2. *The conduct of the study*

As has already been pointed out, case study uses a variety of techniques,
often 'sociological' in character. It should be reiterated that the research
methods chosen in a particular study will determine, as much as depend
upon, the scope and nature of the case being studied.

In general, the means of collection of data cited or summarized in the
report of a case study should be made explicit. The kind of *in-depth*
portrayal produced by the case study aspires to credulity of account, but the
reader should be allowed to reconsider for himself the relationship between
assertion and evidence. The overheard should be distinguished from hear-
say, primary evidence from secondary, description from interpretation,
verbatim accounts from summaries. The principle can be extended: the
'raw' data needs to be accessible, as well as the 'cooked' account; the
accuracy of transcripts should be open to independent check; and the
reactivity of the researchers should be assessed or at least 'assessable' in
principle. Some case study workers, like some photographers, encourage
reactivity and make the subjects' response to their presence an integral part
of the data; others seek social invisibility, aspiring to a 'fly-on-the-wall'
presence.

The advantages of a particular technique for collecting witnesses'
accounts of an event – *triangulation* – should be stressed. This is at the heart
of the intention of the case study worker to respond to the multiplicity of
perspectives present in a social situation. All accounts are considered in part
to be expressive of the social position of each informant. Case study needs to
represent, and represent fairly, these differing and sometimes conflicting
viewpoints. Arguably it can only do so if its own principles of representation
and interpretation are made explicit to its informants and built into the
'research contract'. To the case study worker the issue is in part a simple one

of internal consistency, a careful explication of which 'facts' are agreed and which are open to diverse interpretation.

Having begun to collect information, the case study worker will find that the data raises further problems familiar from experimental research as questions of reliability and threats to internal and external validity. For instance, people, places and issues mentioned in one interview may need to be followed up in subsequent interviews, observations, or document collection; discrepancies between accounts will need pursuing; 'facts' need cross-checking; critical incidents must be identified; and the kind of evidence by which working hypotheses may be refuted or reformulated must be sought out.

A major issue is that of *reporting*. In principle at least, the notion of case study allows such a variety of forms of reporting as collage, film documentary, mixed-media presentations, role-play simulations, oral feedback, quasi-journalistic reports, as well as the more usual written reports. Photography, documentary-film making and journalism in particular, were explored by the conference since these fields can provide models for case study work both in terms of products and procedures.

Another issue which attracted attention at the conference was that of *training*. Nobody is too sure how case study workers should be trained. In a field where all the research problems must be solved 'on the ground', learning by example and by experience seems called for. The good and bad habits and research styles of different case study workers might well be discussed in any scheme of preparation for case study work.

3. *The consequence of the research*

Case study research and evaluation, because it is rooted in the practicalities and politics of real life situations, is more likely to expose those studied to critical appraisal, censure or condemnation. The uses to which in-depth case study reports are put are typically beyond the control of the case study worker. His findings may be used to support cases or arguments propounded by the reader, whose standards and assumptions will always be his own. As was suggested earlier (in reference to the research contract) an argument can be put for *limiting* either access to data or its release except under controlled conditions. The case study worker will be party to many inside stories not all of which will be negotiable currency in discussion outside the group under study. He knows more than he should tell. The limiting consideration is that the case study worker acknowledges that *others* must live with the consequences of his findings.

One conventional device for handling these problems is the anonymization of reports. That this is a nonsolution in most situations is easily demonstrated. If the anonymization is sufficiently impenetrable to disguise the identity of the participants even from those close to the situation, then, it is doubtful whether it can feed reflection and action within the situation itself. If on the other hand, the anonymization works only for outsiders, those with most to gain or lose are scarcely protected by it. Also the logic of anonymization presupposes that the primary interest in case study is in the *generalization* not the *case*. The distortion involved in anonymizing reports so that they become unrecognizable even to insiders is a heavy price to pay for the privilege of 'going public'. Even so, the price may be worth paying: in a world where those who participate in research are so often at a significant disadvantage, the marginal advantages of anonymization may be worth having. It can protect participants from significant political figures distant from the immediate context of the research, and the protection increases with time (as the case study becomes less true of the contemporary situation and as its findings are used in contexts distant from the original one). At the very least anonymized reports have the value of fiction: what they lack in authenticity (in the strongest sense of that term) they may restore to the reader by illustration.

As we have indicated, it was felt that a 'victim's charter' might formulate what those being researched might be entitled to ask the research worker. Such a charter might contribute to an increased awareness of what is at stake in inviting in the case study worker. Another possibility is the development of a 'code of practice' for case study workers, backed by sanctions from the professional community. One problem is that the codes of practice adopted by professions outside education offer equivocal models, in that they are frequently self-serving, safeguarding the profession rather than those coming into contact with it, and reinforcing rather than challenging the imbalance of power between professional and nonprofessional interests in the community.

One focus for the discussion of the ethics of case study evaluation and research at the conference was the SAFARI principles of procedure, (MacDonald and Walker 1974; 1975), emphasizing the *negotiation* of access to and release of sensitive data. The SAFARI principles allow informants the right to 'edit' the researcher's accounts of their views and actions. In this way informants can share in the controlled release of data to audiences within and outside the research situation. [. . .]

Possible advantages of case study

Case studies have a number of advantageous characteristics that make them attractive to educational evaluators or researchers:

(a) Case study data, paradoxically, is 'strong in reality' but difficult to organize. In contrast, other research data is often 'weak in reality' but susceptible to ready organization. This strength in reality is because case studies are down-to-earth and attention holding, in harmony with the reader's own experience, and thus provide a 'natural' basis for generalization. A reader responding to a case study report is consequently able to employ the ordinary processes of judgement by which people tacitly understand life and social actions around them.

(b) Case studies allow generalizations either about an instance or from an instance to a class. Their peculiar strength lies in their attention to the subtlety and complexity of the case in its own right.

(c) Case studies recognize the complexity and 'embeddedness' of social truths. By carefully attending to social situations, case studies can represent something of the discrepancies or conflicts between the viewpoints held by participants. The best case studies are capable of offering some support to alternative interpretations.

(d) Case studies, considered as products, may form an archive of descriptive material sufficiently rich to admit subsequent reinterpretation. Given the variety and complexity of educational purposes and environments, there is an obvious value in having a data source for researchers and users whose purposes may be different from our own.

(e) Case studies are 'a step to action'. They begin in a world of action and contribute to it. Their insights may be directly interpreted and put to use; for staff or individual self-development, for within-institutional feedback; for formative evaluation; and in educational policy making.

(f) Case studies present research or evaluation data in a more publicly accessible form than other kinds of research report, although this virtue is to some extent bought at the expense of their length. The language and the form of the presentation is hopefully less esoteric and less dependent on specialized interpretation than conventional research reports. The case study is capable of serving multiple audiences. It reduces the dependence of the reader upon unstated implicit assumptions (which necessarily underlie any type of research) and makes the research process itself accessible. Case studies, therefore, may contribute towards the 'democratization' of decision making (and knowledge itself). At their best, they allow the reader to judge the implications of a study for himself.

References

Festinger, L., Riecken, H.W. and Schauchter, S. (1964) *When Prophecy Fails: a social and psychological study of a modern group that predicted the destruction of the world.* New York, Harper and Row.

MacDonald, B. and Walker, R. (eds.) (1974) *Innovation, Evaluation, Research and the Problems of Control – Some Interim Papers.* SAFARI Project, Centre for Applied Research in Education, University of East Anglia.

MacDonald, B. and Walker, R. (1975) Case study and the social philosophy of educational research, *Cambridge Journal of Education,* 5, pp. 1–11.

Stake, R.E. (1975) *The case study method in social inquiry.* Centre for Applied Research in Education, University of East Anglia (mimeo). The 'naturalistic'/'formalistic' distinction was introduced in Stake's paper for the conference.

Clem Adelman, David Jenkins and Stephen Kemmis *Towards a Science of the Singular,* edited by Helen Simons, Centre for Applied Research in Education, UEA Norwich, Occasional Publication No. 1, pp. 47–61.

Clem Adelman is Research Coordinator at Bulmershe College, Reading. Stephen Kemmis is Assistant Professor at the Curriculum Studies Centre, Deakin University, Victoria. David Jenkins is Professor of Arts Education at the University of Warwick.

CHAPTER 7

PEDAGOGIC RESEARCH: ON THE RELATIVE MERITS OF SEARCH FOR GENERALIZATION AND STUDY OF SINGLE EVENTS

Michael Bassey

Critics of the case study method frequently point to the fact that generalization is not usually possible and that a study of a single event has limited value. The 'generalization problem' is referred to in Chapters 5 and 6. In this chapter, Michael Bassey suggests that we should eschew the pursuit of generalizations and instead, should actively encourage the descriptive and evaluative study of single events. In his view, 'the relatability of a case study is more important than its generalizability'. He makes the distinction between what he calls 'open' and 'closed' generalization, claims that open generalizations are rare and gives reasons to support this claim. He provides guidance to investigators on the dangers of generalization on insufficient evidence and makes the case that a thorough study of a single event can make a useful contribution to the improvement of practice.

Recent British writings on the nature of educational research seem to agree on two expectations: (a) that educational research should result in generalizations which will coalesce into educational theory, and (b) that educational research should contribute in some way to improvement of educational practice. Evidence that these are the twin expectations of many (but not all) members of the educational research community, is presented in the first section.

The main purpose of the paper is to explore the question as to whether these two expectations are compatible. Does contemporary educational research provide generalizations which are useful to teachers? In order to consider this question it is necessary to examine the concept of generalization. I shall draw a distinction between 'open' and 'closed' generalizations and conclude that while 'open' generalizations are the more useful in pedagogic practice, they also seem to be the more scarce. This will lead to my contention that the study of single events is a more profitable form of research (judged by the criterion of usefulness to teachers) than searches for generalizations. I shall also suggest that the merit of study of single events lies not in the extent to which it can be generalized, but in the extent to which a teacher reading it can relate it to his own teaching.

In making these assertions, I am concerned with the usefulness of research to teachers. The argument is located in the domain of pedagogic research and does not necessarily refer to all educational research. It may be that the search for generalization can help administrators to improve educational practice.

Pedagogic research is a sub-set of educational research; it is research into the processes of teaching and learning, and as such necessarily focuses on individuals rather than populations.

The prevailing expectations that educational research should provide generalizations and that these should be useful

In 1968 Butcher introduced the series of books entitled *Educational Research in Britain*, of which he is editor, by stating that educational research is to be interpreted as 'empirical research, based on experiment, on social surveys and on the clinical study of individuals'. This definition identifies the field of enquiry as empirical, but gives the enquiry no intention or purpose. It is noteworthy for its reference to the study of individuals.

In a reaction against the assumption 'that educational research is a branch of psychology or social science', Peters and White (1969) suggest that 'educational research is sustained systematic enquiry designed to provide us with new knowledge which is relevant to initiating people into desirable states of mind involving depth and breadth of understanding'. This broadens Butcher's definition to include philosophical and historical study, and gives the purpose of 'initiating people into desirable states of mind'.

In 1970 Nisbet and Entwistle published *Educational Research Methods*, which became a standard textbook for undergraduates studying educational research. They described a seven-stage strategy for doing research in which the key is 'to design a situation which will produce relevant evidence to prove or disprove a hypothesis or give answers to a specific question'. They said, 'It is necessary throughout to work by the light of some general idea or hypothesis.' In a paper written in 1973 they gave a definition which included the concept of 'efficiency': 'Educational research consists in careful, systematic attempts to understand the educational process and, through understanding, to improve its efficiency.'

Simon (1978), addressing the British Educational Research Association in 1977, expressed the view 'that the focus of educational research must be *education*, and that its overall function is to assist teachers, administrators, indeed all concerned in the field, to improve the quality of the educational process – and, in so doing, enhance the quality of life'.

Eggleston (1979), addressing the same Association in the following year and attempting to 'map the domain' of educational research, cited Simon's view and suggested how 'descriptions of schooling . . . could be generalized'. He said,

> we are still ignorant of the strategies teachers use such as the selection of facts to be taught, the experiences given to pupils to advance concept development or to train them in specified skills. We do not know how teachers sequence experiences, design and use diagnostic procedures and instruments to monitor pupils' progress, of the strategies they use to maintain motivation or other conditions for learning or even to make the classroom a congenial place to be.

Stones (1979), in his textbook *Psychopedagogy*, says 'although teachers are undoubtedly different, there is an important basic core of sameness which does enable us . . . to make some generalizations about the nature of teaching'. He expects that the joint activity of teachers and researchers will lead to 'a theory of teaching' which will entail 'new regularities in the form of theoretical principles'.

Stenhouse (1980) suggests that

> educational research has as its overriding aim the support of educational acts . . . Yet it must also support the planning of research acts in educational settings. Our problem is to find approaches to research which produce theory which is of use both to practitioners of education and to practitioners of educational research and which enables both to act in the light of systematic intelligence.

He goes on to assert that 'the most important distinction in educational research at this moment is that between the study of samples and the study of cases'. Linking his 1980 paper with one written in 1978 it is clear that he expects both the study of samples and the study of cases to lead to generalizations.

Stenhouse distinguishes between predictive generalizations, which arise from the study of samples and are the form in which data are accumulated in science, and retrospective generalizations, which can eventually arise from the analysis of case studies and are the form in which data are accumulated in history. He writes 'while predictive generalizations claim to supersede the need for individual judgement, retrospective generalizations seek to strengthen individual judgement where it cannot be superseded'.

Cohen and Manion (1980) in their introductory text *Research Methods in Education* put particular stress on scientific methods of enquiry, and indicate that 'the ultimate aim of science is theory'. They see the scientist as concerned 'to generalize his findings to the world at large', although they recognize that the human scientist, including the educational researcher, has 'to exercise great caution when generalizing his findings'. In describing the nature of research they cite, with evident approval, the view of another writer: 'Research is best conceived as the process of arriving at dependable solutions to problems through the planned and systematic collection, analysis and interpretation of data.'

Nisbet, in an address to the inaugural meeting of the British Educational Research Association in April 1974, expressed a contrary view to that of educational science and problem solving. He said,

> I think that recent years have seen a move away from the naive idea that problems are solved by educational research; that is the old 'Educational Science' idea, and it is a myth. Educational research can strengthen the information base of decision-making; its procedures of inquiry and evaluation can inject rigour . . . investigation into teaching and learning sharpens thinking, directs attention to important issues, clarifies problems, encourages debate and the exchange of views, and thus deepens understanding . . . Research of this kind aims to increase the problem-solving capacity of the educational system, rather than to provide the final answers to questions.

Although there are differences of outlook, I think it reasonable to infer that these British commentators on research more or less concur on two points: (a) that educational research should result in generalizations which will coalesce into educational theory, and (b) that educational research should contribute in some way to improvement of educational practice.

On the other side of the Atlantic, similar views have been expressed by some writers while others have quarrelled with them.

Thus Gowin (1972) has challenged the 'assumption that educational research is to be like research in natural sciences – to search for generalizations (laws) which are expected to hold in a variety of situations'. He argues that since educational phenomena are man-made events, changes in educational practice will invalidate educational generalizations.

The concern for the usefulness of educational research for finding solutions to problems has been totally rejected by Kerlinger (1977).

> Most people assume that educational research can solve educational problems and improve educational practices. The assumption is false. And it creates expectations that cannot be fulfilled. Educational research does not lead directly to improvement in educational practice.

His argument is that research should be concerned with fundamental development of theory which in the long run 'may have beneficial though indirect effects on educational practice'.

Does contemporary educational research provide generalizations which are useful to teachers?

(a)

A large volume of research has been conducted on the possibility of differences occurring between the classroom performance of boys and girls. Maccoby and Jacklin (1974) reviewed 1400 studies in this field and identified only four statements about sex differences in performance and behaviour of children and young people which they considered to be 'fairly well established'. These are: that teenage girls have greater verbal ability, that adolescent boys excel in visual-spatial ability, that adolescent boys have greater mathematical ability, and that males at all ages are more aggressive than females. The first three of these statements are based on a number of studies where tests have been used and which enable the statements to be quantified. The differences vary slightly from one investigation to another but overall the emerging pattern is of differences amounting to about one-third of a standard deviation.

Even if every class contained the same distribution of ability between boys and girls as large-scale samples, the differences are so slight that they are unlikely to provide useful pedagogic knowledge to teachers. In effect these generalizations are likely to be misleading because the differences between large samples of boys and girls are so slight that in small samples (i.e. classes) the differences between the boys and girls will fluctuate from one class to another; sometimes the actual position in the class will be the opposite of that in the large samples, but if the teacher expects one sex to be of higher ability than the other it is possible that his expectation will be fulfilled because of the effect of the expectation on teaching. I submit that these generalizations (arising from 1400 research endeavours) are not useful to teachers.

In general it must be the case that any research investigation which is based on large samples (in order to give confidence to its conclusions) is not going to provide useful predictive information to the individual teacher working in a classroom (where $N = c.$ 30). Of course, it can be argued that the generalization drawn from a large sample may sensitize or alert him to possible differences between the members of his class, but it can also be argued that because the generalization cannot be applied to the class members with surety, it may be counter-productive by causing the teacher to make erroneous predictions.

I must emphasize that my denigration of these generalizations is in terms of their usefulness to individual teachers. For educational administrators, politicians, and polemicists, generalizations about differences between boys and girls may be useful in terms of discussion of the merits of single sex and coeducational schools.

(b)

In 1972 Entwistle and Nisbet published a companion volume to their methodological text entitled *Educational Research in Action*. Their aim was to give examples of 'empirical studies which are intrinsically interesting and which illustrate important research strategies'. A large section of the book is devoted to 28 extracts from research papers in education published mainly between 1966 and 1972.

I have analysed these exemplars in terms of the question:
(i) Does the paper contain what purports to be a generalization (or several) drawn from the empirical evidence?

Of the 28 papers, 15 contain empirical generalizations by way of conclusions. Of these 15 papers I have then asked:
(ii) Could the generalization(s) be helpful to a teacher who is trying to improve his or her teaching?

Clearly this is a subjective analysis. My finding is 'Yes' in only four cases. The statements which I think could be useful to teachers are:

(1) 'Among 11-year-olds, teaching approaches which foster divergent thinking may result in minimal benefits to performance on current tests of mathematical ability' (Richards and Bolton, 1971).
(2) 'Multiple marking by rapid impression of essays written by O-level candidates is likely to be more reliable than individual marking by detailed schemes' (Britton, Martin and Rosen, 1966).
(3) 'Some teachers fail to perceive the pedagogical implications of many of their own uses of language' (Barnes, 1969).

(4) 'Students who have trained in interaction analysis are likely to be more able to control their own classroom behaviour than untrained students' (Wragg, 1971, citing Flanders).

I submit that much husbandry has resulted in little produce as judged by the criterion of generalization useful to teachers. Certainly the examples contain matters of description and discussion which are likely to be of interest to teachers, but few useful empirical generalizations.

The methodological text of Nisbet and Entwistle advocates hypothesis testing in search of generalization, but their textbook of exemplars seems to suggest that much research is not resulting in generalization and that which is, only rarely gives generalizations which could be helpful to teachers. Perhaps it is significant that at the beginning of their methodological text they give a fictitious generalization as a basis for discussion of causality: 'We may find that there is a correlation between colour preferences and school. attainment. Those children who choose garish colours tend to do badly in exams.'

Nisbet and Entwistle use this to illustrate the point that survey data do not establish causality. With the wealth of real research data that they had available, why did they choose a fictitious example? Perhaps this is evidence of the paucity of generalizations which are relevant to classrooms.

(c)

Cohen's (1976) textbook *Educational Research in Classrooms and Schools* provides another approach to the question as to whether contemporary educational research provides empirical generalizations which are useful to teachers. The purpose of the book is set out as: (a) to introduce the reader to the purpose and techniques of observing pupils and teachers in school and classroom settings; (b) to provide the reader with research tools to assist his observations and his systematic recording of data; (c) to develop an understanding of techniques of analysis by way of interpreting observations; (d) to suggest research topics that the reader himself can undertake; and (e) to introduce relevant empirical studies that help illuminate those suggested topics of research. Over 300 research papers are cited, mainly from British and American journals, and about 120 'research tools' are described in sufficient detail for the reader to use; examples are Maw and Maw's 'Curiosity Measures', Dommert's version of the 'Rokeach Dogmatism Scale', Oliver and Butcher's 'Manchester Survey of Opinion Scales about Education', Rutter's 'Child Behaviour Scale' and McQuitty's 'Linkage Analysis' for identifying staffroom cliques.

I have identified 68 specific suggestions for research investigations in Cohen's book. Of these, 64 are expressed in a form which hints at a hypothesis which could lead to a generalization. For example:

(a) 'Study the relationship between personality variables and rigidity in goal-setting behaviour in pupils or college students' (p. 16).
(b) 'What is the effect of "modern" as opposed to "traditional" methods of mathematics teaching upon junior school children's ability to think divergently?' (p. 27).
(c) 'Explore the association between classroom climate, teacher values, and teacher pupil contacts and the incidence of curiosity in classroom settings' (p. 37).
(d) 'Do Machiavellian teachers more readily identify Machiavellian pupils?' (p. 72).
(e) 'What is the difference in the incidence of cheating behaviour in extreme traditional and progressive classroom regimes?' (p. 81).
(f) 'Test the proposition that feelings of superiority are more generally found among those bearing unique names' (p. 95).
(g) 'Design a study to explore the relationships between teacher satisfaction, bureaucratic orientation, and school organisation' (p. 158).
(h) 'Do teachers hold stereotypic views about the personalities of their pupils from features of their handwriting?' (p. 181).
(i) 'How does class size affect the quality of teaching and learning?' (p. 232).
(j) 'Test the proposition that headteachers behave differently according to the status of the teacher group with whom they are interacting' (p. 282).

There are a number of serious methodological issues raised by some of these research proposals – matters of definition, of uncontrolled variables, of sample size and of ethics, but, supposing that it were possible to formulate empirical generalizations from them, how many of these research investigations would help teachers in the business of teaching? Perhaps (b), (c) and (i) would be useful; is it coincidence that these would be the most difficult of the ten items to investigate and would require large-scale research efforts if any valid generalizations were to be made; certainly they are not suitable for inclusion in Cohen's list of 'topics that the reader himself can undertake'.

I submit that Cohen's book gives further evidence of the scarcity of generalizations which are useful to teachers in their teaching.

Open and closed generalizations

(a)

What is an empirical generalization? In the simplest terms it is a collation of observed results, or findings, or conclusions. If a *result* arises from the study of one set of events, then a *generalization* is a statement which collates the results from a number of sets of events.

It is necessary to distinguish between empirical generalizations which are grounded in facts and logic, and normative generalizations which are grounded in value judgements. Thus statements such as 'the nation needs more engineers' and 'teachers ought to be punctual' are normative generalizations, based on someone's value judgements, and not empirical generalizations.

A distinction can be made between empirical generalizations which are open and those which are closed. A closed generalization refers to a closed set of events; an open generalization to an open set of events. An open generalization is a statement in which there is confidence that it can be extrapolated, beyond the observed results of the sets of events studied, to similar events, with the expectation that it will be similarly applicable. A closed generalization is a statement which refers to a specified set of events and without extrapolation to similar events. A closed generalization is descriptive; an open generalization is both descriptive and predictive.

Figure 1 gives a visual representation.

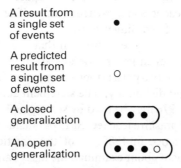

Figure 1   The concepts of closed and open generalization

These terms seem to be closely related to the terms 'retrospective generalization' and 'predictive generalization' used by Stenhouse (1978). He uses 'retrospective generalization' to refer to 'attempts to map the range of experience' and 'predictive generalization' to refer to attempts to perceive within the range of experience 'the operation of laws in the scientific sense'.

(b)
The following is an example of a closed generalization.

'In 1976 in 281 Nottinghamshire infant classrooms the major ways in which the teachers organized the learning of mathematics were:

work with mathematical apparatus	37%
work written into each child's book	19%
work from teacher's work cards	19%
oral work with teacher	18%
work from printed books or cards	6%
work written on the chalkboard'	1%
	100%

This is an example of an open generalization:
'Examinations motivate students to learn subject-matter which is to be examined.'

Both of these are empirical generalizations, that is generalizations based on factual evidence. The first one is 'closed' in space and time; it relates to a particular group of teachers at a particular time. The second one is 'open' because it lacks these fixed dimensions.

It must be admitted that the distinction that closed generalizations are only descriptive while open generalizations are both descriptive and predictive, is more a case of two polarizations along a continuum rather than, as suggested here, a rigid dichotomy. The statement about infant teachers in Nottinghamshire in 1976 may be used by some people to make predictions about other Nottinghamshire teachers in 1976 outside the sample, or of the Nottinghamshire practice in 1980, or of the practice in other parts of England. The statement about examinations makes an accurate prediction for many students, but for some it makes a false prediction – for example in the case where fear of the examination inhibits learning. Likewise the description of a statement as 'valid' or 'invalid' is again a case of imposing a dichotomy where a continuum might be more appropriate. My excuse for using these dichotomous labels is that they are a reasonable approximation to reality and thus contribute to the intelligibility of the argument.

(c)

Researchers tend to value open generalizations more than closed generalizations. Indeed, the sub-set of researchers who call themselves 'scientists' are, with rare exceptions, only concerned with open generalizations.

I suspect that in education there are many opportunities for making closed generalizations, for example about a particular set of schools at a particular time, but few opportunities for open generalization.

(d)

The following statements are open generalizations which I take to be useful to teachers.

The extent to which somebody learns, depends upon factors including:

whether he is in an affective state conducive to learning (whether recent events, or the physical context, or the social context promote or inhibit positive feelings towards the subject matter);

whether his interest is aroused and maintained (whether the subject matter gives him a sense of purpose or challenge in learning it);

whether the subject matter is meaningful to him (whether it is communicated clearly for him, whether it relates to his existing knowledge and experience, whether the parts of the subject matter integrate into a coherent pattern for him);

whether the subject matter is presented to him in quantities and at rates which are appropriate to him;

whether he has opportunities actively to use the new learning and to obtain rapid feedback on the success of his learning.

The above statements can be taken to be applicable to learning in any human being, today, in the Stone Age and in the twenty-fifth century AD. Thus they are open generalizations. I believe them to be rare.

Hosford (1973) has prepared a listing of 133 pedagogic statements mainly of this kind which he considers to be capable of empirical testing. He describes them as 'postulates' which were gathered from a wide range of educational writings and hammered into shape in series of seminars with teachers. Not all of Hosford's statements are empirical.

Hosford does not claim that his listing is exhaustive, but to me it gives the impression that it is comparable to a listing of the known chemical elements in 1900 AD rather than an explorer's map of the world in 1500 AD.

(e)

The arrogance and implication of my suggestion that there are few open generalizations in education is bothersome. Nevertheless, it seems a succinct way of describing the problem of which many people engaged in educational research are aware. The following quotations show some of the ways in which this problem has been expressed by others.

Travers (1973) in his editorial introduction to the *Second Handbook of Research on Teaching*, says,

> In many cases, after reviewing the literature, the author made the decision that the material was such that he could not write a chapter bringing the findings together – the complaint being that the research consisted of a patchwork of unrelated items that neither fitted together nor yielded a useful set of generalizations.

Rosenshine and Furst (1973), writing in the *Second Handbook of Research on Teaching* about the use of direct observation to study teaching, say: 'It is possible that the patterns of effective teaching for different ends are so idiosyncratic that they will never be isolated.'

Entwistle (1973) writing for the Open University says,

> As far as educational research is concerned, the paradigm of the hypothetico-deductive method is an ideal rarely achieved. The complexity of children's behaviour in a classroom often leaves research workers still at the stage of hypothesis hunting. Elaborate theories with accurate prediction lie in the future . . . Science provides important guidelines, but here is the uneasy realization that social science may, after all, be different in kind from natural science.

Beard, Bligh and Harding (1978), in a monograph for the Society for Research into Higher Education on research into teaching methods in higher education, come to the following conclusion.

> The growth of educational research [into teaching methods in higher education] has been accompanied in recent years by a growth in criticism of its methods and consequently of its results. There are so many variables that it is impossible to control all of them; even obviously important variables may sometimes remain uncontrolled. In addition, there are unpredictable effects. Human subjects when assigned to experimental and controlled groups differ from the biologists' wheat grains in being autonomous. They may choose to remove themselves, to compare notes with other students who are subjected to a different treatment; or they may so resent, or enjoy, a new method that their motivation and performance are significantly affected while it retains its novelty. Fatigue, pressure from other work, or some kind of distraction may also affect results. Even when experiments seem to be conducted successfully,

the results usually apply only to certain groups of students. They provide little information about individuals and rarely establish causal relationships and it is often difficult to draw conclusions having general application. While it is true that we seem almost as far as ever from developing a theory of instruction, there is at least a fairly substantial body of information to provide ideas for teachers who wish to try new methods, and to indicate possible outcomes.

Some writers take the view that these difficulties are not inevitable, but are simply attributable to education research being at an early stage of development. Thus Burroughs (1975) says:

> Not all educational research is hypothesis orientated. This is principally for two reasons; first, this science is still in its early exploratory days, concerned with the assembly of data and with the answering of questions . . . in this respect it is in the same position as other sciences in their early stages . . . Secondly, a number of research workers have not yet realized the importance and power of the hypothesis and do not conceive their projects in such a way as to use them.

In my view, Burroughs is unjust to the research workers who reject hypothesis hunting.

(f)

In *What's the Use of Lectures?* Bligh (1971) summarized his analysis of 68 research reports on the effectiveness of lectures compared to other methods for transmitting information in this statement: 'The lecture is as effective as other methods for transmitting information.'

This purports to be an open generalization. In fact it is not a valid generalization at all. In his analysis he found 16 reports in which lectures were more effective than other methods in transmitting information, 14 reports in which lectures were less effective and 38 reports in which the results showed no significant differences between lectures and other methods. I submit that this type of finding should be expressed in the form of a closed generalization, namely: 'In the studies carried out up to 1971, the lecture is as effective as other methods for transmitting information.'

This form of statement makes it quite clear that the generalization refers to certain events of the past and that although this may give an indication of the effectiveness of lectures in the future it does not necessarily predict accurately. This is not pedantry but rigour. I would also wish to see more of the variation of results expressed in the statement of findings, as the scale of the statement, namely:

> In 68 studies carried out up to 1971 it was found in over a half that the lecture is

no more and no less effective than other methods for transmitting information. However, in just under a quarter of these studies the lecture was found
to be more effective and in a similar number it was found to be less effective.

(g)

In *Teaching Styles and Pupil Progress*, Bennett (1976) formulated conclusions in the form of open generalizations, namely:

> The results form a coherent pattern. The effect of teaching style is statistically
> and educationally significant in all attainment areas tested. In reading, pupils
> of formal and mixed teachers progress more than those of informal teachers,
> the difference being equivalent to some three to five months' difference in
> performance. In mathematics formal pupils are superior to both mixed and
> informal pupils . . .

It would have been more rigorous (and less open to abuse by the popular
newspapers) had he expressed these conclusions in the form of closed
generalizations, namely:

> The results *from 37 teachers (selected from 468, 4th year junior school teachers in
> Lancashire and Cumbria in 1974 to make three groups characterized as 'formal',
> 'mixed' and 'informal')* form a coherent pattern. The effect of teaching style
> *was* statistically and educationally significant in all attainment areas tested. In
> reading, *the* pupils of *the* formal and *the* mixed teachers progressed *on average*
> more than those of *the* informal teachers, the difference being equivalent *on
> average* to some three to five months difference in performance. In mathe-
> matics, *on average the* formal pupils *were* superior to both mixed and informal
> pupils . . .

The insertion of 'on average' is important because, as Bennett makes
clear, not all of the thirteen informal teachers had worse results than the
other teachers.

> The results presented so far portray a fairly dismal picture of achievement in
> informal classrooms. Nevertheless there was one such classroom which was
> categorized by high gain in every achievement area; indeed in one area it was
> the highest gain class.

It follows that his statements about formal and informal styles are not
useful in predicting for *any particular teacher* the outcomes of these styles.
There are other factors operating in the classroom; these statements may be
helpful if seen as thinking points, but are unhelpful, if not worse, if seen as
having the predictive power of open generalizations.

There is an important point to be made here about averaging. The
fundamental unit in education is the individual person, but in educational

research the common procedure in analysing data is to obliterate tł
vidual and to consider averages and standard deviations from the av
It is said that this is necessary in order to draw meaningful conclusions from
data, but inevitably this conceals the evidence of individuals who are
different from the majority. Perhaps researchers should publish scatter-
grams showing the results from every individual as well as the averages.
This would draw attention to any anomalies.

(h)
Gowin (1972), in the paper cited earlier, refers to the so-called 'two-thirds
rule'. This expresses the findings that 'two-thirds of the time in a classroom
someone is talking, and during the two-thirds of that time it is the teacher
that is doing so'. Gowin comments in these terms:

> This regularity in educational phenomena has been consistently observed and
> recorded over decades. It looks like an empirical generalization that will hold
> up like generalizations in chemistry or some other science. But change the
> educational concept from self-contained classrooms to open learning centres,
> from group instruction to personalized instruction – change the education
> concepts which direct the educational practice and the regularity expressed in
> the two-thirds rule will vanish from the educational scene.

In my view the 'two-thirds rule' is an empirical generalization, but one of
the closed variety. It should be expressed in terms of the classrooms which
have been studied and not in terms of any classroom.

In what ways are generalizations useful to teachers?

Open generalizations give reliable predictions and so are obviously valuable
in the making of classroom decisions. But, in my view, they are scarce in
number and so once these few have been mastered, and have become an
integral part of a teacher's way of operating, they appear obvious and no
longer valuable. Thus it is self-evident to a competent teacher that unless
the interest of his pupils is aroused, or unless the subject is meaningful to
them, little will be achieved. Perhaps the value of open generalizations is
primarily to student-teachers.

Closed generalizations serve a different purpose in the making of classroom decisions. Because they do not necessarily predict what will happen
in his classroom the teacher cannot use them as prescriptions. A closed
generalization can be used by a teacher trying to *relate* what has happened in
other classrooms to what is happening in his. The closed generalization can

stimulate his thinking about possible lines of action and it can alert him to possible consequences; it can influence his judgement on the best way of acting: it can assist him in deciding what to do, but it cannot tell him.

It follows from this, that in formulating a closed generalization, the more information which is given that helps a teacher to relate the teaching situations of the generalization to his own, the more likely it is to be useful to him. But in seeking to generalize, one is looking for similarities rather than differences, and so much of the information which might be helpful is not recorded. This leads to the view that perhaps the thorough study of single events may be more valuable than the extraction of common factors from a series of single events. In other words, perhaps the case study is potentially more useful to teachers than the closed generalization.

It is noteworthy that Cronbach (1975) advocates placing less emphasis on generalization than has been the traditional practice of educational psychologists.

> Instead of making generalization the ruling consideration in our research, I suggest that we reverse our priorities. An observer collecting data in our particular situation is in a position to appraise a practice or proposition in that setting, observing effects in context. In trying to describe and account for what happened, he will give attention to whatever variables were controlled, but he will give equally careful attention to uncontrolled conditions, to personal characteristics, and to events that occurred during treatment and measurement. As he goes from situation to situation, his first task is to describe and interpret the effect anew in each locale, perhaps taking into account factors that were unique to that locale, or series of events. As results accumulate, a person who seeks understanding will do his best to trace how the uncontrolled factors could have caused local departures from the modal effect. That is, generalization comes late, and the exception is taken as seriously as the rule.

Relatability or generalizability?

Walker (1980), in a paper on the conduct of educational case studies, raises what he calls the 'generalization problem'.

> This is seen in terms of the limited reliability and validity of the case study and is often framed in terms of two questions: how can you justify studying only one instance; even if it is justifiable theoretically, what use can be made of the study by those who have to take action?

If the purpose of educational research is to produce generalizations which will coalesce into theory, it is clear that the only justification for a case study is that it is one more brick contributing to the construction of a large building. This seems to be the view of Stenhouse (1978) in his call for four levels of data organization: case data, case record, case study and analytic survey; the last of these 'is an attempt to draw together data from case records to make retrospective generalizations across cases'.

On the other hand, if the purpose of educational research is to contribute in some way to improvement of educational practice it may not be necessary to fit case studies together into one edifice.

I submit that an important criterion for judging the merit of a case study is the extent to which the details are sufficient and appropriate for a teacher working in a similar situation to relate his decision making to that described in the case study. The relatability of a case study is more important than its generalizability.

As an example consider the Cosford Cube (Taplin, 1969). The Cosford Cube was developed by Taplin, an RAF instructor, as a simple way of obtaining feedback in the classroom from trainees. It consists of a 2½ inch wooden cube painted with a different colour on each face. The instructor, in the course of his teaching, poses a multiple-choice question with the possible answers colour coded. To indicate his answer each trainee rests his elbows on the desk with the cube cupped in both hands and with his colour code answer showing to the instructor. Trainees cannot see each other's answers, but the instructor can see them all.

This was developed for RAF trainees. To what extent could it be applied in other teaching situations? The kinds of questions which a teacher reading a case study on the use of the Cosford Cube might ask are these:

How was the procedure introduced to students?
Could I do it?

What were the students like in the experiment?
How far were they motivated to learn?
Would it be suitable for my students?

How frequently was the procedure used?
Would I use it as often or more, or less?

How did the students respond to the procedure?
Did they see it as worthwhile?
Would my students appreciate it?

How much gain in learning occurred?
Did students who disliked it, learn less?
How would my students fare?

These questions are attempts to relate the reader's situation to that of the experiment.

Research forms which are alternatives to quests for generalizations

If there are few opportunities for research leading to open generalizations of pedagogic interest and if the opportunities for research leading to closed generalizations tend to have little relevance to the improvement of teaching (cf. Cohen's examples), what alternative forms of pedagogic research are there? As suggested above, the answer lies in research into single sets of events, in other words, case study research. Unfortunately the current esteem of the research community is very high for searches for open generalizations and low for the description of single events. Table 1 gives a simplistic analysis of the prospects for pedagogic researchers in terms of opportunities, potential impact and current esteem of the research community. There are signs however that the esteem of research into single sets of events is rising.

Table 1 Prospects for pedagogic researchers in terms of three kinds of research

	Opportunities	Potential impact on teaching	Current esteem of research community
Research leading to open generalization	Few	Large	Very high
Research leading to closed generalization	Many	Small	High
Research into single sets of events	Many	Large	Low

Research into single sets of events can be descriptive, or evaluative, or both, namely:

Description of the various ways in which individual teachers carry out some particular task, in order to broaden the base from which a teacher reading the research report can make his own decisions on how to tackle the task.

Evaluations of the above by (a) collection of comments from children, teachers, experts and observers; and (b) classroom observations such as time studies, interaction studies, analyses of children's work, attainment tests, etc.

If studies such as these are carried out systematically and critically, if they are aimed at the improvement of education, if they are relatable, and if by publication of the findings they extend the boundaries of existing knowledge, then they are valid forms of educational research. I submit that the educational research community, including those who engage in research, sponsor research, train new researchers, validate research degree proposals, examine research degrees theses, and preside over research publications, should distinguish between pedagogic research and other forms of educational research, and in relation to pedagogic research should eschew the pursuit of generalizations, unless their potential usefulness is apparent, and instead should actively encourage the descriptive and evaluative study of single pedagogic events. In this way pedagogic research will contribute effectively to the improvement of pedagogic practice.

References

Beard, R.M., Bligh, D.A. and Harding, A.G. (1978) *Research Into Teaching Methods in Higher Education*, 4th edition. Surrey, Society for Research into Higher Education.

Bennett, N. (1976) *Teaching Styles and Pupil Progress*. London, Open Books.

Bligh, D.A. (1971) *What's the Use of Lectures?* London, UTMU.

Burroughs, G.E.R. (1975) *Design and Analysis in Educational Research*, 2nd edition. University of Birmingham.

Butcher, H.J. (ed.) (1968) *Educational Research in Britain*, Vol. 1. University of London Press.

Cohen, L. (1976) *Educational Research in Classrooms and Schools*. London, Harper & Row.

Cohen, L. and Manion, L. (1980) *Research Methods in Education*. London, Croom Helm.

Cronbach, L.J. (1975) Beyond the two disciplines of scientific psychology, *American Psychologist*, Vol. 30, No. 2, pp. 116–127.

Eggleston, J. (1979) The characteristics of educational research: mapping the domain, *British Educational Research Journal*, 5, pp. 1–12.

Entwistle, N.J. (1973) *The Nature of Educational Research*. Open University course on Methods of Educational Enquiry.

Entwistle, N.J. and Nisbet, J.D. (1972) *Educational Research in Action*. London, Hodder & Stoughton.

Gowin, D.R. (1972) Is educational research distinctive?, in Thomas, L.G. (ed.) *Philosophical Redirection of Educational Research*, 71st Yearbook of the National Society for the Study of Education. Illinois, University of Chicago Press.

Hosford, P.L. (1973) *An Instructional Theory: a beginning.* New Jersey, Prentice-Hall.

Kerlinger, F.N. (1977) The influence of research on education practice, *Educational Researcher*, September, pp. 5–11.

Maccoby, E.E. and Jacklin, C.N. (1974) *The Psychology of Sex Differences.* Stanford University Press.

Nisbet, J.D. (1974) Educational research: the state of the art, in Dockrell, W.B. and Hamilton, D. (eds.) *Rethinking Educational Research.* Kent, Hodder & Stoughton, 1980.

Nisbet, J.D. and Entwistle, N.J. (1973) The psychologist's contribution to educational research, in Taylor, W. (ed.) *Research Perspectives in Education.* London, Routledge & Kegan Paul.

Nisbet, J.D. and Entwistle, N.J. (1970) *Educational Research Methods.* London, Hodder & Stoughton.

Peters, R.S. and White, J.P. (1969) The philosopher's contribution to educational research, in Taylor, W. (ed.) *Research Perspectives in Education.* London, Routledge & Kegan Paul, 1973.

Rosenshine, B. and Furst, N. (1973) The use of direct observation to study teaching, in Travers, loc. cit.

Simon, B. (1978) Educational research: which way?, *British Educational Research Journal*, Vol. 4, No. 1, pp. 2–7.

Stenhouse, L. (1980) The study of samples and the study of cases, *British Educational Research Journal*, 6, pp. 1–6.

Stenhouse, L. (1978) Case study and case records: towards a contemporary history of education, *British Educational Research Journal*, 4, No. 2, pp. 21–39.

Stones, E. (1979) *Psychopedagogy.* London, Methuen.

Taplin, G. (1969) The Cosford Cube: a simplified form of student feedback, *Industrial Training International*, 4, pp. 218–219.

Travers, R.M.W. (1973) *Second Handbook of Research on Teaching.* Chicago, Rand McNally.

Walker, R. (1980) The conduct of educational case studies: ethics, theory and procedures, in Dockrell, W.B. and Hamilton, D. (eds.) *Rethinking Educational Research.* Kent, Hodder & Stoughton.

Michael Bassey *Oxford Review of Education*, Volume 7, No. 1, 1981, pp. 73–88 (Appendix pp. 88–94 excluded).
Dr Michael Bassey is Reader in Education at Trent Polytechnic, Nottingham.

CHAPTER 8

ETHICAL PRINCIPLES IN SCHOOL SELF-EVALUATION

Helen Simons

This chapter is of particular interest to teacher-evaluators not only because of the author's approach to school self-evaluation, but also because she discusses in some detail ethical problems which may arise in such an exercise. She discusses problems of impartiality, confidentiality/control, negotiation, collaboration and account-ability and lists procedures derived from each of these principles.

She makes two suggestions which some researchers may query. In the section on impartiality, she states that the role of the evaluator is to describe what happens, not to recommend what should happen. She is describing a method of self-evaluation based on democratic principles and takes the view that it is not the role of one teacher to pass judgement on colleagues. This seems reasonable enough, but in many investigations, the purpose of the exercise *is* to provide recommendations for improvement of practice or change of policy. The purpose of the investigation will dictate the nature of the conclusions.

In the section on confidentiality/control, she suggests that pseudonyms or role designation should be used in reports, rather than real names. This is a practice commonly adopted, but not always. Most Open University case studies name real people and real institutions. The important point is that if names are to be used, the people involved must be willing to be named.

[. . .] School-based evaluation is not a new concept and has been used to refer to quite different practices. It may be useful to indicate how the term has been interpreted in the past and why a different approach, namely school self-evaluation based on democratic principles, merits investigation.

Informal evaluations undertaken by heads and/or staff as part of their 'normal practice' or curriculum renewal or policy change are based in and usually remain private to the school or, perhaps, a few within the school. Formal evaluations conducted by outside researchers using the school as a base may become public but are usually conducted and presented in terms defined by the researchers and subject to their control. Both kinds of evaluation do not necessarily involve or reflect the views of a large number of staff. In the case of external evaluations power to control what is made accessible to others lies, with certain exceptions, in the hands of the researchers even though in many cases they have consulted over access, aspired to reflect issues relevant to teachers and sought agreement for publication.

The proposal suggested here accepts the need for schools to present accounts of their work to the public but shifts the basis of control for how this should be done to the people within the school. Giving teachers control over their own evaluation respects their autonomy, protects their 'right to privacy' and, paradoxical though it may seem, provides a process for making the policies and practices of schools more public. School-based evaluation in the context defined here is not a defensive reaction to accountability demands from the centre or outside the school but a positive means for institutional self-development. It will, at the same time, provide a document of self-accountability. The prime aim of the self-evaluation is to assist staff to monitor policies and practices within their school to inform their own decision making; the secondary aim is to produce accounts of their work which can be made accessible to outside groups such as parents, governors, the LEA and the community.

Principles

The aim of the democratic approach to evaluation is to open up the work of the school to discussion while finding some way of protecting the individual's 'right to privacy'. This is a particularly delicate exercise to carry out within an institution bounded in time and in one building and where the principal evaluators are the teachers themselves. The principles and procedures below may help to create conditions where this might be possible. Each teacher/evaluator would be asked to adopt these principles of procedure in conducting research in their schools. These are safeguards to the participants, the teacher/evaluator, the school and the objectivity of the evaluation. They should be explicit and all staff and students, whether involved directly or indirectly in the evaluation, should be informed of them. The procedures, summarized at the end, are derived from the following principles.

I. *Impartiality*

In a school where the evaluation of a policy issue is initiated and co-ordinated by a member of staff the principle of impartiality is both problematic and essential. It is problematic because the member of staff may have vested interests in the issue and wish to see these represented. It is essential for precisely the same reason. If the evaluation is to be perceived to be objective and the evaluator impartial, this principle is crucial to:

(a) Safeguard the evaluation against bias and the participants against the evaluators using the evaluation as a platform for the promotion of their own views. It is not possible for the teacher/evaluator to be entirely free from bias. What is important is that the person be aware of these biases and be prepared to subject them to internal checks and criticism. If the teacher/evaluator can find a person outside the school acceptable to the participants and him/herself it might be possible to have an outside check as well.

(b) Protect the evaluator and the evaluation against cooption by particular groups within or outside the school. The evaluation should not advocate one group's position, that is teachers, pupils, heads of departments, at the expense of others, for example heads or junior staff; it should treat everyone's point of view as open to justification and attempt to represent different perspectives impartially. To this end the teacher/evaluator should forgo putting forward his view. In the event his view may be represented by others but even if it is it should not receive undue emphasis.

(c) Establish the credibility of the evaluation outside the school. Self-reports have low credibility. If the evaluation can demonstrate that through the procedures it has checked for bias and reported impartially it will be more likely to be regarded as nonpartisan to inside critics and credible to outside critics who dismiss such internal reports as 'too subjective'.

II. *Confidentiality/Control*

The principle of confidentiality is equally problematic in a school where the evaluator is also a member of staff. Certain information will already be public knowledge. But there will also be information private to the individuals. So much that is taken for granted in normal day-to-day practice is open in a self-evaluation to critique. What is private may become public, if even to a few, and this may be threatening to some of the staff. Important decisions, it is often claimed, are made during the 'chat in the staff room over a cup of tea' or informally outside of school. Such occasions should not be jeopardized by the evaluation. The line between 'gossip' and informal chat may be perceived to be a narrow one and needs to be checked if informal conversations and observations provide data for the evaluation. Some procedures are necessary to ensure that business carries on as usual and that teachers and pupils are not put at risk by openly and frankly discussing their work or policy issues.

Information that is private to the individual should be governed by the principle of confidentiality. Information that is already public knowledge within the school should be subject to controlled release. The onus is on the researcher to aspire not to gossip and on the participants to take control over their own data. If participants have control over what data are given and released they are more likely to offer accurate perceptions and to respond honestly to the issue under discussion.

Giving control also helps to ensure that participants are not made vulnerable by their cooperation and contribution; it reassures them that the person documenting the account and facilitating the information exchange cannot misuse information from any one individual.

Giving control, in summary, protects their 'right to be discreet' and allows them to pace the flow of any information they decide to share. It should not be used, however, to censor relevant information. (Relevant information will be agreed upon by those contributing to the study.) There would be little point in undertaking the evaluation if the aim was not to produce some useful information. Confidentiality, if necessary (and in some cases it might not be) should be seen as a stage in a process of making information that is useful accessible to further discussion. Control should not be used to protect confidentiality. Once accurate and relevant accounts have been negotiated and presented in ways that do not threaten participants [. . .] this protection should no longer apply.

III. *Negotiation*

Negotiation is a central principle in democratic evaluation, protecting participants from the evaluators taking total control over the data and using them for their own purposes. Confidentiality may be some protection for the individual in some situations but it is no guarantee. Once information has been given the participant has been made vulnerable, while the evaluator, now privy to certain information, gains power. Without other principles the evaluators could use their position to gain clearance of that information for wider release. After all, they have the initiative throughout for generating the data. It is the participant who is more at risk. The fact that the evaluators claim to be trustworthy and operating on the principle of impartiality does not necessarily help. It may set up a sense of false security where participants may be quite prepared to give over control of the data to the evaluators. All this serves to do is reverse the situation and put the evaluators at risk. Participants also deny their responsibility to take control over 'their' data.

Negotiation helps to ensure that a balance is maintained between the 'public's right to know' and the individual's 'right to be discreet'. The evaluators should negotiate with participants to set the boundaries of the study in terms of accessibility, relevance of issues and feasibility of procedures and approach. They should negotiate clearance of information offered by participants and used as data for the evaluation before distribution to anyone else.

Negotiation does not lead to a 'watered down' account, as some people have claimed. On the contrary. It encourages people to participate; gives them room to contribute equally and fairly; improves the impartiality of the account by inviting checks on biases and improves the reliability and validity of the accounts. Aware that other participants are presenting their perspectives participants are encouraged to put their views honestly. Documenting different people's perspectives on the same issue is also a further reliability check.

IV. *Collaboration*

[. . .] Given the current pressures on schools to 'go public' internal evaluation is likely to raise anxieties about the use of information, control of data and appropriateness of techniques of assessment. However harmonious relationships in a school appear to be, however democratic the organization, trust does not automatically exist between professionals. It has to be created. In any institution people will choose their confidants and keep their secrets. School self-evaluation demands a degree of openness which on the face of it might seem to threaten individuals' or small groups' right to privacy to keep their classroom practices within the confines of the classroom and school policies within the confines of the school.

The principles already cited go some way to ensure that participants' 'rights to privacy' are protected while information is gradually shared. But an additional, perhaps prior, principle is collaboration. To engage in the evaluation at all demands a commitment to sharing data relevant to an understanding of the school's practices and policies. The principle of collaboration ensures that teachers begin to share their work with others in the school; the other principles give them control over how and at what pace they do this.

To take account of initial anxieties each participant may wish to choose to collaborate with one or two persons in the school asking them to check self-reports for fairness, accuracy and relevancy. Once a degree of confidence is gained and reliability and validity attributed to the data and procedures, these can gradually be extended in the interest of presenting fair accounts to facilitate policy discussions in the whole school. The procedures are designed to promote self-reflection in the school as a whole but can only do so to the extent that participants are willing to cooperate in the study.

V. *Accountability*

That schools should be accountable to the public is not at issue in a democratic society. The public have a right to know what is going on in schools which they help to support and to which they send their children. The question is how, in what terms and to whom, in particular, should they be accountable. It is this question which has in recent years come under the microscope of the education profession and lay community alike in terms of who maintains control over the running of our schools.

It should not be assumed [. . .] that schools are the most closed of institutions in our society. There are many ways in which schools already provide information about themselves. They keep records of pupil achievement. Parents receive report cards of pupil progress. Examination results are public. Parents and the public may also have access to information on issues such as school rules, staff policy on options, academic and pastoral organization, roles of staff, transfer from primary to secondary, remedial teaching, career guidance, extra-curricular activities. What are less open to view are the decision-making processes for determining policies of teaching practice, curriculum changes, allocation of resources, etc. But it should be noted that in these respects schools do not differ from many institutions.

The proposal here suggests that schools take the initiative for further ways of reporting to the public by first accounting to themselves. By opening up their own practices to internal criticism and documenting their perspectives and aspirations on issues central to their development, teachers can facilitate self-reflection within their own school. In so doing they might also produce accounts which meet outside accountability demands. But such reports would be defined in the school's own terms and their distribution to any other group controlled by them.

That the evaluation should also be accountable to individual participants and the school is also not at issue. The procedures help to ensure that the teacher/evaluator meets this responsibility.

Procedures

Set out below are lists of the procedures derived from each of the principles just discussed.

I. *Impartiality*

1. The teacher/evaluators' role is to collect the judgements of others and represent a range of views on policy issues. They should withhold their own judgement in description and keep their own view out of reports.
2. Their role is to describe what happens in policy meetings, staff meetings, the classroom, etc., to report accurately and fairly whatever transpires, not to recommend what *should* happen: i.e.
   they should inform decisions without prejudging them;
   they should present options without prescription;
   they should come to no final judgement;
   they should present a range of perspectives on the issue;
   they should not press particular viewpoints.
3. Self-reports by one person within the school should also be descriptive adhering to the procedures above. 'Critical friends' within the school should check for biases and respond on criteria of fairness, accuracy, and relevancy. It is not their role to pass judgement on colleagues.
4. Conditions are the same for all. All participants should have equal access to the data once it has been negotiated. No one has the right to veto what is reported and cleared by participants.

II. *Confidentiality/Control*

1. Conversations are confidential to the individual person; knowledge within the school is subject to release by them.
2. The evaluator will not report anything or examine documents relevant to a particular person without his/her consent.

3. Interviews, discussions, staff meetings, committee meetings, written statements are all potential data for the evaluation. But individuals have the right to restrict parts of the exchange or to correct or improve their statements.
4. Contributors to the evaluation have control over to whom it is released.
5. Reports should aspire to be issue- not person-orientated.
6. Pseudonyms or role designation should be used in reporting if attributing quotations to people. While this does not offer anonymity it depersonalizes issues that may be critical to discuss and which, if contentious, might become 'too personal'.
7. Clearance need not be sought for information summarizing findings or reporting general perspectives on issues which involve no specific detail about persons or groups.
8. Where details are included which do identify the person or source, clearance is necessary.

III. *Negotiation*

1. The teacher/evaluator should negotiate the boundaries of the study with participants.
2. The teacher/evaluator will seek access only to those data sources relevant to the issue under discussion. There will be no gratuitous reporting. What is relevant needs to be negotiated with the participants. Potential relevant data sources within the school include the head, teachers, pupils, ancillary staff, school records, examples of pupils' work and, outside the school, governors, parents, LEA advisers.
3. Reports/statements should first be checked with the individual or group concerned. Only with their agreement on amendments should reports be made accessible to other people.
4. Reports should be negotiated on criteria of fairness, accuracy and relevancy, not on personal grounds, for example whether the person looks favourable or unfavourable in the report.
5. On occasions one person may negotiate on behalf of a group (e.g. head of department on behalf of department) providing the group delegate this responsibility to that person.
6. If several people are mentioned in a report, information should be negotiated first with those who would be most disadvantaged if it were negotiated with all at the same time. (The question of who would be most disadvantaged in any one setting needs to be discussed.) This helps to

ensure that participants genuinely share control with the teacher/
evaluator and share control and risk with the other participants.
7. Before taking part in negotiation, participants should be aware for whom
the report is intended. If it is subsequently desired for another group its
release has to be renegotiated.
8. The accessibility of any product of the evaluation should be negotiated
with all the participants.

IV. *Collaboration*

1. Every person has the right to participate.
2. Every person has the right not to collaborate.
3. The teacher/evaluator should choose one or two persons within the
school to check reports for fairness, accuracy, and relevancy.
4. The teacher/evaluator may choose one or two persons outside the school
(subject to internal agreement with participants) to help keep biases in
check.
5. The teacher/evaluator should not expect everyone to participate nor
coerce anyone who would prefer not to participate.
6. All collaborators should work to the same procedures.

V. *Accountability*

1. The teacher/evaluator will be accountable to the participants in the ways
outlined in this paper.
2. The evaluation will be accountable to the school by being responsive to
their policy concerns.
3. The evaluation will be accountable to internal criticism and external
checks from time to time if the latter is agreed upon.
4. Other ways in which the evaluation needs to be accountable will depend
upon local settings and the kind of issues discussed.

Concluding comments

Within any institution there are likely to be power imbalances in the
distribution of roles, tasks and information. Increasing the flow of information increases the possibility that the powerful may gain more influence at
the expense, perhaps, of those in the least powerful position. Who is the
more powerful, of course, may differ on different issues. As the teacher/
evaluator begins to document the study he or she may come to be perceived

as upsetting the balance of power. The procedures are necessary therefore not only to protect all participants but also the teacher/evaluator from misusers of information. It is perhaps the case that in a truly open society there would be no need to introduce such explicit procedures. But that does not seem to be the system we work in at present.

Procedures do not, however, provide guarantees. Their effectiveness depends upon the evaluator establishing and maintaining an atmosphere of trust. This is best achieved by demonstrating that the evaluation is responsive to the needs of the school and that the teacher/evaluator is committed to the rights of participants and the procedures. Onus for upholding the principles clearly lies with the evaluator. The ultimate sanction rests with participants. By withholding relevant information, giving the evaluation token support, or refusing to participate, teachers within the school can effectively curtail the school's self-study.

Notes

1. The idea for this type of school self-study stemmed both from evaluation theory and practical experience in studying a school in the SAFARI Project – a Ford Foundation sponsored project looking at medium-term effects of curriculum projects in schools. In this school six teachers reported how their group discussion of a SAFARI issues report stimulated discussion of 'critical' policy issues within the school of a kind which had not been possible at regular staff meetings or in special sub-committees set up to discuss school policy. Their experience pointed out the potential of this approach for continuing self-evaluation and professional development. This paper outlines procedures to the school itself to explore this potential systematically.

2. [. . .] For further details of SAFARI see Innovation, Evaluation and the Problem of Control: Some Interim Papers, Centre for Applied Research in Education, University of East Anglia, 1974.
   [. . .]

Helen Simons. Bulletin No. 3: *Classroom Action Research Network: School-based Evaluation.* Cambridge Institute of Education, Spring 1979, pp. 49–55 (Original title: *Suggestions for a school self-evaluation based on democratic principles.*)
Helen Simons is a Lecturer in Curriculum Studies and Evaluation at the University of London Institute of Education.

CHAPTER 9

SOURCES, RECORDS AND REFERENCES: A GUIDE FOR STUDENTS PLANNING INVESTIGATIONS IN EDUCATIONAL MANAGEMENT

Judith Bell & Sandy Goulding

Many a project has ground to a halt, or been left incomplete because too much time was spent searching for materials and checking sources and references. Judith Bell and Sandy Goulding take us through the steps involved in conducting a literature search, offer advice about record keeping and describe the processes involved in the presentation of references and bibliographies. Every investigator will need the skills and techniques they describe and this chapter will serve as a guide and source of reference for novice and experienced researcher alike.

Any investigation, whatever the scale, will involve reading what other people have written about your area of interest, gathering information to support or refute your arguments and writing about your findings. If you are provided with a topic for investigation, then you will in all probability be provided with lists of books and articles which come under the heading of Required Reading, Recommended Reading, Suggested Reading, Set Books, or something of the kind. That is obviously your starting point and, in a small project which has to be completed in two or three months, may provide sufficient reading for your purposes. If you are selecting your own topic, you will need to find out what has been published in your field, even if time only allows you to read a selection of books and articles and reviews. An extensive study of the literature will be required for a Ph.D., and a critical review of what has been written on the topic produced in the final report or thesis. A project lasting only two or three months will not require anything so ambitious, but you will still need to show you have read as much as time allowed, and that you have some awareness of the current state of knowledge on the subject. The important questions are:

How to find the most relevant published materials quickly?

How to avoid getting bogged down?

How to record information about the literature so that it can be easily found and understood weeks, months, or years later?

What has been done before?

Earlier chapters in this book have stressed the need to adopt a systematic approach to planning an investigation. Whatever the size of the task, the same meticulous planning and attention to detail needs to be adopted in conducting a literature search. The first step is to ensure that you have access to a library; the second to ensure that you fully understand the services that are offered by library staff, and what materials the library holds – on the shelves, in reserve collections, on microfiche or microfilm. Bibliographies, abstracts, indexes and encyclopaedias can save hours of searching for sources, but they are not always easy to find or to understand. Although most libraries in this country follow the Dewey decimal system of classification, libraries do have different views about how some publications should be classified and stored. Government publications are notoriously difficult to find in a library which is new to you and rather than waste valuable time tracing them, it may be best to ask at the library information desk and to seek expert advice at an early stage. All libraries vary to some extent, so some time needs to be invested to become familiar with the geography and the stock before you begin your search for the literature. But first find your library.

Access to libraries
Public libraries

The services of public libraries in the local authority where you live (and possibly also where you work) will be available free of charge, and a good many local authorities have arrangements with neighbouring authorities which allow you to have borrowing rights. Small branch libraries will not generally have stocks which will be of use to research workers, though in some cases special collections have been built up which are of great value to students. Eastwood library in Nottinghamshire, for example, has a good collection of works by and relating to D.H. Lawrence, who lived in Eastwood at one time. However, this is rather exceptional and generally speaking an investigator will need to make use of the large main libraries.

Academic libraries

University, polytechnic or college students normally have full borrowing rights for that institution's library. 'Outsiders' who wish to use the facilities of an academic library will need to obtain the librarian's permission. Most libraries will give permission for bona fide students to use the library for reference purposes and a generous few allow lending facilities. However, you cannot *demand* to use specialist libraries. They are for the use of the students and staff of the institution and demands made on library staff are likely to stretch their resources and patience, particularly at certain times of the year. Teachers and others engaged in educational work in England and Wales are generally entitled to use the libraries of their nearest school or institute of education, though again this may be restricted to reference use, and in recent years a number of institute libraries have been incorporated into main university libraries. Full information about the school or institute of education libraries is outlined in *Study and Library Facilities for Teachers: universities, institutes and schools of education, etc.*, produced annually by the Hull Institute of Education for the librarians of institutes and schools of education.

What are you looking for?

We all think we know how to use libraries and certainly it would not take any of us long to get to grips with the system operating and the stock held by small branch libraries. Finding the way round and discovering what stock is held in main public and specialist libraries in universities, polytechnics and colleges is quite another matter. They can seem like Aladdin's caves for students and researchers. They hold treasures that dazzle; but caves can be dangerous. It is easy to get lost and to become so anxious not to leave any of the treasures behind that it becomes impossible ever to leave. All this is rather fanciful, but many a research project has foundered because the investigator had not defined the area of study sufficiently clearly and so extended the range of reading far beyond what was necessary. Large libraries are complicated places and library staff at the information desk will do their best to help you to come to grips with the way the stock is organized – but first, you need to know *exactly* what you are looking for.

The bewildered student in the cartoon is not so far removed from reality in some cases, so before you embark on an exploration of the library, and as a preliminary to conducting a literature search, you need to decide what you

Reproduced by permission of Colin Wheeler

need to know. That sounds easy enough. But is it?

You will only really get to know what a library can offer and how to use the facilities when you start looking for information yourself. Discussing library use in the abstract means very little until you are on the trail yourself, but there are certain guidelines that will help you to plan a search and certain steps that need to be taken whatever the scale of the operation.

Planning a literature search demands certain skills, foremost amongst which is the ability to define precisely what you mean. Let us say your area of interest is *leadership*. That would be your starting point, but exactly what do you mean by leadership? How will the library classify works which relate to leadership? Are you interested in leadership in schools, or in the steel industry, or government? Do you want references as far back as possible, or only in the past two years? In the UK, worldwide, or only in Halifax? Are there likely to be books and articles of interest to you that are classified under different headings? In fact, what do you mean and what exactly are you looking for?

The following outline takes you through the process of planning. If you are not to waste time, this process needs to be carried out whether you are intending to conduct a large and complex computer search, or whether your time and resources limit you to a study of library holdings and a range of other secondary sources (bibliographies, abstracts, indexes, etc).

Planning a literature search

		Examples
1.	*Select the topic*	LEADERSHIP
2.	*Define the terminology*	Leadership may be sufficient at this stage, but before you continue, do you have a clear idea of what 'leadership' means? Might other countries use a different terminology? If you consider the term 'leadership' is sufficiently explicit, continue to the next stage.
3.	*Define parameters*	
	Language	English?
	Geography	Material published in the UK only? USA? Australia? Where else? (If you only have two months to complete the entire project, you can't do everything. Keep the literature search to the UK and only move overseas if the search reveals nothing of significance.)
	Time period	1980 – present?
	Type of material	Journals, books, theses? (You may not have time to consult theses, which are generally only available for reference or on interlibrary loan.)
	Sector	School? Further education? University?

4. *List possible search terms*

The term 'leadership' is unlikely to produce all the relevant sources. You need to think of synonyms under which works of interest to you might have been classified. It may be helpful to consult a dictionary, or Roget's Thesaurus for ideas. Think of alternatives to 'leadership', or headings which might include aspects of leadership (authority? head teacher? manager?). One approach is to produce a diagram on the following lines, but you may find it easier simply to list all the terms you can think of. Remember, your diagram or list will probably expand as the search proceeds.

The search for terms

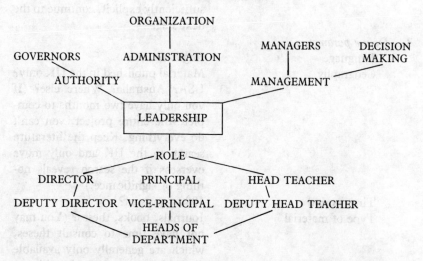

Having selected the topic, defined the terminology and the parameters, selected the search terms and put them into alphabetical order, you are then in a position to start looking for the materials. Your next step is to select sources.

5. *Select sources*

Library catalogue

Use the subject approach with selected terms (leadership, management, authority, head teacher, etc.). Make a note of the appropriate library class numbers. You can then use the classified catalogue, which is in class number order (i.e. in the same order as the books on the shelves) to find out exactly what the library holds on a particular subject. The library catalogue can be consulted again later as further search terms emerge from the bibliographies. You will also need to return to it at the end of your literature search, using an author or title approach, to check whether the library holds any material you discover in the bibliographies and which was missed in your original subject search.

Bibliographies

These will provide you with brief references of published works in your area. Start with books.

(a) Books

The *British National Bibliography* (BNB) has been published since 1950 and is generally available for consultation in public libraries. There are cumulative volumes. Use the index, which will probably list other terms you have not yet thought of. List these, to ensure consistency when searching through each BNB volume. (BNB also covers first issues of journals, monographs and some government publications, but it is concerned mainly with books).

The following extracts illustrate the way in which BNB lists items under subject headings.

From BNB Subject Catalogue	From BNB Index
(Volume 1, 1980)	*(Volume 2, 1980)*

Primary Schools

372.1′2′0120926 — Primary schools. Head teachers. Leadership. *United States. Case studies*
Jentz, Barry C. Leadership and learning : personal change in a professional setting / [by] Barry C. Jentz and Joan W. Wofford. — New York ; London [etc.] : McGraw-Hill, 1979. — xv,181,[1]p ; 24cm.
ISBN 0-07-032497-2 : £6.10

(B80-01592)

372.1′2′0120941 — Primary schools. Head teachers. Role. *Great Britain*
Jones, Roy. Primary school management / [by] Roy Jones. — Newton Abbot [etc.] : David and Charles, 1980. — 159p : 3 ill ; 23cm.
Bibl.: p.155. — Index.
ISBN 0-7153-7843-0 : £4.95 : CIP rev.

(B79-35781)

372.1′2′0120942 — Primary schools. Head teachers. Role. *England*
Waters, Derek. Management and headship in the primary school / [by] Derek Waters. — London : Ward Lock, 1979. — vi,338p : ill, forms ; 22cm.
Bibl.: p.330-335. — Index.
ISBN 0-7062-3865-6 Pbk : £5.95

(B80-24346)

Schools Administration

371.2′00941 — Schools. Administration. *Great Britain*
John, Denys. Leadership in schools. — London : Heinemann Educational, May 1980. — [196]p. — (Organisation in schools)
ISBN 0-435-80468-5 : £8.00 : CIP entry

(B80-05844)

371.2′012′0722 — Schools. Administration. Role of head teachers. *United States. Case studies*
Blumberg, Arthur. The effective principal : perspectives on school leadership / [by] Arthur Blumberg, William Greenfield. — Boston, Mass (London [etc.]) : Allyn and Bacon, 1980. — viii,280p ; 25cm.
Bibl.: p.271-273. — Index.
ISBN 0-205-06812-x : £15.95

(B80-25433)

Head teachers

Head teachers. Primary schools. England
  Role   372.1′2′0120942
Head teachers. Primary schools. Great Britain
  Role   372.1′2′0120941
Head teachers. Primary schools. United States
  Leadership — *Case studies*   372.1′2′0120926
Head teachers. Schools. United States
  Role in administration — *Case studies*   371.2′012′0722
Head teachers. Secondary schools. United States
  Administrative duties   373.1′2′0120973

Leadership

Leadership
  See also
    Captaincy. Sports
Leadership
  — *Conference proceedings*   301.15′53
Leadership. Christian life   248
Leadership. Discussion groups
  Christian life — *Daily readings — For discussion group leadership — Serials*   242′.2′05
Leadership. Group work. Roman Catholic Church   267
Leadership. Head teachers. Primary schools. United States
  — *Case studies*   372.1′2′0120926
Leadership. Management
  — *Manuals*   .658.4
Leadership. Management. Teams. Business firms
  — *Manuals — For construction industries*   658.4′02
Leadership. Politics. Great Britain
  1916-1978. Psychology   301.5′92
Leadership. Students. Schools
  Assessment. Sociometric analysis — *For teaching*   371.8′1

You will note that the Dewey decimal number is given in these BNB extracts. When you look up this number in BNB's classified sequence you will find the full bibliographical details of the work indexed. It is important to use the index and find the Dewey number for each year of BNB that you search, because class numbers change and also vary according to the subject emphasis.

As you scan the items, you will note that some do not fulfil your stipulated criteria. Two of the above items are published in the USA. It would be foolish to suggest that once you have defined parameters you may not move outside them, but bibliographies and indexes make seductive reading. Titles look interesting and before you know it, every title in the bibliography is noted. Try to discipline yourself and take the view that a strong case has to be made for the inclusion of any publication which falls outside your stipulated limits. Remind yourself how much time you can afford on this literature search and the reading which will inevitably follow, and be ruthless.

Having scanned the BNB for books, you move on to journals.

(b) Journals

British Education Index (BEI) has been published since 1954, with annual cumulative volumes. BEI indexes British periodicals concerned with education, and all the details necessary for finding an article on a particular topic are given in the subject list. Remember you are not checking under 'leadership' alone. You will also need to check under your other search terms.

The following extracts illustrate the way in which BEI lists some of the terms which are associated with the topic of 'leadership'.

Leadership

LEADERSHIP. Classroom behaviour. Teachers
The teacher's leadership behaviour in the classroom / Shizuo Yoshizaki. — *Sch. Psychol. Int.*, Vol.1, no.5 : 81. — p13-14

LEADERSHIP. Higher education institutions
Style
Leadership styles in institutions of higher education : a contingency approach / O.A. Ajayi. — *Coombe Lodge Rep.*, Vol.14, no.4 : 81. — p211-222
Bibliography: p221-222

LEADERSHIP. Managers
Training
Leadership development — towards an interpersonal skills
training programme / Beverly Alban Metcalfe. — *J. Eur. Ind.*
Train., Vol.5, no.1 : 81. — p23-26

LEADERSHIP. Principals. Further education institutions
Sustaining leadership / Eric Briault. — *Coombe Lodge Rep.*,
Vol.14, no.3 : 81. — p172-178

Management

MANAGEMENT. Primary schools
1967-1980 — Ireland & Northern Ireland — Comparative studies
The **implementation** of changes in the managerial system in
primary schools in Northern Ireland and the Republic of Ireland,
1967-1980 : a comparative study / Michael McKeown. — *Ir.*
Educ. Stud., Vol.1 : 81. — p275-295

MANAGEMENT. Recreation facilities. Community schools
The **management** of recreational facilities in community schools /
Michael McDonough. — *Ir. Educ. Stud.*, Vol.1 : 81. — p376-394
Bibliography: p393-394

MANAGEMENT. Schools
Decision making. Participation of teachers. Attitudes of trainee
teachers
Personal variables in student-teacher attitudes towards teacher
participation in school decision-making / G.A. Richardson. —
Durham Newcastle Res. Rev., Vol.9, no.47 : Autumn 81. —
p285-292

Deputy head teachers

DEPUTY HEAD TEACHERS. Primary schools
In-service training. Courses — Case studies
Primary school management : an in-service course / B.J.
Leatherbarrow. — *Br. J. In-serv. Educ.*, Vol.7, no.3 : Summer 81.
— p176-178

(c) Abstracts

Abstracts are invaluable and can
save weeks of effort, so it is always
worth investigating what is available. They provide summaries of
books, articles, etc. *School Organis-*
ation and Management Abstracts have
been produced quarterly since 1982
and are available for reference in
major libraries. *Research into Higher*
Education Abstracts is produced by

the Society for Research into Higher Education. *Sociology of Education Abstracts*, published by Carfax Publishing Company, has been produced since 1965 and a number of American and Canadian abstracting services provide international coverage of books, journals, reports, etc.

You can find out what abstracts are available in your area of interest by consulting *Ulrich's International Periodicals Directory*, and library staff will tell you which abstracts are in stock.

The following is an example of a journal abstract in *School Organisation and Management Abstracts*, Volume 2, No. 2, 1983, p. 96.

830/144   Leadership and the effective school. STEVE MURGATROYD & HARRY GRAY, *School Organization*, 2(3), 1982, pp 285—296.

The authors argue that effective schools require effective leadership. Four qualities are regarded as essential—empathy, warmth, genuineness and concreteness—for possession of leadership skills, which are regarded as essential. A picture is given of a school with both ineffective leadership and defective interpersonal relations, in which leadership was aloof, invisible, poor at communication, rejecting of others, closed, problem avoiding and responding to problems in a punitive fashion. Various methods of training and support for leadership are outlined.   —DR

(d) Theses

The *British Education Theses Index 1950–1980* (BETI) provides information on microfiche on a subject basis. Most theses can be obtained through interlibrary loan, but this always takes time and involves a charge. An example of the BETI subject list (still on the theme of 'leadership') is given below. If you are preparing for a higher degree, it is important to give yourself an idea of style, format, length, etc., but if you are working on a more limited project, you may not have time to spend obtaining and reading theses.

D 04*   COPYRIGHT LISE, 1981 BETI SUBJECT LIST
LEADERSHIP
An analysis of discussion leadership skills among
   student teachers,   by T.L. Kerry
Nottingham,   M.Phil.,   1976/77
10-067507

LEADERSHIP
Cohesion, satisfaction, leadership and
   output,   by F.J. Shatwell
Birmingham,   M.A.,   1957/58
10-076536

LEADERSHIP
The dynamics of leadership in adolescent school
   groups,   by   L.W. Shears
London, Institute of Education,   Ph.D., 1951/52
10-061523

LEADERSHIP
An ethological study of dominance behaviour in
   young children,   by K.A. Krebs
Oxford,   D. Phil.,   1972/73
10-022784

LEADERSHIP
The idea of education for leadership,   by J.L.
   Harrison
Manchester,   Ph.D.,   1967/68
10-008359

MANAGEMENT IN EDUCATION
The role of the housemaster in comprehensive day
   schools in the light of current thinking about
   management,   by P.C. Connor
Liverpool,   M.Ed.,   1971/72
10-036307

MANAGEMENT IN EDUCATION
The staff meeting in the structure of secondary
  school management,   by J.C. Chilton
Manchester,   M.Ed.,   1972/75
10-025897

MANAGEMENT IN EDUCATION
Teacher participation in school management,
  by R.D. Hurdman
Aston,   M.Phil.,   1976
10-056659

MANAGEMENT IN EDUCATION
Towards a socio-semantic framework for the analysis of
  the language of teachers, with special reference to
  management situations,
  by N.J. Maynard
Dundee,   M.Ed.,   1972/73
10-023156

MANAGEMENT IN EDUCATION
see also related heading ADMINISTRATION;
  COMPUTERS; EDUCATION; POLICY;
  EDUCATIONAL PLANNING; INSPECTION;
  NETWORK ANALYSIS; OPERATIONS RESEARCH;
  PRIMARY EDUCATION; RESEARCH IN
  EDUCATION; SCHOOL ORGANISATION;
  SECONDARY EDUCATION; STATISTICAL
  METHODS; SYSTEMS ANALYSIS
10-049446

Conducting an extensive literature search for a Ph.D. or a book is a
lengthy and quite complicated task. The above outline does not include
many of the sources that are available to a researcher, but it is likely to be
sufficient for most individual investigators working within a limited time
scale and with little or no funding. If you wish to know more, there are many
publications to help you. Dale (1981) in *Management and the School: using
the literature,* and Haywood and Wragg (1982) in *Evaluating the Literature*

produce an extensive range of information about bibliographies, glossaries, encyclopaedias, reviews, indexes, abstracts, current awareness services, theses and a good deal more. Haywood and Wragg also give guidance about using a computer link to retrieve information. You will only need to make use of a computer search if you need to conduct a very thorough study of the literature. If you or your institution can afford computer searches, they will reveal sources quickly, but they may produce more information than you can deal with in the time available. They require the help of library staff, can only be conducted where the library has access to a terminal, and they cost money. You can quickly run up a large bill, particularly if your enthusiasm gets the better of you. Valuable though computer searches are, most small-scale investigators will still depend on the library catalogue and the range of secondary sources (bibliographies, abstracts, indexes, etc.) to lead them to primary sources – the published books and articles.

The indexes, bibliographies and catalogues will provide you with information about what is available, but the next step is to obtain the primary material – the books and articles relating to your area of interest. Return to the library catalogue to find out what is in stock and where, either on the library shelves, in a reserve store or on microfiche. A brief scan can sometimes be enough to tell you whether the book or article is likely to be worth thorough study. Look at the preface and the chapter headings and see if there are summaries to chapters. Journal articles will generally have brief abstracts which give a clear idea of content and approach. If the material is not in stock, you may have to order it on interlibrary loan, but remember that this is not a free service. Either you or your library will have to pay, so make sure you have exhausted all the sources in your own library before you turn to outside stocks and check the information you have about the material before placing the order. Look at the date of publication. Is it likely to have been superseded? Does the reference in the bibliography or index give any clues? Might it relate to a context sufficiently different from your own to make it of only marginal interest? Have you seen a reference to this book or article in another work? Checks of this kind are unlikely to be foolproof but they can help in drawing up a short list of requirements.

Keeping records

Finding information in the first place can be hard enough. Finding it again, some time afterwards, can be even harder unless your methods of recording and filing are thorough and systematic. We all think we shall remember in the early days of an investigation. After several weeks of reading, analysing and selecting, memory becomes faulty. After a few months, we may vaguely recall having read something some time about the topic being studied, but when and where escapes us. After a longer period, the chances of remembering are remote.

Some writers on research methods recommend that a special research notebook should be kept, in which all activities relating to the investigation should be recorded – the dates letters were written and telephone calls and visits were made, good ideas, likely questions, dates when questionnaires were sent out and when returned. Such a notebook provides a chronological account of the progress of the investigation. Whether you keep a notebook or not, complete records should be kept of *all* sources (even those which prove to be of no interest) and the meaning of acronyms and jargon words, as you come across them.

The card index

Every student needs to keep a card index and the sooner some means of systematic record keeping is started the better. In the early days of an investigation, it may seem enough to jot down a reference on the back of an envelope, but old envelopes thrown into a box will not provide you with a reliable resource and the likelihood is that references will be incomplete and difficult to track down at a later stage. If you are only going to need half-a-dozen references, then scraps of paper may serve, but as your investigation proceeds you will accumulate many sources of information and an orderly system is necessary from the beginning. Most research workers will acknowledge that they have wasted valuable time tracing books, periodicals, quotations because they forgot to note the reference at the time, or because they inexplicably left off the name of the journal, the author or the date. The advantage of cards is that you can insert later entries and can re-sort if necessary. You can use the 5 x 3 inch size cards normally used in library catalogues, the 6 x 4 inch size or the 8 x 5 inch which give more room for notes.

Library card catalogues can serve as an example of the sort of basic information you should include and the type of layout that will suit your purposes, but if your cards are to serve as a research resource, you may need more information, either written on the back of the cards, or even extra sheets stapled to the cards.

The cards should be complete references and should include all the information you are likely to need for interlibrary loan applications and for drawing up the references or bibliography for your project report. They may include useful quotations, notes about the content of the book or article, reminders that a certain chapter or page had useful information about some topic. They will be your stock-in-trade and you should start building up your stock as soon as you begin your studies. It is a good idea to keep model cards which remind you about items that should be noted, together with punctuation and layout. You will always need the following:

BOOKS	ARTICLES
Author's surname and forename or initials	Author's surname and forename or initials
Date of publication	Date of publication
Title (underlined)	Title (in inverted commas)
	Source of the article, namely: Title of journal (underlined); Volume; Issue and page numbers

Titles of books and articles are not abbreviated, but titles of journals may be. Bibliographies normally abbreviate the titles they index in the standard way, but you can check the *British Education Index* for the standard abbreviation of most of the journals you are likely to use. If journals you are using are not listed in the *British Education Index,* the *British Standards Institution* (BS 4148) (usually available for consultation in libraries) sets out the con-

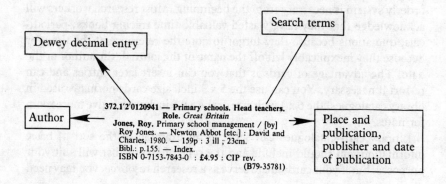

Dewey decimal entry

Search terms

Author

Place and publication, publisher and date of publication

372.1'2'0120941 — **Primary schools. Head teachers.**
Role. *Great Britain*
Jones, Roy. Primary school management / [by]
Roy Jones. — Newton Abbot [etc.] : David and
Charles, 1980. — 159p : 3 ill ; 23cm.
Bibl.: p.155. — Index.
ISBN 0-7153-7843-0 : £4.95 : CIP rev.
(B79-35781)

ventions and you can then work out an abbreviation for yourself. Do not make up own abbreviations, so if in doubt reproduce the title in full.

It may not be necessary to include all the information found on library catalogue cards and, for example, on BNB references. Consider the information on the BNB entry below on p. 148.

What information do you need from this entry? You will obviously need the author, the title of the book, the place of publication, name of publisher, and date of publication. You may feel it is of little importance to remember that this book has 159 pages, but the price may be useful, if you or the library wish to purchase a copy of the book. The ISBN number (International Standard Book Number) which is a number unique to the publication concerned, is useful if you are requesting a book on interlibrary loan, so it is worth adding to your card. You may not feel it is of much interest to know that the bibliography appears on p. 155, nor that there is an index. The Dewey decimal number should only be recorded from the catalogue in your own library, so there would be no reason to transfer the number from a BNB entry. You may need to know where you originally found the book, so you should always record the source of reference (e.g. BNB 1979, BEI 1980, Sheffield University library catalogue, etc.). Your own card would then be on the following lines:

```
Jones, Roy (1980)
Primary School Management
Newton Abbot: David and Charles

(BNB 1979)
ISBN 0–7153–7843–0          £4.95
```

When you have read the book, you may wish to attach notes or quotations to your card, to draw attention to particularly interesting parts, or even to note that the book is of no particular interest to your project, with reasons why. You should always make a note of any book, article or report you have consulted, even if you did not find it particularly useful. There must have been some reason why you decided to look at it in the first place. The title may have sounded interesting, or you may have read other works by the same author that impressed you. It would follow then that, some time ahead, the title may still sound interesting and the author may still be remembered as having produced quality work in another context. You may come across the reference again, and ask to borrow the book again. All this is a waste of time and in any investigation, whether small or large scale, there is never enough time to do everything that has to be done. A note to remind you why you decided the work was of no interest would be enough to jog your memory and to enable you to abandon that particular line of enquiry.

Noting quotations

A particularly perceptive observation by an author may often illustrate a point you wish to make in an assignment or report, and add an extra dimension to your argument.

Making a note of quotations at the time you read them is as important as recording the full bibliographical information about the source. When you are writing up your final report, you will not have time to recall books from the library, nor to search in the used-envelope box. If a particular sentence or paragraph strikes you at the time of reading as being a potential quotation, note it carefully, record the chapter and page number, show clearly if you have left out any word and file it where you know you will be able to find it, even if this requires some cross-referencing in your card index. If you have the facilities, it is an even better idea to photocopy the extract, adding details about source in the usual way, and attaching it to your card. (Library staff will advise about copyright regulations.) If you are unable to photocopy, then make it quite clear which is the quotation and which is your paraphrase or, when you come to write up your report, you may find you are committing the sin of using someone else's words as your own.

Bibliographies and references

The term 'bibliography' has several meanings. It can be used to mean a publication listing the details of material about a subject, place or person. It can be a list of sources consulted during the preparation of an essay, project or dissertation, or it can be a list of works by a specific author. So far in this chapter we have been concerned with bibliographies which list details of materials about leadership, but in this section we are concerned with the second definition, that is a list of sources consulted during the preparation of a project. Most project reports will need to have a bibliography of this kind and/or list of references. The difference between the two lies in the fact that references give specific details of particular books or articles which have been cited or referred to in the report, essay or dissertation, whereas a bibliography is a list of works you have consulted during the course of your investigation – whether or not you refer to them in the text. Page numbers are not included in bibliographies, but they are included, where appropriate, in references. The amount of time it takes you to produce either or both in your final report will depend on how meticulous you were when you first made out your reference cards.

In an essay or report, all sources should be acknowledged in a sufficiently precise way for the reader to be able to find the material. Quotations must always be acknowledged, and if you are drawing heavily on someone else's ideas in part of your report, these should also be acknowledged. The question is how to do it.

Two main approaches are in common use, namely the Harvard system and the British system (based on the British Standards Institution). Most educational institutions will have a preferred style and will usually issue instructions about how referencing is to be done. But if no such guidance is provided, you will need to decide which method you prefer.

The British system places the author's initials before the surname, and the date appears after the volume, part or issue number (for journals) and after the publisher (for books), as follows:

S D Sieber 'The integration of fieldwork and survey methods' *American Journal of Sociology*, Vol 78, (1963), pp. 335–59.

M J Wilson *Social and Educational Research in Action: a book of readings* London: Longman/The Open University Press, (1979).

The disadvantage of this method is that when works are referred to in the main body of the text, references have to be supplied either by means of footnotes (which make difficulties for typists), or by end notes, for example. In the main text,

'M J Wilson, in his discussion of styles of research[1] . . .'
and at the end of the chapter or in a footnote,

[1] M J Wilson *Social and Educational Research in Action: a book of readings* (London: Longman/The Open University Press, 1979), p. 42

The Harvard method has a number of advantages over the British system. It avoids footnotes, does not interrupt the flow of the text and yet provides information for the reader about sources without the necessity of referring to end notes. The principle is that in the text, the author's surname and date of publication is included (e.g. 'As Fox (1984) says . . .' The full details of Fox's 1984 publication will then appear in the alphabetical list at the end of the chapter or report. Page references are given in the text, for any quotations or where the writer is drawing heavily on another writer's ideas.

Sources appear in alphabetical order at the end of the chapter or report, not in the order in which they appear in the text. If an author has more than one entry, then the publications are listed in chronological order. If an author has more than one publication in the same year, then suffixes 'a' or 'b' are added, e.g. Youngman (1979a) and Youngman (1979b). Where more than one author is involved, the first name determines the order.

The Harvard method of referencing provides a simple way of coping with references in the main text and also in bibliographies. [. . .]However, as long as you are consistent throughout, and follow a recognized method, it does not matter which style you select. Referencing can take an irritatingly long time if you have to keep checking back, so good habits established early in your investigations will pay off at this stage. If your cards are in good order, drawing up your bibliography will only be a matter of transferring the information from card to paper, but it must be done in a consistent way. It is not permissible to use the Harvard system for one reference, the British system for another and a method of your own for a third.

It takes a little time to remember all the detail of what is underscored and what appears in inverted commas, where dates appear and how to deal with quotations. Once you have mastered the detail, it becomes automatic to record *all* sources as soon as you come across them, *in the format of your choice*. Because the detail is difficult to remember, it is wise to keep model cards for your card index, to remind you what should always be included and also to keep an example of a list of references in a published work, so that you can check your punctuation and detail are consistent. Something on the lines of the examples opposite would serve the purpose quite well.

There is a thriving publishing business offering advice to authors and guidance to students preparing theses and dissertations. Some go into great detail and require considerable time and expertise to master the intricacies of the systems proposed. For most purposes, the suggestions offered in this chapter will suffice. Attention to detail and consistency are the two most important qualities. Taking a lead from the way references are handled in published works is a reasonable approach, but producing references and

BOOKS

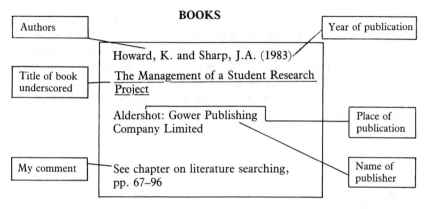

Authors

Year of publication

Howard, K. and Sharp, J.A. (1983)

Title of book
underscored

The Management of a Student Research
Project

Aldershot: Gower Publishing
Company Limited

Place of
publication

Name of
publisher

My comment

See chapter on literature searching,
pp. 67–96

ARTICLES IN COLLECTIONS

Castner, B.M. (1950)

'Language development'
in
Gesell, A. (ed) The First Five Years of
Life: a guide to the study of the
pre-school child

London: Methuen

ARTICLES

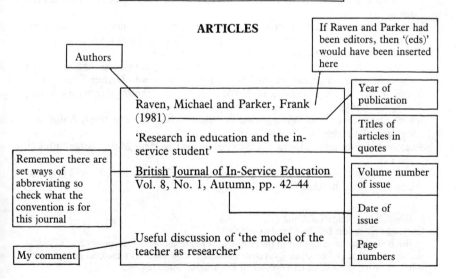

If Raven and Parker had
been editors, then '(eds)'
would have been inserted
here

Authors

Raven, Michael and Parker, Frank
(1981)

Year of
publication

'Research in education and the in-
service student'

Titles of
articles in
quotes

Remember there are
set ways of
abbreviating so
check what the
convention is for
this journal

British Journal of In-Service Education
Vol. 8, No. 1, Autumn, pp. 42–44

Volume number
of issue

Date of
issue

My comment

Useful discussion of 'the model of the
teacher as researcher'

Page
numbers

bibliographies is not something you do at the end of your project. The task is begun the first time you consult an index, a bibliography or abstract and continues throughout the whole of the period of the investigation. All sources should be recorded as soon as they are located. If your card index is in good shape, preparing references or a bibliography will merely be a matter of sorting cards into alphabetical order and presenting them in a list at the end of your report. What could be easier?

References

British Education Index (1954 on), quarterly. London, British Library Bibliographic Services Division.

British Education Theses Index 1950–1980 (1980). Leicester, Librarians of Institutes and Schools of Education.

British National Bibliography (1950 on), weekly. London, British Library Bibliographic Services Division.

British Standards Institution (1970) *Abbreviation of Titles of Periodicals Part 1. Principles,* (BS 4148). London, British Standards Institution.

British Standards Institution (1978) *Citing Publications by Bibliographical References,* (BS 5605). London, British Standards Institution.

Dale, S.M. (1981) *Management and the School: using the literature.* Milton Keynes, Open University Press.

Haywood, P. and Wragg, E.C. (1982) *Evaluating the Literature.* Nottingham, Nottingham University School of Education (Rediguide 2: guides in educational research).

Hull Institute of Education (annual) *Study and Library Facilities for Teachers: universities, institutes and schools of education, etc.* Hull, Hull Institute of Education for the Librarians of Institutes and Schools of Education.

Research into Higher Education Abstracts (1966 on), three per year. Abingdon, Carfax Publishing Co. on behalf of the Society for Research into Higher Education.

Roget, P.M. (1970) *Thesaurus of English Words and Phrases.* Harmondsworth, Penguin Books.

School Organisation and Management Abstracts (1982 on), quarterly. Abingdon, Carfax Publishing Co.

Sociology of Education Abstracts (1965 on), quarterly. Abingdon, Carfax Publishing Co.

Ulrich's International Periodicals Directory (1982) 22nd edition. New York and London, R.R. Bowker Co.

Judith Bell and Sandy Goulding.
Copyright © Judith Bell and Sandy Goulding.
Judith Bell is a senior counsellor in the North West Region of the Open University. In 1983/84 she was seconded to The Open University, School of Education, as a member of the course team preparing the Advanced Diploma in Educational Management.

Sandy Goulding is a Senior Lecturer in Quantitative Methods at Luton College of Higher Education, having been seconded during 1983/84 to the Open University as a member of the course team preparing the Advanced Diploma in Educational Management.

CHAPTER 10

DESIGNING QUESTIONNAIRES

M.B. Youngman

Questionnaires are probably the most common method of collecting information. They are cheap to administer, can be sent to a large number of subjects and, provided they are well designed, are relatively easy to analyse. However, questionnaires are difficult to design. Finding the right words, the best layout and the method of distribution most likely to yield a good response is skilled work. Mick Youngman has helped many research students at the University of Nottingham to design and analyse questionnaires. In this chapter, he provides advice about planning, question writing, design, piloting and distribution. It is essential reading for anyone contemplating the use of questionnaires in a survey.

1 The importance of planning

The relative effort associated with different stages of research depends very much on the type of research being undertaken. Experimental approaches necessarily demand very careful selection of design, samples and measures, but the subsequent analysis then tends to be almost automatic. When research uses questionnaires, the balance of effort is often assumed to be reversed. Certainly to compile and distribute a large number of questionnaires may seem, and indeed sometimes be, a straightforward clerical exercise requiring very little research skill. Unfortunately, this simplicity is too often exaggerated, to the extent of assuming that analytical considerations are irrelevant at the initial stage. Such an approach will almost inevitably result in the introduction of difficult, and even insurmountable, problems during analysis. The solution lies in accepting that the initial and concluding stages of a survey are not independent; the questionnaire structure must include all the facilities deemed to be necessary for a successful analysis. For example, the treatment of various types of non-response (questions refused, pages missed, or even whole questionnaires not return-ed) should be considered from both the coding and analysis standpoints. Similarly the role of open-ended questions should be decided in advance; failure to do so may result in the loss of essential factual information. Probably the simplest safeguard is to plan the questionnaire coding, before distribution, to take into account as many of the analyses as can be antici-pated. Inevitably some will depend upon the outcome of preliminary tests, but the majority of analytical requirements can be accommodated with a reasonable amount of prior thought.

Before proceeding to the essential steps in questionnaire usage it should be mentioned that researchers must satisfy themselves that this method is likely to be more effective than other approaches such as interviews, observation or some combination of them. [. . .] The remainder of this article assumes that the decision has been made in favour of questionnaires although many of the issues covered [. . .] could quite likely apply to structured interview schedules as well.

2   Question specification

The variety of question structures, and the numerous problems associated with them, makes it vital to give careful consideration to all aspects of question specification. Failure to appreciate the degree to which the research outcome may hinge upon the strengths or weaknesses of individual questions could easily invalidate an entire study.

2.1   *Source of questions*
Dreaming up interesting questions might seem an enjoyable and acceptable approach to determining questionnaire content, but for worthwhile results a much more rigorous procedure is necessary. As with any other attempt to isolate pertinent research data, the prime source must be the working hypotheses and the literature survey that contributed these hypotheses. This implies two possibilities; either the literature study will have revealed specific questions, or more generally it will have suggested important areas needing more detailed investigation. Either way, there should be some theoretical justification for including a particular question, beyond super-ficial appeal.

2.2 *Fact or opinion*

Fact and opinion can usefully be taken to represent two extremes of question content and as a result they often require different formats. Frequently factual information can be elicited using a simple YES/NO question.

EXAMPLE 1

Do you have a child at Higginthorpe Primary School?	YES	
	NO	

Assuming that the respondent does not confuse the three terms Infant, Primary and Junior, and assuming also that 'child' has been suitably defined to allow for stepchildren, foster children and so on, it should not be difficult to produce a reliable answer. But what about:

EXAMPLE 2

Does your child regularly do homework?	YES	
	NO	

The interpretation of 'regularly' is extremely arbitrary, and there is no indication regarding who supplies the homework. To turn this into a factual question both of these ambiguities must be removed. Even more doubtful is a question like this:

EXAMPLE 3

Does your child expect to stay at school after 16?	YES	
	NO	

The potential factuality of this question is very carefully disguised! At the other extreme, opinion or attitude questions are easily spotted:

EXAMPLE 4

Do you consider your child's school to be cooperative?	YES	
	NO	

From this example it should be clear that opinion is usually a matter of degree, making it unlikely that a simple YES/NO response will be satisfactory. One final warning about factual questions is that although in *theory* a question may be factual, in *practice* it may not be so. A good example concerns school size:

EXAMPLE 5

How many children are in your school?

Given that school numbers fluctuate, at what time is the count to be made? More important, though, is the hint of precision in the question. Few teachers would know the answer to within 10 and the apparent need for an exact answer may be confusing. Since it is likely that broad size bands would be sufficient, the question should be phrased accordingly.

2.3 *Structured or open*

To some extent the deliberation over whether open or structured questions are required will have already occurred. In opting for a questionnaire rather than an interview approach, the assumption must be that the *bulk* of the information to be collected is accessible via structured questions. Consequently an open question like:

EXAMPLE 6

What are the essential skills
education should provide?

should tend to be used as an adjunct to the main theme of the questionnaire. For example, it could allow the respondent to elaborate upon an earlier more specific question, such as:

EXAMPLE 7

Is modern education suited to the
needs of Britain today

for all children?	
for most children?	
for many children?	
for few children?	
for no children?	

Another valuable use for the more open type of question is to put the respondent at ease. Excessive structure can progressively generate a feeling of repression or even resentment, simply because the respondent feels he is not doing justice to his opinions. Open questions inserted at the end of major sections, or at the end of the questionnaire, can act as safety valves, and possibly offer additional information. However, they should not be used to introduce a section since there is a high risk of influencing later responses.

The area where open questions are especially valuable is in pilot studies. Many researchers use a more extended approach at the pilot stage, on the understanding that subsequent refinement will allow a more convenient structure to be used in the main study.

2.4 *Question structure*

Questionnaires can encompass a multitude of response formats although many of these are best treated as specific but separate methods. So a series of scaled attitude questions may be included in a questionnaire, but the analysis would need to bear in mind the principles implicit in scaling methods. [. . .] Nevertheless, at the stage of questionnaire design it would be unnecessarily restrictive to assume that questionnaires only contain YES/NO questions, or indeed, only questions.

Statement or question. In question form Example 7 above seems rather awkward. Particularly where opinions are involved, it may be better to ask for an indication of degree or agreement with a statement.

EXAMPLE 8

Modern education suits the needs of Britain today	for all children	
	for most children	
	for many children	
	for few children	
	for no children	

Not only is the item structure less complicated, often it is shorter, making design and response that much easier.

Descriptions. The apparent simplicity of an item of the form:

EXAMPLE 9

Describe your school _____

_____

belies the considerable difficulty of analysing the responses it generates. Even though analytical difficulty is not a sufficient reason for avoiding a technique, the value of purely descriptive items should be considered carefully beforehand.

Lists. After descriptions the next level of structure is listing.

EXAMPLE 10

List what you feel are the GOOD and BAD things about your school.

            GOOD   BAD

    _____   _____

    _____   _____

    _____   _____

    _____   _____

However, similar problems remain, particularly those of classification, completeness (what can you deduce about something not mentioned?) and the varying lengths of the lists suggested. A simple solution to the last problem is to ask for a fixed number of comments.

Checklists. The first two problems in listing can partly be overcome by supplying the statements to be checked off (that is, answered YES). Because of the large number of items needed, [. . .] the subsequent classification may be a substantial undertaking. [. . .]

Categories. If certain important categories of response can be identified sufficiently early in a research design then it should be possible to improve the rather loose structure of the checklist by formulating more direct questions incorporating these broader response categories.

EXAMPLE 11

Which of these things do you DISLIKE about your new school?	1	BUILDINGS	
	2	TOO MANY CHILDREN	
	3	TOO MANY TEACHERS	
	4	THE NEW SUBJECTS	
	5	HOMEWORK	
	6	SPORT	

Since a relatively small number of categories (up to 20) is usually sufficient for most questions, some simplification is achieved compared with the earlier structures. Further benefits are achieved if the number of choices is fixed (for example, 'indicate the WORST THREE things' . . .). In many cases it will be legitimate to ask for a single choice, although this will normally only apply to factual questions.

EXAMPLE 12

What type of school do you attend?	1	COMPREHENSIVE	
	2	GRAMMAR	
	3	SECONDARY	
	4	INDEPENDENT	
	5	OTHER*	

* If other, please specify

YES/NO questions: These are really no more than an alternative way of describing some of the methods already described. So in Example 11, when an unspecified number of choices is allowed, another way of obtaining the same information would be to treat the six categories as six separate YES/NO questions. This would certainly make most statistical analyses easier. The important benefit from the YES/NO formulation is that both possible responses, YES and NO, are explicit. This is particularly valuable in scale construction because some of the problems of response bias (for example, people's stronger tendency to agree than to disagree) can be overcome by a judicious grading of positive and negative constructs.

EXAMPLE 13

(a) Are the teachers helpful?

| YES | | | NO | |

(b) Is it easy to consult teachers?

| YES | | | NO | |

A parent with reservations about school contacts would be more likely to disclose this via the second question than the first.

Partial agreement. When the starkness of a YES/NO response becomes too restrictive, some gradation of response is necessary. The commonest rating system uses levels of agreement, usually with five response categories. It is the Likert scale.

EXAMPLE 14
Teachers are usually helpful

Strongly agree	Agree	Neutral	Disagree	Strongly disagree

Notice that the wording of the question needs to allow for the possibility of varying levels of agreement. If the statement had been presented in the form: 'Teachers are *always* helpful', then responses would be forced towards the disagreement end purely through logicality. A further consideration in choosing response categories concerns the *intermediate response*. If it is included, it must be clearly differentiated from responses such as failure to understand the question, disagreement with the possibility rather than the tenor of the statement, or pure indecision. With a carefully piloted questionnaire it should be possible, and analytically preferable, to do without an intermediate response *so long as* it is made clear to the respondent how nonresponse is to be indicated.

Semantic differential. Here the level of agreement is elaborated even further in that even more gradations are offered, and the constructs themselves are finer and usually more personal. The respondent indicates his level of support for a construct defined in terms of opposites.

EXAMPLE 15

SCHOOL IS

difficult	1	2	3	4	5	6	7	easy
important	1	2	3	4	5	6	7	unimportant
long	1	2	3	4	5	6	7	short
useless	1	2	3	4	5	6	7	useful
interesting	1	2	3	4	5	6	7	boring

The more personal nature of such items makes the semantic differential a useful device for examining individual reactions over a broad range of personal involvements. As with the previous method, the instructions supplied to the respondent are an important part of the instrument. Anywhere from five to twelve categories have been used, but again a middle point may cause problems of interpretation.

Ratings. A slightly more conventional form of the semantic differential arises when a single, relatively common place, construct is used to evaluate a range of situations:

EXAMPLE 16

Rate the IMPORTANCE of the following, using 1 to indicate of little or no importance, 5 as very important.

IMPORTANCE FOR PROMOTION	LOW				HIGH
Education	1	2	3	4	5
Intelligence	1	2	3	4	5
Specialized training	1	2	3	4	5
Qualifications	1	2	3	4	5
Personality	1	2	3	4	5
Luck	1	2	3	4	5

Instructions are again important, especially regarding the numerical link. As the rating method is largely arbitrary, a general rule in coding is to associate high numbers with positive constructs (that is, 5 = very important) since this produces a more natural interpretation at the analysis stage, particularly when correlations are involved.

Rankings. These should *not* be confused with ratings. For rankings the responses are placed in *order*. However, the treatment of rankings does raise response and analysis problems and preference should usually be for ratings. [. . .]

This summary of question structures is by no means exhaustive. The general benefit of such an outline is that many of the points relating to the methods covered apply equally well to other question forms.

2.5 *Difficulty*

When questions are formulated in such a manner that response becomes difficult, the reliability of the whole questionnaire can become suspect. For a start an intelligence dimension may be introduced unintentionally, and this could distort the responses of low-ability children. Difficulty also has the effect of alienating the respondent, often to the extent of producing flippant or even aggressive responses. Almost inevitably an ambiguous question will be unreliable through a tendency to generate random responses. One effective way of detecting potentially difficult questions is to pilot them by administering the questionnaire personally, *timing* each response. Any questions which take substantially longer to answer than others quite likely are too complicated. They should be reworded, or broken down into separate parts.

Response overlap. This is a common error particularly with factual questions, but it is also easily remedied.

EXAMPLE 17

What is your age?

1	2	3	4
UNDER 20	20–25	25–29	OVER 30

What answer does a 25-year-old give? Category 2 should really be 20 – 24. There is, however, the opposite possibility, namely of leaving a gap. Categories 3 and 4 omit age 30. Probably category 4 should be 30 and over. [. . .]

Excessive precision. The danger of implying excessive precision has already been mentioned. Usually any numerical answer is best categorized within the question, rather than at the analysis stage. Simply ensure that minimum precision is achieved.

Impossible questions. Even though certain questions may seem to request straightforward information, often it can be impossible to supply an answer, either because the wording is too precise or because the information is inaccessible. An example of an excessively precise question has already been offered in relation to school size, but any numerical answer is prone to this difficulty. Age, distance, salary or IQ are all cases where banding is a more appropriate structure. Inaccessibility occurs when the respondent does not have access to the information sought. Usually this involves attitudes, especially other people's, rather than factual data [. . .]

Complexity. Excessively complex questions can usually be reduced to two or more simpler questions, thereby improving response ease and reliability.

EXAMPLE 18

What course in education are you currently studying?

PGCE   B.Ed F/T   B.Ed P/T   Dip.Ed F/T   Dip.Ed P/T   M.Ed F/T   M.Ed P/T

☐   ☐   ☐   ☐   ☐   ☐   ☐

A better form would be:

(a) What is your mode of study?   Full-time   Part-time
                                             ☐   ☐

(b) What is your course?   PGCE   ☐
                                  B.Ed   ☐
                                  Dip.Ed   ☐
                                  M.Ed   ☐
                                  Other   ☐
                                  If other, please specify

Double negatives. Most adults experience difficulty in handling double negatives and so there is little chance of children coping reliably with them.

EXAMPLE 19

(a) Having a parent-teacher association
    makes it more difficult to get all types
    of parents to help in school activities   SA   A   N   D   SD

(b) The whole of your life is affected by
    your education   SA   A   N   D   SD

(c) Teachers deserve great praise for the
    way they manage such large classes   SA   A   N   D   SD

(d) Without a parent-teacher association
you cannot talk things over as equals   SA   A   N   D   SD

(e) Schools should use religious education
to help children learn what is right and   SA   A   N   D   SD

Question (d) of Example 19 is a relatively common double negative but it does require some care in answering. Occasionally people tackle a double negative by switching *both* negatives (i.e. *with* a PTA you *can* . . .) and then assuming that the same answer applies. Clearly that tactic would not necessarily be logically valid.

Double questions. Questions sometimes contain two separate propositions and then there is the problem of knowing to which the answer refers.

EXAMPLE 20

Education after 15 is too specialized and
should only be compulsory for clever
children   SA   A   N   D   SD

This is rather obvious in its extremity but more subtle double-barrelled questions are common. Question (c) of Example 19 is not explicit in what is meant by 'the way they manage large classes' – management can be good or bad. Question (e) is another one where there is a distinct danger of only part of the question being answered.

Excessive elaboration. The principle of parsimony is a very effective rule of thumb for question design. The longer a question is, the greater the chance of introducing some of the problems already discussed. Question (a) of Example 19 offers an instance of an unnecessarily elaborate question, gradually compounding difficulty. 'Having a . . . more difficult . . . all types of parents . . . to help in' are all grammatical and semantic formulations that are not immediately obvious by themselves, never mind in association. There is often a good case for sacrificing a degree of literary finesse if the meaning of the question can be made more accessible. For instance, with school children, colloquial expressions such as 'get on', 'OK', 'sweets' and 'bike' are likely to communicate more effectively than their more grammatical equivalents.

Consistency. Whilst it is reasonable, and indeed useful, to vary the structure of different sections of a questionnaire, there is a danger of confusing the respondent if variety is carried to extremes.

EXAMPLE 21

(a)	I find a lot of school work difficult to understand	Yes, often	Sometimes	Hardly ever
(b)	I should like to be one of the cleverest pupils in the class	Yes	Not sure	No
(c)	I work and try very hard in school	Always	Mostly	Sometimes
(d)	I am very good at sums	Always	Sometimes	Hardly ever
(e)	I don't always get on well with some of the children in my class	Yes, true	Not sure	False

Within the space of five questions the child is expected to cope with five different response systems. Each requires extra thought and quite likely introduces an element of uncertainty in the child, for little real benefit. Better to forgo some of the specificity and instead to devise a more universal set of answer categories, such as YES/SOMETIMES/NO.

In addition to difficulty resulting from the form of individual questions, there is a further likelihood of confusing the respondent within the overall design of the questionnaire. Before dealing with that topic there is the trap of impertinence.

2.6 *Impertinence*

Literally, impertinence refers to question content that is not pertinent to the main research theme. At the extreme questions of this kind also become impertinent in the everyday sense because respondents may take personal offence, and react accordingly. Questionnaire designers need to be aware of both possibilities, not only because response rate and reliability may be affected, but also because respondents do have rights which should be respected [. . .]

2.7 *Suggestion*

The risk of suggesting suitable responses is not so strong in questionnaires as it is with interviews. Nevertheless it is wise to be aware of the possibility of subconsciously implanting your own wishes in the question structure. This is most likely to arise as a result of not offering a sufficiently broad range of options in response categories [. . .]

3   Questionnaire design

Placing this section after Question Specification does not imply that design need not be considered until late in the research; the reality is that the design cannot be finalized until some idea of the content is known. Having examined the range of possible question structures, it then becomes easier to produce the overall questionnaire form.

3.1 *Theme*

The general theme of the questionnaire should be made explicit, either in the covering letter, or in the questionnaire heading, or both. This ensures that the respondents know what they are committing themselves to, and also that they understand the context of their replies.

3.2 *Appearance*

The surest way of deterring a potential respondent is to send out a hastily constructed and untidy questionnaire. Appearance is usually the first feature of the questionnaire to which the recipient reacts. A neat and professional look will encourage further consideration of your request, increasing your response rate. In addition careful thought to layout should facilitate both completion and analysis. There are a number of simple rules to help improve questionnaire appearance.

1. Liberal *spacing* makes reading easier.
2. *Photoreduction* can produce more space without reducing content.
3. *Consistent positioning* of response boxes, usually to the right, speeds completion. It also avoids inadvertent omission of responses.
4. Choose the *type face* to maximize legibility. If photoreduction is to be used capitals, being bigger, are more legible.
5. *Differentiate* between instructions and questions. Either lower case and capitals can be used, or responses can be boxed.
6. Allow space for any *computer coding* if it is intended.

3.3 *Size*

There may be a strong temptation to include any vaguely interesting question, but this should be resisted at all cost. Excessive size can only reduce response rates. If a long questionnaire *is* necessary then even more thought must be given to appearance. Photoreduction helps, if only by making the task of completion look smaller. Pages are best left unnumbered; to flick to the end and 'see page 27' can be highly disconcerting.

3.4 *Mixture*

Mixing questionnaire content is another way of encouraging responses. A continuous sequence of YES/NO questions can be very tedious. By switching between two or three different question structures and topics, interest is more easily maintained. However, the danger here is of excessive variation. If the respondent never has time to adjust to a particular response format frustration may be induced, along with the accompanying unreliability. The semantic differential is especially valuable since it is intrinsically appealing, and at the same time it allows a lot of information to be supplied quickly.

3.5 *Order*

Probably the most crucial stage in questionnaire response is the beginning. Once the respondents have started to complete the questions they will normally finish the task, unless it is inordinately long or difficult. Consequently the opening questions need to be selected with care. Usually the best approach is to ask for biographical information first. This tends to be the easiest because the respondents should know all the answers without much thought. Furthermore, interest should immediately be aroused since most people enjoy talking about themselves.

Another benefit is that an easy start provides practice in answering questions. On the other hand there are situations where biographical data can have the opposite effect. For example, some teachers are sensitive about their qualifications. A rather more important consideration, however, is whether the insertion of biographic content will disturb the continuity of points made in the covering letter. If the theme has been clearly established in this letter, it may be advisable to continue that line of questioning in the opening sections of the questionnaire itself. Once the introduction has been achieved the subsequent order will depend on many considerations, some of them such as mixture having already been mentioned. One possibility to be aware of is the varying importance of different questions. Essential information should appear early, just in case the questionnaire is not completed. For the same reason relatively unimportant questions can be placed towards the end. If any questions are likely to provoke the respondent (questions about race for example) these too may best be left until the end, in the hope of obtaining answers to everything else.

3.6 *Instructions*

Anyone who has played the game where you describe an object such as a bicycle, using only words, will know how difficult it is to provide clear and unambiguous verbal instructions. The questionnaire designer cannot avoid this problem. Within most questionnaires there are *general instructions* and *specific instructions* for particular question structures. It is usually best to separate these, supplying the general instructions as a preamble to the questionnaire, but leaving the specific instructions until the questions to which they apply. The response method should be indicated (circle, tick, cross, etc.). Wherever possible, and certainly if a slightly unfamiliar response system is employed, an example helps greatly in confirming that the verbal instructions have been understood.

One trivial but effective instruction is to ask the respondent to complete the questionnaire using a *colour* other than black (assuming that the form is printed in black). Bright colours such as red or green make the subsequent coding and analysis substantially quicker.

The importance of questionnaire instructions is often underestimated. Certainly the piloting should test the clarity of the instructions as well as the questions and method.

3.7 *Automation*

Much as the arrival of piles of completed questionnaires might seem to signal the end of the road, in reality there remains considerable work to be done. This can be alleviated if proper care is given to question structure and response provision. In particular, respondents can often be asked to supply an answer code, substantially reducing coding time. [. . .]

3.8 *Thank you*

Respondents to questionnaires rarely benefit personally from their efforts and the least the researcher can do is to thank them. Even though the covering letter will express appreciation for the help given, it is also a nice gesture to finish off the questionnaire with a further thank you:

THANK YOU FOR COMPLETING THIS QUESTIONNAIRE

If at all possible some information should also be made available to interested participants. A final comment to the effect that a summary of the findings is available on request is evidence of genuine gratitude.

4 Piloting

Piloting is an integral part of any research and a questionnaire survey is no exception. Indeed, the strong dependence upon the instrument rather than the researcher makes pilot assessments even more necessary. These need to evaluate the instructions, the questions and the response systems. Also, if a novel distribution method is to be adopted (see next section) that too must be tested. And on top of all that it is likely that more than one pilot will be needed because any changes suggested by the first pilot will themselves require testing, albeit less extensively.

Although the piloting of a questionnaire might seem rather laborious, it would be wrong to assume that the effort is unproductive. The information collected at the pilot stage can itself be of value. For example, if everyone says YES to a question, then that question can usually be dropped from the main study because the answer is known, and because it has no discriminatory value. A second benefit is that the pilot data can be used to test the coding and analytical procedures to be performed later. Indeed, wherever possible all the anticipated coding and analytical procedures should be tested using the pilot data. Any alterations resulting from this test can then be incorporated in the final form of the questionnaire. To try out the analytical procedures it will be necessary to select appropriate statistical methods [. . .]

Pilot procedures normally involve a small-scale application of the main method, but with questionnaires some modification of this pattern may be desirable. In particular it is usually advisable to administer some questionnaires personally so that the respondent can be observed, and questioned if necessary. By timing each question it becomes possible to identify any questions that appear inordinately difficult, and also a reliable estimate of the anticipated completion time can be obtained for inclusion in the covering letter. The standard concepts of *reliability* and *validity* have limited relevance in questionnaire design. Validity is typically assessed in terms of face validity, more often than not a euphemism for doing nothing. If any more objective measure is available (for example, groups of respondents expected to show different responses) then it should be considered. Reliability is slightly more accessible. Often some of the information is available elsewhere (on school records, for example) and checking may be practicable within the small pilot sample. Alternatively the respondents can be questioned personally to see how far these more lengthy responses match their earlier questionnaire answers. In general, piloting is far too often ignored, and the resultant disaster becomes all too predictable.

5   Distribution and return

[. . .] The researcher using questionnaires for data collection remains heavily dependent upon response rates. Since the best guarantee of efficient sampling is a high response rate, distribution and return arrangements become vital parts of the research design.

5.1 *Method*

Cost, effort, delay and willingness are just a selection of the factors affecting choice of distribution method and therefore no single ideal procedure can be offered. Usually relative advantages and disadvantages will have to be offset and a compromise solution reached. However, it is possible to isolate three main considerations.

Personal or postal. Although postal distribution is perhaps the most popular method, there may be situations where it becomes preferable or even essential to deliver the questionnaire personally. Two obvious examples are where the sample is small, making a high response rate vital, or as a follow-up after postal circulation has failed to produce a response. Whilst postal circulation is usually cheaper, personal contact is often quicker.

Direct or indirect. Where the sample members fall into convenient groups such as schools, classes or colleges, it may be possible to contact them indirectly using an agent within the group. This can be particularly helpful at the return stage, since the agent can usually be enlisted to remind or encourage some of the less cooperative participants. However, the indirect contact may not be possible if anonymity is an important consideration. The general problem of anonymity is discussed later in Section 5.5.

Nominated or chance. In most instances the subjects will have been identified individually beforehand. Occasionally, however, all that is required is a suitable number of responses and then it may be possible to avoid the effort and expense of nominating specific subjects. Instead, chance respondents are obtained, either one-by-one, or by distributing batches of questionnaires to suitable collection centres. The main disadvantage of the chance method is that being self-selected, chance respondents may not be representative in respect of the characteristics the sample was intended to cover.

In specifying the precise method to adopt these three considerations are taken independently, so that, for example, the final choice might be for a *postal indirect nominated distribution*. Furthermore, the return can be different from the distribution. Thus the above distribution example might favour an alternative return method, say *postal direct*. The distribution and return procedures are separate, and should be considered on their own merits.

5.2 *Contents*

As well as the *questionnaire* itself it is normal to send a *covering letter* and possibly a *stamped addressed return envelope*. If the questionnaire is especially complicated it may also be necessary to supply a separate set of *instructions*. The questionnaire should be checked for *completeness* to ensure that all pages are present and that none is blank or illegible. The covering letter should be reasonably explicit regarding the aim of the inquiry. It should admit that the request does make certain demands of the respondent's time, offering an estimate if possible. The letter should not be effusive or ingratiating. Instructions for *return* should be included but those for completion should be on the questionnaire. The *return date* must be obvious; the easiest solution is to print it in block capitals on a separate line:

'. . . It would be appreciated if you could return the completed questionnaire by:

TUESDAY 17th JANUARY
if at all possible . . .'

Notice that both day and date are given since the day of the week acts as a stronger reminder. It is rarely worth allowing more than two weeks from receipt of the questionnaire because longer times only encourage procrastination. The covering letter should also include an assurance of *confidentiality,* specifying the range beyond which the information will not pass (usually the research team only). Also if *official permission* or support has been sought, for example from the Local Education Authority, it is advisable to mention this. Certainly where parents are involved, they are unlikely to cooperate fully in a survey which does not have the blessing of the school head or the Authority. They may not be interested in helping even if they are aware of official support, but that is a different matter.

5.3 *Returns*

Returned questionnaires, completed or otherwise, usually show an initial surge, followed by a gradually decreasing flow, the later ones often taking four or five times as long to arrive as the early ones. To make best use of this period processing should begin as soon as the first ones are received. Arrival date should be noted and the questionnaire numbered, unless it is already. The contents should be checked for completeness since it may be possible to return a questionnaire if any sections have been inadvertently missed. [. . .]

5.4 *Follow-up*

It will rarely be possible to accept the initial response as sufficient without some effort to increase it. The follow-up request should not be left too long otherwise what little interest the nonrespondent had will have disappeared altogether. The tone of the follow-up letter should acknowledge the difficulty that person might have in complying with your request, but it needs to emphasize the importance of every single questionnaire. A replacement questionnaire should be included 'in case of misplacement or loss'. Occasionally, as a last resort, it may be practicable to supply a shorter follow-up questionnaire, covering only the essential parts.

Should the response rate still be unsatisfactory, even after the follow-up, it may be worth considering a personal visit or telephone call, rather than a further letter. Follow-up requires some form of respondent identification and therefore if an agent is used for distribution, or if anonymity is essential, special arrangements may be required. In extreme cases follow-up may not be possible at all.

5.5 *Anonymity*

Some form of identification must be devised initially if only to enable any necessary follow-up to be made. There may also be a need to link data collected on different occasions. Usually, however, all that is required during processing is an index number. Consequently it is preferable to limit recorded identification to this number, apart from maintaining a private master list relating these numbers to individuals.

Questionnaires should be kept secure, and destroyed at the earliest opportunity, although the practicability of this will depend on the efficiency with which the responses can be coded. [. . .]

6 Concluding comment

The later stages of a questionnaire survey are often characterized by a reduction in the amount of control the researcher maintains. It is advisable to take all reasonable steps to minimize the effects this change might have on the quality of the outcome. In general, a continuous and systematic handling procedure is recommended. For example, a clear record of the returns should be kept, and processing should be carried out as soon as possible after receipt of the questionnaires. Even storage should be treated with the same degree of care; I recall one research study that lost a quarter of its responses because a carelessly stored box of questionnaires was thrown away by the cleaners!

References

Kerlinger F.J. (1973) *Foundations of Behavioral Research* 2nd edition. New York, Holt, Rinehart & Winston.
Oppenheim A.N. (1966) *Questionnaire Design and Attitude Measurement*. London, Heinemann.
Tuckman B.W. (1972) *Conducting Educational Research*. New York, Harcourt Brace Jovanovich.

M.B. Youngman, Rediguide 12: *Guides in Educational Research*. University of Nottingham, School of Education.
March 1982
Copyright © TRC (Oxford) England.
M.B. Youngman is a Senior Lecturer in Educational Research Methods at the University of Nottingham.

CHAPTER 11

CONDUCTING AND ANALYSING INTERVIEWS

E.C. Wragg

A major advantage of interviewing is its adaptability. A skilful interviewer can follow up leads, probe responses, investigate motives and feelings, which a questionnaire can never do. There are problems of course. It is time-consuming and a highly subjective technique, so there is always the danger of bias. Analysing responses can present problems and question wording is as demanding for interviews as it is for questionnaires. Professor Wragg discusses some of the pitfalls of this technique, offers helpful advice and provides a checklist of questions to ask 'before', 'during' and 'after'.

Introduction

Interviewing is the oldest and yet sometimes the most ill-used research technique in the world. Person A wishes to find out information, Person B has a point of view, is in possession of relevant facts or has undergone certain experiences. What could be more straightforward than Person A simply seeking out Person B, asking him a direct face-to-face question and noting down the answer?

Yet consider the following pitfalls which describe but six out of countless opportunities for inaccuracy or distortion in interviewing.

Pitfall 1: Interviewer bias
An interviewer's question can lead the respondent in a certain consciously or subconsciously desired direction. For example: 'Is there too much sex and violence on television and what are you going to do about it?'

Pitfall 2: Sample bias
An investigator interviews mothers in a shopping centre and concludes that 'few parents understand ITA'.

178 Conducting Small-scale Investigations in Educational Management

Pitfall 3: Hired interviewers
Some studies of people hired to conduct interviews show that they may fake answers when subjects are uncooperative.

Pitfall 4: Race bias
It is frequently the case that black pupils respond differently to a black interviewer than to a white one.

Pitfall 5: Straitjacket interview
Some tightly structured interview schedules permit little latitude. For example: 'Are you in favour of corporal punishment?' YES/NO

Pitfall 6: Respondend bias
Respondents frequently give the interviewer an answer which is more public relations for their own group than an accurate response. For example when Mildred Collins (Students into Teachers (1969)) interviewed heads and asked what they did for probationers they tended to say they were always helping, ever a cheery word. The probationers during interview reported lack of interest and few contacts.

1 Why interview?

Researchers need to begin not so much by saying, 'I am doing research into home/school relations so I shall interview 50 parents', but rather by carefully outlining questions to which answers are sought, and then deciding which data-gathering techniques are most appropriate. In some cases questionnaires or tests will be better than interviews; in other cases interviews may be *complementary* to other modes of enquiry.

Suppose, for example, you are studying teachers' praise and children's learning, arguing that the better readers in the class receive more praise than the poorer readers. You might interview teachers, ask them who are the best readers and who are the poorest readers, and then require them to tell you how often they praise various children. A much more effective strategy, however, would be to use reading scores derived from an objective test, classroom behaviour description obtained from live observation or lesson transcripts, and use interviews to supplement this information.

Equally, if you have a lot of simple questions requiring short answers or ratings on five or seven point scales, a mailed questionnaire might reach a much wider audience and produce much more information. Alternatively if your questions are such as to require a great deal of careful thought or research rather than an off-the-cuff reply you should elicit a written response.

On the other hand, if your target population consists of small children, illiterates or poorly educated people, you may obtain better results from talking to them rather than expecting them to write.

2 Where to interview?

Environment is most important in our daily lives. Even professional people, used to meeting officials, attending meetings, using telephones, feel on their guard when interviewed in an office with the questioner behind a desk. Such things usually only happen in a crisis or in the Income Tax Office.

Much more relaxed is the interview in a home or in comfortable chairs. Not that this is always perfect, as many people are kings in their own home and may be so overconfident as to give false information. What you need to ask yourself is what location, given the nature of your interview, makes most sense.

Confidentiality is also an important element. Few people will be frank if they are in earshot of an 'audience'. If you interview parents in a school, for example, it should be, whenever possible, away from other parents, teachers and their own children, unless their presence is desirable. When interviewing children, especially adolescents, it is also important to do this away from their peers, in whose company they often feel they must play a certain role. Investigators studying adolescents often find that in a group interview they strike a strong 'anti-school' note, whereas in individual interviews they are more likely to admit to being interested in their work and resenting their colleagues' attempts to disrupt lessons. Small children, however, may not communicate at all unless in the company of their parents or friends.

3 Whom to interview?

Sampling is a problem throughout educational research. A single or a few respondents may be atypical, and a cast of thousands may be equally unrepresentative if badly selected. [. . .]

Basically the choice is between a *random sample* and an *opportunity sample*. An opportunity sample consists of those whom it is convenient to interview, either because they are willing to talk or because they come your way. The group of mothers out shopping referred to in Pitfall 2 above comprised an opportunity sample. The investigator was wrong, therefore, to make inferences about 'parents' when his sample may have been predominantly of one social class or background, and when fathers had not been interviewed at all.

A random sample gives everyone an equal chance of being interviewed. If you were studying 10-year-old children in a school and wished to interview a quarter of them you might, for example, interview every fourth child from an alphabetical list starting with one of the first four children in the alphabet chosen arbitrarily. However, your final sample might, by chance, contain many more boys than girls. You might prefer, therefore, a *stratified random sample*. To obtain a stratified random sample you specify in advance, as part of your research design, which sub-groups of the whole sample might be important. This is usually decided on the basis of previous research findings or professional judgement.

Suppose you are interviewing secondary school children and can manage 60 interviews in a school, you might specify age and sex as being important sub-categories of the whole school population. A stratified random sample might produce the following six sub-groups, allowing you to interview equal numbers of boys and girls and of 11, 13 and 15-year-olds. The ten children in each 'cell' would then be selected randomly from all those in that category.*

	Boys	Girls	Total
1st year	10	10	20
3rd year	10	10	20
5th year	10	10	20
Total	30	30	60

Stratified random sample of secondary pupils

This design would be very simple with six 'cells' each containing ten children. Beware of too many stratifications. If you wish to add colour of eyes, social class, IQ, or personality you could find yourself with a 200 or 300 cell design and either have empty cells (e.g. no pupil in the 'female, 1st year, blue-eyed, middle-class, low IQ, introvert' category) or several thousand people to interview.

* The principle is that you select numbers of children in each cell in proportion to the total. Here, the author has assumed equal numbers of boys and girls in the school population, and also equal total numbers in each year.

One further point to bear in mind is that you need to be open and honest about your sample. When a random sample is selected it is customary to have a 'reserve list' in case anyone drops out of the sample or refuses to be interviewed. Interviewing in some areas invades well-defended privacy, and on topics to do with taboo subjects the refusal rate might be high. Consequently if many people drop out or refuse to be interviewed, and are replaced by others, one has an opportunity sample of people willing to be interviewed, rather than a genuinely random sample.

It should be said that there is nothing wrong with an opportunity sample provided that (a) the investigator states clearly that this is what he has chosen, and (b) he does not make over-bold claims or inferences from his interview data. Many interesting pieces of research based on interviews have used opportunity samples.

4   When to interview?

This may seem a pointless question to ask, and yet it can be a quite critical issue, particularly if the interview is part of a battery of data-gathering devices.

Suppose one is interested in knowing something about how student teachers change during their training. Any preliminary interviews designed to elicit information about their attitudes, experience or behaviour would need to take place immediately before or at the very beginning of their course. If these were left until after the course had commenced important changes might already be underway. People's attitudes and behaviour often do transform over a period of time, a phenomenon which some researchers into personality call 'function fluctuation'.

A second consideration is the frailty of human memory. When respondents are being asked to describe or evaluate events, they should be interviewed as close to those events as feasible. A good example of this occurs in research into classroom interaction. If one tape records a lesson and plays it back to a teacher for discussion, this interview should take place within a very short time of the lesson. Some investigators have returned to the school some days later and been surprised at how little teachers could recall of the lessons in question. Teaching is a busy job and many thousands of incidents occur every day.

A third trap concerns extraneous circumstances, sometimes beyond the investigator's control. Children interviewed about 'authority' might have a quite different view of it if a teacher has just arbitrarily punished the whole class than if they have just returned from a relaxed residential field course. It is not always possible to do anything about such circumstances, but grossly unsuitable timing should be avoided, and people should not be interviewed when markedly upset or euphoric unless this emotional condition is the subject of or central to the enquiry.

A further critical aspect of timing occurs when interviewing is supplementary to other modes of enquiry. Roy Nash, in his book *Classrooms Observed* (1973), interviewed teachers using the Kelly Rep Grid technique for assembling personal constructs [. . .]. He then observed their classes and interpreted his constructs from what took place in their lessons. It might have been better, or at least a valid alternative, to assemble classroom descriptions first, and then interview teachers afterwards. One needs, in particular, to bear in mind that the interview itself can exert quite a significant influence on events. If one interviewed a teacher to elicit, for example, his attitudes to slower learners in the class, he might quite probably behave differently towards these children when subsequently observed.

Other aspects of timing are self-evident. Late evening is a time when both investigator and respondent may be fatigued. Parents who are shift workers are not always accessible at times when other workers can be found at home. Pupils in rural areas may not be available after school because of the prompt departure of school buses. These and other small but significant points of timing should be clarified before any programme of interviewing is undertaken. One experienced interviewer engaged in an evaluation of a national curriculum package made the mistake of interviewing a group of teachers after they had been to a meeting. He found that many used identical phrases in their replies, as these were fresh in their minds from the meeting they had just attended.

5   Using interviews in pilot studies

One common use of interviews is at the early stage of an enquiry which may or may not go on to use interviews in its main phase. Three typical examples are given below.

Example A. An investigator intends to study teachers' attitudes to new curricula. He hopes to use an attitude questionnaire, but in the first instance he interviews a sample of teachers known to be either hostile or particularly receptive to new ideas. He notes down actual phrases used in conversation, and eventually uses these as part of a pool of possible items for an attitude inventory. He also interviews the small group of teachers who respond to the pilot version of the attitude scale to see how they regard it.

Example B. A primary and secondary school head are interested in making the transition from one school to the other as smooth and trouble-free as possible. Their principal intention is to establish and monitor an experimental programme for one year, but preparatory to this they interview a number of pupils, parents and teachers from each school to help them discover more about children's anxieties, any lack of communication between the two schools, teachers' ideas, parents' problems and so on. The experimental programme is then substantially influenced by what was discovered in the interviews.

Example C. A classroom researcher wishes to observe and study probationer teachers at work. One of his concerns is to know what to observe. He interviews several experienced teachers, getting them to describe their job. From these interviews he assembles a checklist of items such as 'marking books', 'preparing materials', 'asking pupils questions', 'dealing with misbehaviour', 'ordering equipment', etc. which he then uses to categorize the type of jobs various probationers find themselves doing in a day.

6 Types of interview

Three kinds of face-to-face interview are commonly distinguished: the *structured*, *semi-structured* and *unstructured* interview.

Structured interviews. These are based on a carefully worded interview schedule and frequently require short answers or the ticking of a category by the investigator. They are often like a written questionnaire in form, and indeed it is common for a sub-sample of people who have been given a questionnaire to be interviewed, partly to amplify and partly to check their written answers. The structured interview is useful when a lot of questions are to be asked which are not particularly contentious or deeply thought provoking. If the area under investigation does require more profound deliberation the respondent may become irritated at being press-ganged into one word or category answers. In such a case the semistructured interview would be far better. Typical items in a structured interview schedule require yes/no answers, some quantification of time such as 'always, often, sometimes, rarely, never' or a demographic grid such as the one below.

Can you give me a few details of the people in this family? How many children are there?

| (pre-school) |
| (at school) |

Can we start with the youngest?

	Christian name	Relationship to informant	Sex M | F	Age on 1.12.77	Name of school	Office use
A						
B						
C						
D						
E						
F						
G						
H						

Demographic Grid

Since this sort of information can so easily be collected by questionnaire method there is no reason to interview unless face-to-face questioning really is a superior method.

Semi-structured interviews. Again a carefully worded interview schedule is assembled, but in this case much more latitude is permitted. Often there is an initial question followed by probes. The schedule may contain spaces for the interviewer to record notes, or a tape recorder may be used. A semi-structured interview schedule tends to be the one most favoured by educational researchers as it allows respondents to express themselves at some length, but offers enough shape to prevent aimless rambling. A typical item from a semistructured schedule used during an enquiry into home/school liaison is shown below.

Since last September, have you or your husband helped _____ at home with arithmetic or other subjects? (circle code as appropriate).

	W	H
Yes, often	①	④
Yes, occasionally	2	5
No, or hardly ever	3	6
No mother/father	7	8

If * YES (1) (2) (4) (5)

(a) what sort of things do you do?

HUSBAND _____

WIFE _____

(b) how does _____ feel about it?

If*NO(3)(6) why not? _____

* Footnote: The numbers in brackets after YES (1) (2) (4) (5) and NO (3) (6) refer back to the codes at the beginning of the item, i.e. if the respondent answers the first question 'yes, often' or 'occasionally' for husband or wife, the interviewer goes on to ask 'what sort of things do you do?'

Unstructured interviews. Depth interviews require considerable skill and in areas such as psychotherapy practitioners receive extensive training in the necessary techniques. Consequently it is not something which can be undertaken lightly or by anyone not well informed about procedures or hazards. Yet, sensitively and skilfully handled, the unstructured interview, sometimes lasting for two or three hours, can produce information which might not otherwise emerge. One national manufacturer of prams once engaged a group of psychologists to give depth interviews to young mothers. Whereas the conventional market research interview might be concerned with price, shape, colour or convenience, the unstructured depth interviews produced information of a different kind. Some young mothers eventually talked about their fears of babies suffocating, their conflicts with grandmothers who preferred coach-built prams and other examples of deep-rooted attitudes or anxieties such as would only emerge during skilful questioning. In general the novice interviewer is best advised not to embark on this kind of interview until he can confidently handle a more structured situation, and not before he is fairly clear about his own value system.

7   Group and team interviewing

So far we have considered the common one-to-one interview, but, despite the warnings given earlier, it is sometimes useful for more than two people to be involved, provided this does not overawe the subjects.

Group interviews. These involve several respondents. Despite the problem of undue prominence being given to the statements of the very articulate or vociferous, an interview with a small group of perhaps three or four people can be quite useful. For example, if an investigator wishes to get a picture of classroom life this can often be assembled quite accurately with a small group. Pupils will correct each other on points of detail until a consensus is established. Nevertheless caution must be exercised. The consensus might still be fiction.

Team interviews. These normally involve two interviewers working in partnership. In some contexts, say a study of sex roles in adolescents, it might be useful to have a man and a woman present. Certainly, it would be extremely unwise in a study of adolescent sex, for example, for a male investigator alone to conduct an interview with a girl adolescent. Similarly in a multiracial context a white and a black interviewer might work in tandem. The advantage of the team interview is threefold. Firstly it may facilitate responses from some subjects; secondly it allows one person to ask questions and the other to make notes, or to observe certain aspects of the respondent's behaviour; thirdly, since interviewing can be such a subjective process, it allows two people to make separate records of the event and then compare their two versions.

8   More than one interviewer

Sometimes, usually in funded research, a group of interviewers might embark on an interviewing programme. This occasionally happens in small-scale research where the investigator has friends or colleagues – fellow teachers, a spouse, a group of student teachers – who are willing to help out and increase the sample being studied. It is most important that training should be given to such collaborators. Ideally they should be given an explanation of the purposes of the research, told how to use the schedule and supervised whilst conducting a pilot interview. All should use whatever form of words is agreed for each question and not improvise. A videotape of an interview can be shown, and each person can use the schedule as if he were the interviewer. Careful scrutiny of the responses should show if different interviewers are misusing the schedule or not recording accurately. Differences between interviewers cannot be entirely obliterated, but they can be minimized. If there are preliminary and follow-up interviews lists can be exchanged so that interviewers do not see the same respondent on both occasions, unless this is desirable on other grounds.

9 Devising an interview schedule

It is a highly skilled job to devise an interview schedule which elicits relevant information, contains no redundant items and eliminates questioner bias. Even a watertight schedule cannot totally excise the kind of bias inherent in tone of voice, gesture and facial expression.

The investigator needs first of all to make a list of areas in which he requires information. These should then be translated into actual questions and probes, bearing in mind the age and background of the respondent. Professional jargon should be left out unless the person being interviewed is fully familiar with it.

Let us take the example of an investigator studying home/school liaison in junior schools in a working class area. Some schools have held meetings for second and fourth year parents to demonstrate and explain teaching methods, and the interviewer wants to know about these. He could ask, 'What did you think of the meetings?', but this might merely elicit non-committal answers such as 'not bad' or 'quite interesting'. He might enquire, 'How do you evaluate the school's attempts to communicate the principles of Science 5-13 to parents?' and receive a blank stare or a polite smile from most respondents. 'Presumably you went . . .' suggests the person must reply in the affirmative. What he should rather do is build up an item until it meets his requirements, bearing in mind the following:

(1) Some parents might not have gone to the meetings because their children never delivered the invitation.
(2) In some cases only one parent might have attended, in others none or both. Why do people not go? Is it shift work, baby-sitting problems, lack of interest?

(3) Some parents might say they were present because it looks negligent not to have attended, so they should be asked to describe what happened. Often people who say 'Yes' in the first instance, retract when asked about the event.

(4) If some of the information is to be coded for later data processing a code might be built in for easy circling and transfer to punched cards. For example:

Yes   ①

No   2

Don't know   3

Consequently the final item, question, probes, data codes and all, would look like this:

In October last, parents were invited to a meeting where the teachers explained their teaching methods – one meeting for the second year pupils and one for the fourth years. Were you invited to either of them?

Yes	1
No	2
Don't know	3

If YES (1) Did you or your husband go?	W	H
Yes, attended second year meeting	4	9
Yes, attended fourth year meeting	5	10
No, did not attend either	6	11
Don't know	7	12
No father/mother	8	13

If YES (4) (5) (9) (10)

(a) What can you remember of it?

(b) How did you feel about the meeting?

(c)   Did you learn anything from it at all?

If NO (6) (11) Why did you not go?
[. . .]

10   Pilot interviews

When you have assembled a schedule always do two things:

(a) *Pass it on to experienced people for comment.* What is straightforward to
you as the investigator may be baffling to another person not fully in the
picture. Sometimes you are too close to something and others can be
more objective.

(b) Do one or more pilot interviews. Try out your completed schedule with
one or two typical respondents. Do not make the mistake of trying it out
on a sophisticated colleague or friend and then using it with children or
less sophisticated people. If necessary ask one other person to use the
schedule and offer comments. Be prepared to modify it, considerably if
necessary, in the light of informed comment. *Pilot the modified version
again.* There are many instances of investigators committed to a round
of interviews who only discover the ambiguity or other inadequacy of
their instrument after the first few subjects have responded. By then it
is often far too late to modify it.

11   Organising time and travel

Pilot interviews can also give you some rough ideas about the amount of
time you will need. Many investigators, even experienced ones, are hope-
lessly unrealistic about the amount of time needed to complete an interviewing programme.

Suppose, for example, someone conducting research into children's
leisure activities cheerfully decides to interview 100 sets of parents to collect
background information. Since it is fairly difficult to conduct an interview
properly in less than an hour, and can take as long as two or three hours,
perhaps one and a half hours should be allowed on average. One then needs
to add travelling time and 'abortive visit' time, when no one is at home and
one has to try the next person on the list.

Consequently it is difficult, particularly for the part-time investigator usually working evenings and weekends, to do more than one interview a day. A full-time researcher might manage up to three. Clearly, therefore, assuming a part-time investigator can give up to three evenings a week, the proposed 100 interviews would take most of a year. In some enquiries it might be undesirable to aggregate data collected in September with that assembled the following March. The plan for 100 interviews would thus be unrealistic in this context. A far better plan would be to select a smaller number of parents for intensive interview and collect the rest of the data in other ways.

Travel time and costs are also a consideration. Funded research usually has travel costs built in, but independent investigators have to pay their own bills. Travel by public transport can be very inefficient and a great deal of time can easily be wasted.

It is well worth the time spent in planning the interview visits carefully. [. . .] Find out when teachers are free if they are to be interviewed, or make sure you know which lesson and classroom the children are in if they are involved. Check that your visits do not coincide with Sports Day, medicals, prize giving or half term. Then if Lassa Fever strikes suddenly, at least you did your best.

12   Analysing interviews

Analysis time is also frequently underestimated even by experienced investigators. Even quantitative data have to be added up or transferred to punched cards, and qualitative analysis is immensely time-consuming.

If one tape records a one-hour interview, play-back time alone will be one hour. Transcribing will take much longer. A skilled audio typist would need about two hours, allowing for stopping and starting the machine, etc. A shorthand typist would need three hours, and a well-meaning two-finger typist more like five hours. Indeed, it might even need as much as seven or ten hours. The investigator then has a transcript containing perhaps 5000 words and running to 15 or 20 pages. These then have to be read and inferences drawn from them. Thus our optimist who earlier embarked on 100 interviews may have as much as 700 hours of transcribing time and lengthy analysis time. By the time he reports, his research may be out of date.

It is not essential to transcribe interviews, and many interviewers rely on handwritten notes assembled during the interview. These need to be subjected to content analysis, a matter too complex to discuss in any depth here. Suffice it to say that it is important for subjective content analysis to be double checked. The first reader might deduce from reading interview transcripts that certain points are being stressed by subjects. A second reader should independently make his list of salient points. Areas of disagreement can then be discussed and analysed further.

It is also useful to think of content analysis as being a two- or three-stage operation. Usually the investigator knows why he is asking certain questions, but when all interviews have been completed other matters of importance often emerge. A first rapid reading of all transcripts by two independent readers can be used to decide how the main analysis should be conducted. There may even be a 'sandwich' model whereby this major analysis is followed by a final rapid reread to see if anything has been missed or become distorted.

13 Validity and reliability

These concepts apply to interviews as much as to any other data-gathering device. [. . .]

Validity. Does the interview measure or describe what it purports to measure or describe? How does the evidence collected compare with other sources of evidence such as written self-reports, questionnaires, test scores, or observation data? Are the constructs employed meaningful ones? (e.g. would experienced practitioners regard them as important? Are they based on the findings of previous investigators?) Is the evidence collected in any way predictive of future behaviour or events?

Reliability. Test-retest and split-half types of reliability are not always feasible or relevant. Nevertheless one should ask: would two interviewers using the schedule or procedure get similar results? Would an interviewer obtain a similar picture using the procedures on different occasions? This latter point can be checked by asking interviewers to code and report on the same videotape after intervals in time.

14   Conducting the interview

A great deal of common sense needs to be employed when interviewing people. The style should be a balance between friendliness and objectivity. The tight-lipped interviewer with a sphinx-like expression can alienate just as readily as the affable, matey interviewer, who too readily agrees with what his respondents say, can distort.

The beginning of an interview is very important. First of all you should carry some kind of credentials, especially as encyclopaedia and magazine salesmen now frequently use the 'I'm doing a piece of research' gambit to gain entry. A letter from the head of the school or from a research supervisor on headed paper explaining that you are a bona fide investigator will usually be sufficient.

Secondly, make sure all the spadework has been done. If a head is writing to parents or telling class teachers, then do not commence your interviews until you know the ground is cleared.

Thirdly, explain to the subject the purpose of your interview. For example: 'I'm interviewing several parents in the area to try to find out what they think about their children's schooling', or 'I'm talking to a lot of children in your class about what they do in their spare time'. Avoid a tendentious opening like: 'Most young people are browned off with school nowadays, so I'd like to know how you feel' or 'There's been a lot of publicity about falling standards lately, so I'd like to know what you think about it'. Incidentally do not be put off too easily if doing home interviews. Many parents, for example, will tell you that they are too busy, and when you explain 'It won't take long' are so glad of the chance to talk they will scarcely let you out of the house. It is not a bad idea to start off with easier personal questions which arouse interest and do not put off people apprehensive of authority figures.

Fourthly, always remember to ask at the end of the interview if there is anything the subject would like to ask you. You have probably asked a lot of questions and it is the least you can do.

Finally, and most important, assure the subject that the interview is confidential. Do not under any circumstances break this promise. Although educational research does not have a professional code which, if broken, leads to dismissal from a profession, it does have a set of ethics which should be followed. For some investigators this code of ethics requires that the interview 'picture' should be given to the respondent for comment. In other words if you conclude that a person is for or against something he should have the chance, subsequently, of amplifying what he has said, or correcting it if it is erroneous. You need to use your judgement about when this is an appropriate procedure. Incidentally many interviewers, particularly when interviewing in a home or a school, write up a little 'scenario' describing in fairly free form the location and the interview. This can be useful supplementary material and refreshes the memory at a later date.

15   Difficult topics

Some topics, particularly to do with sex, religion, politics or private lives, may be too difficult to handle unless you are an experienced interviewer. Others are difficult but not impossible.

Sometimes one needs to use projective techniques or other devices to elicit an accurate picture. These are too involved to describe briefly, so below are four examples where the investigator uses a particular device to get round a difficult problem.

Example 1. 'Guess who' technique. A researcher investigates under-age smoking. He knows that few children will admit to it, so he says, 'Guess who this describes. This person often smokes secretly. Without telling me the names look through this class list and tell me how many people it might be'. If a whole class come up with a number like 12, 13 or 14 the investigator would have a rough idea of how many were involved without anyone having given away his friends.

Example 2. Critical event. When people talk about some issues their language is often vague. For example, teachers often talk about classes being 'busy' or someone 'having a firm grip'. A clearer picture of what this means can emerge if the person is asked to describe a few 'critical events', that is things which happen in a lesson which indicated that the class was 'busy' or that a certain teacher had 'a firm grip'.

Example 3. Rank ordering. Small children often have no idea if you ask them whether they are the best, the fifteenth or the worst reader in a class. Roy Nash in his *Classrooms Observed* gave the children a class list and asked them to say of each member whether that child was a better or a poorer reader. What transpired was a rank order very similar to that assembled by the teacher.

Example 4. Projection. People are often reluctant to talk about their own fears or desires, and projection offers a device which may produce valuable information. With young children the interviewer may say, 'This is a picture of a little boy who looks worried about something. Can you tell me what he might be worried about?' Many children rapidly begin to talk about themselves, some even switching to the first person. This needs skilful handling both in administration and interpretation and the advice of a good clinical psychologist should be sought.

16   Stereotypes to avoid

Interviewing is a complex if enjoyable way of collecting information [. . .] If you decide to do interviews avoid the following stereotypes. They may read like crude exaggerated caricature, but rest assured they are alive and well. Try to avoid swelling their numbers.

The ESN Squirrel. Collects tapes of interviews as if they are nuts, only does not know what to do with them other than play them back on his hi-fi.
The Ego-Tripper. Knows in his heart that his hunch is right, but needs a few pieces of interview fodder to justify it. Carefully selected quotes will do just that, and one has no idea how much lies on the cutting room floor.
The Optimist. Plans 200 interviews with a randomly selected group of secondary school heads by Christmas. Is shortly to discover 200 synonyms for 'get lost'.
The Amateur Therapist. Although ostensibly enquiring into parents' attitudes to lacrosse, gets so carried away during interview he tries to resolve every social/emotional problem he encounters. Should stick to lacrosse.
The Guillotine. Is so intent on getting through his schedule he pays no attention to the answers and chops his respondents short in mid-sentence. (He actually does manage to do 200 interviews by Christmas.)

17   Books to read

There are many books on the topic, some under the heading 'Qualitative Methodology', others on educational or social science research methods. Below are but five of a huge selection.

Borg, W.R. (1963) *Educational Research: An Introduction*. London, Long-mans, pp. 221–236.

Fox, D.J. (1969) *The Research Process in Education*. New York, Holt, Rinehart & Winston. Chap. 18, pp. 524–569; Chap. 22, pp. 646–679.

Good, C.V. (1966) *Essentials of Educational Research*. New York, Appleton-Century-Crofts, pp. 227–242.

Lovell, K. and Lawson, K.S. (1970) *Understanding Research in Education*. London, University of London Press, pp. 115–123.

Tuckman, B.W. (1972) *Conducting Educational Research*. New York, Harcourt Brace, Chap. 8.

18   A checklist

Finally, if you still intend to interview, go through the checklist below. It highlights many of the points brought out in this chapter. If there are too many NOs you ought not to be interviewing. If the answer to question 1 is NO don't bother with the rest.

BEFORE

1. Is interviewing really the best procedure for the research?   YES   NO
2. Is the purpose of the interview clear?   YES   NO
3. Have I made the best decision about whether to use a structured, semi-structured, unstructured or mixed interview format?   YES   NO
4. Have the relevant authorities been consulted and permission obtained?   YES   NO
5. Has the sample, random or opportunity, been properly assembled?   YES   NO
6. Is the time schedule realistic?   YES   NO
7. Is the travelling efficiently planned and manageable?   YES   NO
8. Has the schedule been skilfully assembled?   YES   NO
9. Is the language level suitable?   YES   NO
10. Has a data processing coding been built-in?   YES   NO
11. Are the procedures for administration of the interview clear?   YES   NO

12. If other interviewers are involved, have they been properly trained and their reliability checked?   YES   NO
13. Has the schedule had a pilot run?   YES   NO
14. Have other people used and commented on the proposed schedule?   YES   NO
15. Am I aware of my own possible bias on the issues?   YES   NO
16. Have appropriate analysis and data processing procedures been worked out?   YES   NO
17. Is there a clear relationship between the interview and other data-gathering devices such as questionnaires, tests, or observations?   YES   NO
18. Have I decided whether to record by hand or by tape recorder?   YES   NO

DURING

19. Is the timing of the interview right?   YES   NO
20. Is the location favourable?   YES   NO
21. Is the rapport sufficiently good for the respondent to be truthful and at ease?   YES   NO
22. Does the subject know the purpose of the interview?   YES   NO
23. Is there privacy?   YES   NO
24. Have I asked all the questions?   YES   NO

AFTER

25. Are the schedules properly completed?   YES   NO
26. Is data processing going to take place as soon as possible?   YES   NO
27. Is content analysis properly conceived with safeguards against too subjective an interpretation or report?   YES   NO
28. Should the interview report be fed back to the respondent for comment?   YES   NO
29. Have I respected my promise of confidentiality?   YES   NO
30. Are the interviews properly written up in the research report?   YES   NO

E.C. Wragg, Rediguide 11: *Guides in Educational Research*. Series editor: M.B. Youngman, Nottingham University, School of Education.
TRC (Oxford) England.
Series copyrighted © 1978–1980.
Professor E.C. Wragg is Director of the School of Education, University of Exeter.

CHAPTER 12

KEEPING A RESEARCH DIARY

Robert Burgess

The use of diaries as a means of gathering information about day-to-day activities is, on the face of it, an attractive way of accumulating information about the way individuals spend their time. Such diaries are not, of course, records of engagements nor journals of thoughts and activities of a personal kind, but records or logs of professional activities. They can, in certain circumstances and with certain subjects, provide valuable information about work patterns and activities. Inevitably, as with all data-collecting techniques, there are problems and in this chapter, Robert Burgess describes how diaries can be used in social investigations and indicates ways in which diary records can be kept by research workers and informants.

Recent studies of schools and classrooms by sociologists and by teachers have utilized an ethnographic approach.[1] Ethnography, it is argued, provides a detailed description of the actions and activities of the members of the school and gives an account of their culture. In short, ethnographic accounts allow the researcher to 'get close' to the data. Such an approach raises the question 'what constitutes doing ethnography?' A brief glance at any of the basic texts devoted to ethnography or fieldwork or field research indicates that the main methods of social investigation include: participant and nonparticipant observation and unstructured interviewing.[2] Such a range of materials highlights one major gap in the discussion of field research methods; namely documentary evidence in general and diaries in particular.

This is a serious gap as researchers who engage in ethnographic work use diaries in order to record the observations that they make in the school and classroom. Indeed, diaries may be kept by both researchers who join schools to teach and do research (researcher-teachers)[3] and by teacher-researchers who alongside their full-time teaching duties monitor their own work and the activities in their schools and classrooms by doing research.[4] Furthermore, both the researcher-teacher and the teacher-researcher may get informants, in the form of teachers and pupils to keep diaries over set periods of time so that they can gain access to activities which they do not witness. While both researcher-teachers and teacher-researchers indicate that part of their research activities involves writing notes and keeping research diaries, they do not tell us, in any detail, about how these diaries may be established and maintained. It is, therefore, the purpose of this article to consider the ways in which diaries are used in social investigations and to indicate ways in which diary records can be kept by both the researcher and the informant.

The researcher's diary

Although the focus of ethnographic research is put upon a series of observations and interviews, it is the situations that were observed and the informants that were interviewed that find their way into the pages of the final research report. However, if ethnographers are to provide detailed portraits of the situations that are observed then they require careful recording in the researcher's diary.

There are few accounts that have provided us with actual material from the researcher's diary or provided guidance on how to keep a research diary. Yet such an exercise raises a series of questions concerning the collection and analysis of data: what data do you record? How do you record it? What categories can be used in recording data? Should the diary be supplemented with interview transcripts, tape recordings and photographs?

Experienced researchers[5] advise that diaries and notes should be kept in triplicate and written on loose-leaf paper. This approach allows copies of the diary to be carefully stored in different places to avoid damage and destruction. Furthermore, it allows the materials to be sorted and resorted in relation to different topics and themes that arise during the process of data collection and analysis. As far as the content of diaries is concerned three major elements are involved. Firstly, a substantive account of the events that have been observed and the informants who have been interviewed. Secondly, a methodological account that involves autobiographical details outlining the researcher's involvement in the social situation in addition to an account of the methods of social investigation that were employed in the study. Finally, the diary should contain an analytic account that raises questions that were posed in the course of conducting research, hunches that the researcher may hold, ideas for organizing the data and concepts employed by the participants that can be used to analyse the materials.[6] Furthermore, some researchers have advised that memos should be written throughout the research process outlining the major themes that can be used to organize the data.[7]

I   The substantive account

The substantive account should involve a detailed chronological record of the events observed and informants that have been interviewed and engaged in conversation. These notes may be organized around a series of questions: Where? When? What? Who? In keeping these questions in mind researchers will be forced to write in detail about the location in which their observations occurred, the time they occurred, the actions and activities that took place and the people who were involved in the situation. In this respect, the records that are kept on an individual lesson might include details of what the lesson is about, what members of the group (including the teacher) say and do (or do not do). Furthermore, details might be kept on what one or two pupils (selected at random) do in the course of the lesson.

Such substantive notes can be supplemented by systematic notes including charts and diagrams. In a school a record can be kept of teachers and pupils with whom the researcher works. Such a chart allows some preliminary classification of the individuals involved in the study and allows the researcher to check on any biases involved in that study in terms of the age, status, and gender of the informants.

In addition, diagrams may be used as a means of summarizing situations in which the researcher has been involved and to reveal in graphic form the pattern of social interaction and spatial relationships in classrooms, in meetings, and in situations such as morning assembly.[8] This substantive record, therefore, provides a continuous description of the situations observed, and persons interviewed. While such records form the main material out of which the final report is produced, they may also be supplemented by charts and diagrams, that allow for further review and analysis. Furthermore, such accounts can be supplemented by tape recordings and photographs that can extend the written records.[9]

II The methodological account

While it is widely acknowledged that ethnographic research involves observation and interviews there are still further questions that need to be raised. Firstly, under what circumstances were observations made? Secondly, what role was taken by the researcher? Thirdly, what informants were selected for study? Finally, how were the informants selected?

If the researcher attempts to record answers to these questions they will provide an autobiographical account of the research process and details of the researcher's involvement in that process. Such an account will complement the substantive materials and in turn provide some suggestions about data analysis that can be done.[10] Furthermore, accounts of methodology can help the researcher to reflect on the philosophical, practical, ethical and political aspects of the research process.[11]

III The analytic account

The analytic account might include a series of jottings that are maintained over the course of the study. Here, researchers record their initial questions and the ways in which these questions were modified over time by the collection of data and by the informants that were utilized in the study. In this respect, Lacey[12] outlines the various 'stages' through which his project passed and the various themes that arose in his study. In short, a continuous record can be maintained of the questions that were used to orientate data collection and that can be used to start data analysis.

A further source of suggestions for data analysis may come from the informants themselves. On some occasions, informants may provide their own analysis of a situation which will provide researchers with a series of concepts that can be used in the study. For example, the terminology that pupils use to classify their peers such as 'swot', 'creep', 'comic', and 'dunce' can be used in the course of data collection and data analysis to build up a pupil typology and to establish the ideal type characteristics associated with these individuals. Secondly, researchers might discuss their observations with informants. In this instance, workshops can be established where materials from the researcher's observations and interviews can be discussed and evaluated by informants. In these circumstances, the informants may suggest ways in which the data that has been collected can be augmented, modified and extended.[13]

Finally, researchers may develop hunches and insights throughout the course of their research. If these ideas are kept on record it allows researchers to look at the ways in which social science concepts, professional concepts, and common sense/everyday concepts can be employed in the analysis of data.

The informant's diary

Ethnographic research involves the study of people *in situ*. It involves the study of informants, their actions and their activities as they occur. Such an approach presupposes that the researcher can gain access to informants and their activities. However, it is evident that in a situation such as a school it is impossible for the researcher to observe all the activities that occur. This arises for a number of reasons. Firstly, the size of the school prevents the researcher being present at all locations. The researcher has to select which classrooms to enter, and what groups to study. Secondly, there are some situations that the researcher may not be allowed to directly observe, such as meetings restricted to high status members of the institution, meetings in the head teacher's study and activities in particular classrooms. Finally, a researcher might be denied access to some classrooms when teachers are concerned that their work will be judged or evaluated during the course of the research.

In these circumstances, the researcher needs to obtain accounts from the participants which will yield a further series of observations and first hand accounts. Researchers might, therefore, ask informants to keep diaries about what they do on particular days and in particular lessons. Teachers and pupils could be asked to record the activities in which they engage and the people with whom they interact. In short, what they do (and do not do) in particular social situations. In these circumstances, subjects of the research became more than observers and informants: they are co-researchers as they keep chronological records of their activities.

The diarists (whether they are teachers or pupils) will need to be given a series of instructions to write a diary. These might take the form of notes and suggestions for keeping a continuous record that answers the questions: When? Where? What? Who? Such questions help to focus down the observations that can be recorded. Meanwhile, a diary may be sub-divided into chronological periods within the day so that records may be kept for the morning, the afternoon and the evening. Further sub-divisions can be made in respect of diaries directed towards activities that occur within the school and classroom. Here, the day may be sub-divided into the divisions of the formal timetable with morning, afternoon and lunch breaks. Indeed, within traditional thirty-five or forty minute lessons further sub-divisions can be made in respect of the activities that occur within particular time zones. (cf. Flanders interaction analysis).[14]

Using informants' diaries gives further detailed data. Firstly, these diaries provide first-hand accounts of situations to which the researcher may not have direct access. Secondly, they provide 'insider' accounts of situations. Finally, they provide further sampling of informants, of activities and of time which may complement the observations made by the researcher.

The diary-interview

The diary suggests a written record, which may vary in depth and in detail. In these circumstances, the researcher may still require further data on which to base an analysis. Here, the diary may hint at the actions and activities of informants but may lack the telling detail that characterizes the ethnographic record. For example, pupil diaries may contain details of 'messing around' in particular lessons and reports of 'doing nothing'. The researcher, therefore, needs to explore the meaning of these statements when a diary-interview is conducted. In this way, a detailed picture can be established about the activities that pupils associate with 'messing around' and 'doing nothing'.

The diary may, in this instance, be used as a data resource which the researcher uses to raise a series of questions and queries that may provide further data. In both the case of the researcher's diary and the informant's diary an interview may be used with the diarist to provide more detailed data. When team research is employed, members of the research team may exchange diaries in order that questions can be raised about the material recorded by each individual. Team members can question each other about the observations they have made so that comparisons can be made between the different sets of data that have been gathered. These discussions can be taped and transcribed as they can be used to provide further data for analysis. Meanwhile, in cases where the researcher obtains an informant's diary, it may be scanned for data that needs to be elaborated, discussed, explored and illustrated; all of which are tasks that can be conducted in an interview.[15]

The uses of a research diary

Research diaries (whether kept by researchers or by informants) can be used in a number of ways:

1. As a means of recording field notes: substantive, methodological and analytic.
2. As a means of providing participants' accounts of situations.
3. As a means of generating further data to complement observational and interview material.
4. As a means of comparing data collected by researchers and by informants.

In this respect, diaries provide first-person accounts of social situations. They provide insights into situations and activities and they provide access to situations in which outsiders cannot go. However, diarists need to make careful records of the situations in which they are involved, as these records are used to explore and explain the social world of schools, classrooms, teachers and pupils.[16]

Notes and references

1. For recent studies of schools and classrooms by sociologists see King, R. (1978) *All Things Bright and Beautiful? A Sociological Study of Infants' Classrooms.* Chichester, Wiley; and Woods, p. (1979) *The Divided School.* London Routledge & Kegan Paul. For accounts of ethnographic studies that have been conducted by teacher-researchers see Burgess, R.G. (1980) (ed.) Symposium on teacher-based research. A special issue of *Insight*, Vol. 3, No. 3; and Elliot, J. and Whitehead, D. (1980) (eds.) The theory and practice of educational action research, *Classroom Action Research Network.* Bulletin No. 4.
2. For a detailed discussion of ethnography or field research see Schatzman L. and Strauss A., (1973) *Field Research.* Englewood Cliffs, N.J., Prentice Hall; and Wax, R. (1971) *Doing Fieldwork.* Chicago, University of Chicago Press.
3. For examples see Hargreaves, D.H. (1967) *Social Relations in a Secondary School.* London, Routledge & Kegan Paul; and Lacey, C. (1970) *Hightown Grammar: the School as a Social System.* Manchester, Manchester University Press.
4. For discussions of the distinctions between researcher-teachers and teacher-researchers see Burgess, R.G. (1980) The role of the teacher-researcher, *Insight*, Vol. 3, No. 3, pp. 31–34; and Burgess, R.G. (1980) Some fieldwork problems in teacher-based research, *British Educational Research Journal*, Vol. 6, No. 2, pp. 165–173.
5. See for example Webb, B. (1926) The art of note-taking, in Webb. B, *My Apprenticeship.* London, Longmans, pp. 364–372.
6. For an account based on research in education see Geer, B. (1964) First days in

the field, in Hammond P. (ed.) *Sociologists at Work*. New York, Basic Books, pp. 322–344.

7. For a discussion of this point see Glaser, B.G. and Strauss, A.L. (1967) *The Discovery of Grounded Theory*. London, Weidenfield and Nicolson.

8. For illustrations of the way in which diagrams can be used in research diaries see Bogdan, R. and Taylor, S.J. (1975) *Introduction to Qualitative Research Methods*, London, Wiley; and for the way in which diagrams can be used in research reports on classroom observation see Stebbins, R. Physical context influences on behaviour: the case of classroom disorderliness, in Hammersley, M. and Woods, P. (eds.) (1976) *The Process of Schooling*. London, Routledge & Kegan Paul, pp. 208–216.

9. For an account that provides a good background on the use of visual and audio-visual recordings in schools and classrooms, see Walker, R. and Adelman, C. (1975) *A Guide to Classroom Observation*. London, Methuen.

10. The way in which methods of social research are linked to the questions posed and the analysis used in the study of schools and classrooms is revealed in Nash, R. (1973) *Classrooms Observed*. London, Routledge & Kegan Paul.

11. For a series of reflections on educational research see Shipman, M. (ed.) (1976) *The Organisation and Impact of Social Research*. London, Routledge & Kegan Paul.

12. See Lacey, C. Problems of sociological fieldwork: a review of the methodology of 'Hightown Grammar', in Shipman, M. (ed.) (1976), *The Organisation and Impact of Social Research*, London, Routledge & Kegan Paul, pp. 63–88.

13. For an account of the way in which links may be made between observations and interviews and subsequent comments made by teachers see Nickerson, J. and Scrimshaw, P. (1980) The biology lesson or Some processes of interpersonal education: a draft analysis, *Classroom Action Research Network*, Bulletin No. 4, pp. 56–65.

14. For a discussion of Flanders Interaction analysis see Flanders, N. (1970) *Analyzing Teacher Behaviour*. New York, Addison-Wesley; and for a commentary on this approach see Delamont, S. (1976) *Interaction in the Classroom*. London, Methuen.

15. For a discussion of diary-interviews see Zimmerman D.H. and Wieder, D.L. (1977) The diary: diary-interview method, *Urban Life*, Vol. 5, No. 4, pp. 479–498.

16. Many of the issues raised in this article concerning ethnographic research and the keeping of research diaries are discussed in more detail in Burgess, R.G. (ed.) (1981) *Field Research: A Sourcebook and Field Manual*. London, Allen & Unwin.

Robert Burgess, *Cambridge Journal of Education*, Lent Term 1981, Vol. 11, No. 1, pp. 75–83.
Dr Robert G. Burgess is a Lecturer in Sociology at the University of Warwick.

CHAPTER 13

OBSERVING AND RECORDING MEETINGS

G.L. Williams

A great deal has been written about classroom observation but very little about the observation of meetings. Yet meetings take up substantial periods of time in any educational organization. Decisions are reached in meetings which have profound effects on the organization and the people who study and work in it. The processes by which decisions are reached, the content of meetings and the kind of behaviour engaged in by the participants are of great importance to education managers. In this specially commissioned chapter, Graham Williams introduces us to a range of methods for observing and recording the content and process of meetings, which will be useful for research workers wishing to understand the behaviour of participants and also for individuals and groups who wish to improve their own performance in meetings.

As members of organizations we all participate in a variety of meetings from informal discussions with colleagues to formal committee meetings with a chairperson and secretary. Rarely do we take the opportunity to observe what is going on in a meeting and work out why participants in the meeting are behaving in the way they are. Most of us complain about committee meetings and staff meetings but if you want to improve both individual and group performance in meetings then observing and analysing what is happening is the first stage in bringing about improvement.

Those carrying out research into behaviour or roles may also be interested in what happens in meetings. If you are observing a meeting as part of a project you need some way of recording your observations. But what should you observe? What sort of things should you look for? What affects the effectiveness of the meeting?

Content and process

A fundamental distinction can be made in looking at a meeting between content issues and process issues. Content refers to what the group of people comprising the meeting is doing in terms of its purposes and objectives; process refers to the way in which the group goes about achieving its formal task – how it is carrying out its tasks.

Content issues

When observing a meeting, it is important first to identify the type of meeting and then to decide what objectives are held by the members for the meeting, though objectives may vary from person to person and sometimes may be kept well hidden. As a result, observations tend to be incomplete. The main types of meetings are:

1. **Command meeting.** A meeting called by a manager to instruct, co-ordinate or control his subordinates. The objectives specified for the meeting are those of the manager. Others may have conflicting objectives.

2. **Selling meeting.** A meeting where one person or a group is trying to persuade or convince the other group members about some issue. The objectives are concerned with persuasion. A sub-set of this type is where a person tries to 'sell' himself, that is by boasting or showing off in more or less subtle ways.

3. **Advisory meeting.** A meeting called for the exchange of information or the seeking of opinions. The purpose may be stated either in terms of giving or receiving information or both. If it is seeking opinions, the purpose may be either to help the leader to make a decision after consultation or to test a decision already formulated.

4. **Negotiating meeting.** A meeting aimed at reaching a compromise/agreement, or making a decision by bargaining, between two or more opposing sides with different points of view. Each side will have different objectives but some overlapping mutual interests arising from their interdependence.

5. **Problem solving meeting.** A meeting concerned with tackling a particular problem or problems. Usually the problem belongs to the whole group and all concerned are able to contribute towards the process. The meeting may have a limited focus on some aspect of problem solving, that is planning or decision making. Also the decision may be made outside the meeting following its recommendation or deliberations.

Meeting		
Type (Complete where necessary)	**Tick as** **appropriate**	**Objectives of** **the meeting**

1 Command
  – instruct
  – coordinate
  – control
  –
		(a) whose
		(b) what they were
		(c) extent to which achieved
		(d) adverse effects

2 Selling
  – ideas
  – self
  –		

3 Advisory
  – giving information
  – receiving information
  – seeking opinions
  –		

4 Negotiations
  between –
  –
  –		

5 Problem solving
  – planning
  – recommending
  – decision making		

6 Support
  – emotional
  – learning
  – problem solving
  – team building
  –		

7 Other – specify		

Fill in the title of the meeting. Then decide which of the six types of meeting it is, and put a tick in the centre column against the appropriate sub-type. Additional types and sub-types can be added if necessary. Finally, answer (a), (b), (c) and (d) in the objectives column.

Figure 1 Types of meeting form

6. **Support meeting.** A meeting where the individual group members come together to give each other support in terms of such things as their emotional needs, learning and development, or individual problem solving. Usually each individual would have his own personal objectives although there would be more overlapping of objectives if this were a team building session.

Some meetings may be of more than one type. In observing a meeting, details of the type of meeting and objectives or purposes can be recorded using the form in Figure 1.

It is also interesting to record the types of meeting that a staff group holds over a period of time, and the balance between the different types of meeting. Do some types of meeting not occur? (or only infrequently). If not, why not? Could the balance between the different types of meeting be improved?

Further analysis of content

Having analysed what type (or types) a meeting is, and what the objectives are, further analysis of the content of the meeting can be carried out by looking at how and/or how well the purposes of the meeting were achieved and what the various contributions were from members that influenced the achievement of objectives and purposes. Further analysis can be carried out by general checklists or by specific checklists for each type of meeting.

General checklists

The starting point for analysis can be either the issues covered or the persons.

(a)
> For each issue in turn:
> – who speaks on that particular issue?
> – for how long?
> – what is the nature of their contribution?
> – how effective is their contribution – particularly in helping to achieve the objectives of the meeting?
> – what helped progress on the issue?
> – what hindered progress on the issue?

(b)
> For each person in turn:
> – what did they contribute to the discussion?

- what was the nature of their contribution?
- how did they help in achieving the purposes or objectives of the meeting?
- how did they hinder the achievement of purposes or objectives?

Checklists for each type of meeting

Checklists can be drawn up for each type of meeting, but every meeting is different so the checklists given should be freely adapted to suit the particular meeting you are observing.

1 Command meetings

1.1 *Instruct*
- what was the group supposed to learn?
- what exactly did the group learn?
- what got in the way of their learning?

Preparation
- how well were the group put at ease?
- did they know what to expect?
- how well was previous knowledge and experience checked?
- to what extent and how was interest created in them?

Presentation
1.1.1 Before the situation
- how well were they prepared for learning from the situation?

1.1.2 During the situation
- how was learning helped during the situation?

1.1.3 After the situation
- how clearly was the situation explained?
- how well was the group helped to learn?

Checking
- how well did the presenter check what was learned?

1.2 *Coordinate*
- what information was gathered and how?
- what information was lacking?
- how was the information integrated?

- did everyone understand its integration and coordination? – if not, why not?
- what are individuals' commitment to future cooperation and co-ordination?

1.3 *Control*
- what was required of people?
- how well did they understand this?
- how acceptable were the requirements to them?
- if they were not acceptable – why weren't they?
- how able were they to comply?
- to what extent did they/will they follow the requirements and why?

2 Selling meetings

2.1 *Selling ideas*
- what preparation had gone into the presentation and how did it show – what effect did it have?
- to what extent did the seller show awareness of the client's needs? – which needs and how was awareness shown?
- how was the attention of clients gained?
- how was their interest generated?
- what obstacles occurred and how were they dealt with?
- how was desire to embrace the idea aroused?
- what was done to obtain action on the part of the clients?
- how successful was the selling of ideas?

2.2 *Selling self*
- how did the individual attempt to create a favourable impression?
- how acceptable was this to the group?
- what attempts were made to maintain a favourable impression?
- what effect did these have?
- what attempts were made to reverse a perceived unfavourable impression? – and to what effect?
- what were the effects of the self-selling effort?

3 Advisory meetings

3.1 *Giving information*

- what information was given and by whom?
- to what extent was this what was required/needed/wanted by the receivers?
- what information that was not given could have been useful and who should have supplied it?
- how was understanding checked (a) by the information giver, (b) by others?

3.2 *Receiving information/seeking opinions*

- were information/opinion givers put at their ease? – by whom and how?
- what information/opinion was given and by whom?
- was this what was required and if not what was missing?
- who seemed to withhold information/opinion and why?
- how was it made clear that the information/opinions were useful/ beneficial?
- are the givers more likely or less likely to respond favourably in future to similar requests and why?

4 Negotiating meetings

- what were the different parties and their positions in the negoti- ations?
- how clear was each side's position and their requirements to others in the meeting?
- how were these made clear?
- what was the pattern of attacking and defending?
- what proposals helped to move the negotiation forward and from whom were they received?
- how and by whom were specific proposals blocked or built on?
- what were the compromises which emerged?
- how did they emerge?
- how did they become acceptable?
- what were the final outcomes of the negotiation meeting?

5   Problem solving meetings

5.1   *Planning/recommending meetings*

(A plan is a detailed expression of a predetermined course of action. The pre-planning stage usually considers alternative courses of action and would often be part of a planning meeting.)

- how were alternative courses of action determined? – by whom and how well?
- how were alternatives compared and one or more chosen? – using what criteria and who was involved in making the comparison?
- how well were the consequences of alternatives judged and by whom?
- how specific was the plan and who contributed (and how) to the specification of the plan?
- what consideration was given and by whom to those who will be responsible for implementing the plan?
- how acceptable is the plan/recommendation?
- who has what reservations?

5.2   *Decision-making meetings*

- how well were the facts obtained and used?
- how well was the nature of the problem or situation analysed and by whom?
- who was actively involved in making the decision and what contribution did they make?
- what was the quality of the decision making?
- what was the quality of the final decision?
- how acceptable was the decision? – who accepted the decision? – who had what reservations?
- how well did individuals understand the reasons for taking the decision?
- was the decision reviewed? – how and by whom?

6   Support meetings

- how clearly could individuals perceive and state their difficulties?
- how well did people express themselves?

- was there the right balance between expression of feelings and expression of content?
- what evidence was there of attention to others, that is attentive relaxed posture, eye contact and verbal following rather than inappropriate abrupt changes of topic?
- what advice, suggestions or reflections were given, by whom and with what effect?
- what was the balance between directive and nondirective responses and were they given appropriately?
- what interpretations were made and how well did members use interpretations? (An interpretation is the bringing of an alternative framework of reference which has the possibility of leading to a breakthrough in dealing with a situation.)
- how and by whom was help given and received?
- what was the degree of openness of communications?
- what was the level of acceptance of ideas and criticism?
- how helpful was the meeting in terms of the support needs met?
- which needs were met, how and how well?

The above are just some examples of possible checklists focusing mainly on the content of meetings. They can be easily adapted to suit specific meetings or new checklists can be devised where these are inappropriate.

Process observations

Having looked at what the meeting is about, let us now consider the different ways a group in a meeting goes about achieving its formal task. There are many different types of processes that we can focus on. Some examples are:
- communication
- decision making
- problem solving
- direction
- functional roles (task and maintenance)
- self-oriented behaviour
- norms

Communication

The communication process is one of the most important processes in any meeting. Basically communication is the transfer of information between people. However, the process itself is complex and in an apparently simple message a mixture of facts, feelings, opinions, insults, etc. can be communicated. In a face-to-face meeting verbal communication is always accompanied by non-verbal communication and the two types of communication may contradict each other. Some aspects of communication are easy to observe, others are more difficult and may have to be mainly inferred rather than observed directly.

Some of the simple-to-observe aspects of communication are:
- the relative contributions of individuals
- who talks after whom
- who interrupts whom
- who individuals talk to

Relative contributions

Here what is observed is the relative frequency and duration of verbal communication. All that is needed for these observations is a list of group members and a mark placed against each name each time that person speaks. A different checkmark can be made if the same person is still speaking after a set period of time (i.e. half-a-minute) so that the length of communication is also measured (see Figure 2).

Participants	
Alex	\\\⁼
Barry	\
Carol	\\\\\ \≡ ⁻
David	\\\≡\\ \\\\⁼
Elaine	
Multiple speaking	\\\

‌\ indicates contribution
‌⁻ indicates communication continuing beyond a set time

Figure 2 Relative contributions

This type of analysis can be useful in highlighting the extent to which certain members may be dominating the meeting and indicating which members are not contributing very much.

Who talks after whom

The analysis above can be easily extended to analyse who talks after whom and to plot the sequence of communication by using squared paper. After each communication a square to the right of the last square completed is used (see Figure 3).

Alex		|		|		|=												
Barry												|						
Carol		|		|		|		|		|				|≡			
David					|		|	|=			|						
Elaine																		
Multiple												|				|	

Figure 3   Sequence of communications

There are often patterns of speaking so that one person tends to be followed by another particular individual. The next level of analysis is to identify what is happening between the two people. For example, is the second person supporting and encouraging the first or trying to undo the point made by the first person? This sort of information can also be entered onto the chart in Figure 3.

Who interrupts whom

This is a particularly important category of behaviour which can also be plotted on the grid in Figure 3. Alternatively, a separate note can be made of instances of interruptions. This simple analysis usually needs to be supplemented with inferences about the causes of interruptions, usually using evidence from other observations such as nonverbal behaviour.

Interruptions often give us clues as to how people perceive their own power or status in a meeting relative to the others at the meeting. People who perceive themselves as of higher power or status or more important often feel free to interrupt those whom they perceive as of lower status. At a meeting of apparent equals, interruptions may indicate that one person feels that they are more important than certain, or all, others and this may lead to dysfunctional consequences.

Who individuals talk to

A useful way of plotting who talks to whom is to use the system shown in Figure 4.

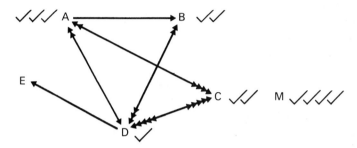

Key A B C D and E are group members   M is multiple speaking

Figure 4 Who talks to whom

The letters represent group members. Each communication from one person to another is represented by an arrow or an additional arrowhead. Communications to the whole group are represented by a tick next to the person's initial. This gives an easy-to-read record of who has communicated to whom as well as the number of contributions from each person. Instances of multiple speaking can be recorded alongside the diagram.

This type of analysis can identify a type of pairing between individuals. If one person almost always addresses communications to another specific individual, the next level of analysis is to examine what is going on between the member of the pair. For example, Carol may talk to David because he usually agrees with her or tries to be supportive. This may imply a coalition or sub-group within the larger group. Further analysis may look at the way this coalition affects the functioning of the meeting.

Another reason for people addressing their communications to a particular person is that they expect the most resistance or criticism to come from that person and they are trying to judge that person's reactions. A deeper level of analysis would be concerned with the relationship between these two individuals.

Non-verbal communication

There is a very complex code by which we communicate non-verbally and it is difficult to do justice to this area in a small section here. It is interesting

that people on the receiving end usually understand the non-verbal message often without realizing how the message has been transmitted. It is more difficult for an observer to understand what is being communicated non-verbally. Channels of non-verbal communication include:
- facial expression
- gestures
- changes in direction of gaze
- eye contact patterns
- tone of voice
- posture
- relative orientation between individuals
- distance between people
- touching
  etc.

Mehrabian (1972) has suggested that there are three dimensions which are particularly relevant in nonverbal communication. These are:
1. Positiveness
2. Potency or status
3. Responsiveness

The first dimension, positiveness, refers basically to liking and disliking. Potency refers to dominant and controlling versus submissive and dependent attitudes. Responsiveness refers to awareness of and reaction to another. Indicators of these three dimensions are as follows:

1. The like-dislike dimension is shown by the degree of immediacy or closeness between individuals in interaction. This can be in terms of physical closeness and/or perceptual availability (eye contact, orientation, etc.). Approach and immediacy indicate preference, positive evaluation and liking. Avoidance and non-immediacy indicate the opposite.

2. Potency or status can be thought of in terms of strength as opposed to weakness. Strength is implied by large versus small (expansive movements as against small and controlled movements), high versus low (standing upright as against bowing) and fast versus slow movements. Another indicator is the degree of relaxation or tenseness. The greater the relaxation the greater the potency or status.

3. Responsiveness is indicated by greater non-verbal activity. In observing individuals in a meeting notes can be made about the three dimensions of non-verbal behaviour and in particular any differences in a person's behaviour to different individuals in the group.

Decision making processes

It is not only on large issues that decisions are made. Decisions are made in meetings all the time, often without participants being aware of the process. It is important to be aware of what decisions are being made (often implicitly) and the way these decisions are made.

What are the different ways in which decisions are made in a meeting? There are a number of possibilities varying from very little involvement of group members through to total involvement of all.

1. Lack of decision
   – even making no decision can be a type of decision
2. Decision by one individual
   – i.e. the expert or autocrat
3. Decision by minority group
   – i.e. power group (inner cabinet) or sub-committee
4. Voting
   – taking a majority vote as to what to do
5. Consensus
   – giving everyone a chance to have their full say and to feel that they have made their position clear so that each individual can at least go along with the group decision to some extent even though they may not be in total agreement.
6. Total agreement

Further analysis might look at the quality and acceptability of the decisions that are taken by the meeting. The way that decisions are made tends to affect the quality and the acceptability of the decision. For example, in voting there is often a polarization in terms of acceptability. Those who voted for the decision may find it very acceptable but the minority who 'lost' the vote may feel that the group has made the wrong decision, and that they were right all along and thus they are not really committed to the decision made by the meeting and may even try to subvert it.

Problem solving

Does the meeting tackle a problem in the best way? Some problems are best solved using a logical approach, other problems may be better tackled using creative techniques such as brainstorming. Many complex problems require both logical and creative approaches but used at the appropriate stage in the problem solving process.

Does the group jump to quick solutions without finding out first what the real problem is?

Does the problem-solving process follow a reasonable sequence such as the following:

- identifying the real problem
  where are we now?
  where do we want to be?
  how can we get there?
  what is problem and what is symptom?
- agreeing on the problem
  checking everyone understands the problem
- defining the problem
  factors contributing to the problem
  factors affected by the problem
- generating alternative possible solutions
  encouragement of differences
  no evaluation or criticism at this stage
- evaluating possible solutions
  forecasting outcomes using good judgement
  looking critically at the alternatives
- taking the decision
  being decisive
- action planning
  appropriate involvement of those who will implement
  considering how to deal with adverse reactions and consequences
- action
- monitoring and evaluation of outcomes

In recording problem-solving behaviour you can check the stages as they occur, indicating the sequence of stages and giving an effectiveness rating for each stage (see Figure 5).

Using the centre column identify the sequence in which the stages of problem solving occurred. Put a 1 by the first stage to occur, 2 by the second and so on. Often a meeting will not pass through all stages so some will be left blank. Using the 4 point rating scale, rate how well each stage that you have marked was carried out.

Stages of problem solving	Order of stages	Rating			
		1	2	3	4
Identifying real problem	3	√			
Agreeing on problem	2			√	
Defining the problem	1			√	
Generating alternatives					
Evaluating solutions	4		√		
Taking the decision	6			√	
Action planning	5				√
Action	7		√		
Monitoring and evaluation	8	√			

Key 4 Carried out well
       3 Fair
       2 Attempt made but done badly
       1 Not done at all

Figure 5 Rating of problem solving

Direction and rate of progress

Two of the main complaints about meetings are they often lack direction and take up far too much time. The two are often related in that if you are travelling in the wrong direction for part of the time it takes longer to reach your destination. In observing a meeting these two factors can be plotted together using a series of small arrows for set periods of time (i.e. three minutes) starting from S (for start) and hopefully (but not necessarily) ending up at G (for goal). The direction of the arrows indicates the direction of the discussion relative to the goal and the value given to each arrow indicates the speed of progress towards the goal on a 5 point scale (minus values are possible). Figure 6 gives an example of a meeting plotted in this way.

Functional roles

Behaviour in a meeting can help the group in two different ways. It may help the group to achieve its task (task roles) or it may help the relationships

indicates trying to go in several directions at once

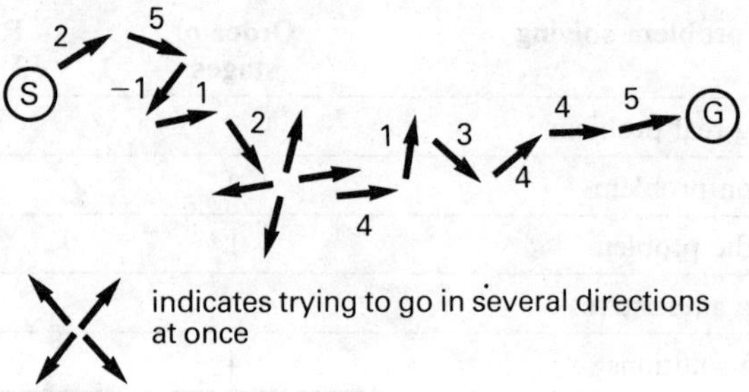

Figure 6   Direction and rate of progress

between members or affect the climate of the meeting (maintenance roles). Both types of roles are important if the meeting is to be effective both in the short term and the long term. The roles can be played by anyone in the group and it is best if most roles are performed by most group members.

Types of behaviour concerned with the group achieving its task:

1. Proposing: Proposing tasks or goals; defining a group problem; suggesting a procedure or ideas for solving a problem.
2. Building: Making suggestions that build on or add to others' proposals.
3. Presenting information or opinion: Offering facts; providing relevant information about group concerns.
4. Seeking information or opinions: Requesting facts; seeking relevant information about group concern; asking for expressions of feeling; requesting a statement or estimate; soliciting expressions of value; seeking suggestions and ideas.
5. Testing and clarifying: Testing for understanding and agreement; interpreting ideas or suggestions; clearing up of confusions; defining terms; indicating alternatives and issues before the group; testing of the quality of the group's procedures or achievements.
6. Keeping group on course: Highlighting diversions and bringing the group back on track.
7. Summarizing: Pulling together related ideas; restating suggestions after the group has discussed them; offering a decision or conclusion for the group to accept or reject.

Behaviours concerned with maintaining the group:

1. Supporting/encouraging: Being warm, friendly and responsive to others; indicating by facial expression or remarks the acceptance of others' contributions.

2. Gatekeeping: Helping to keep communication flowing freely; helping others to participate (bringing in); stopping others from monopolizing or disrupting (shutting out.)
3. Harmonizing: Attempting to reconcile disagreements, getting people to explore differences.
4. Tension releasing: Reducing the build-up of tension where it is becoming dysfunctional, by joke or other mechanism.
5. Showing attention: Indicating interest verbally or by body language, in what the group is doing, listening attentively.

These categories have been developed from Benne and Sheats (1948) and Bales (1950) and can easily be adapted to suit particular types of meetings.

Task and maintenance behaviours can be recorded using the form in Figure 7. It takes quite a lot of practice to be able to use the form for all group members and it is probably best to start by practising observation of just one or two group members until you have familiarized yourself with the categories.

Where categories are under-utilized the next stage of analysis is to look at the reasons for and consequences of this. Would the meeting be more effective if these behaviours were more prevalent?

Self-oriented emotional behaviour

In addition to the task and maintenance behaviours described above some behaviours may be aimed at meeting a personal need or goal without consideration of the group (self-oriented behaviours) and this type of behaviour will often hinder the group's achievement.

Some of the basic causes of these self-oriented behaviours are:

1. Identity
   - what is my place in this group?
   - in this meeting how should I present myself?
   - what role have I got in this context?
   - what role should I play?
2. Goals
   - which of my needs and goals can be met in this meeting?
   - how can the meeting best help me to achieve my objectives?
   - which of the group's goals do I want to support?
3. Power and control
   - how much power, control and influence have I got in this group?

	Group members				
Task roles					
Proposing					
Building					
Presenting: information or opinion					
Seeking: information or opinion					
Testing Understanding Agreement Quality					
Keeping group on course					
Summarizing					
Maintenance roles					
Supporting/Encouraging					
Gatekeeping: Bringing in Shutting out +ve Shutting out −ve					
Harmonizing					
Tension releasing					
Showing attention (give comments)					

Fill in the group members' names at the top of each column. Each time a group member takes a particular role, put a tick alongside the category in the column for that individual.

Figure 7 Functional roles observation form

- how much do I want?
- how do I increase my power and influence?
4. Acceptance and intimacy
   - how well am I accepted and/or liked by others at the meeting?
   - do I accept and like them?
   - how emotionally close do I want to be to them?

These causes can lead to a further series of roles termed individual roles and these are aimed at satisfying individual needs. They are often irrelevant or dysfunctional to the task and maintenance functions. The type of roles that might be observed and identified are:

1. Identity and goals
   - Special interest pleader
   - Playboy
   - Attention seeker
2. Power and control
   - Dominator
   - Aggressor
   - Blocker
   - Recognition seeker
   - Submitter
   - Withdrawer
3. Acceptance and intimacy
   - Help seeker
   - Self-discloser
   - Self-confessor

You will probably come up with some additional categories. As the group develops and members' needs become more integrated with group goals, the proportion of self-oriented behaviour should decrease and there should be more task and maintenance behaviour.

Where you observe self-oriented emotional behaviour in a meeting, the categories above may help to give a possible interpretation of what is happening and why the individual is behaving in that particular way.

Norms

Some examples of the types of behaviour which might be classified as norms are:

- way of speaking (swearing, rudeness, politeness)
- following of procedure
- dress
- amount of participation
- punctuality
- innovativeness (or lack of it)
- aggression
- rational approach

  – formality
  etc.

Norms are shared expectations and attitudes. They are agreements about what should be thought, felt or done and the way in which actions should be carried out. The agreements may be explicit (verbalized) or implicit, and the implicit agreements may be either conscious or unconscious. In addition, norms may be static or dynamic. Static norms are those that are accepted by everyone in the group and dynamic norms are the ones for which it is necessary for the group to bring pressure to bear on some individuals to make them conform to group norms. So in observing a meeting we can classify any norms that we see into the matrix in Figure 8.

Type of norm	Explicit	Implicit	
		Conscious	Unconscious
Static			
Dynamic			

Figure 8   Classification of norms

The norms can be additionally classified by putting the letters U, H or N (unhelpful, helpful or neutral) after them depending on whether they help the group in its task or not.

The formation of norms often occurs around critical incidents. For example, someone may challenge the chairperson of the meeting concerning how the meeting is being run. What happens next may help to form group norms concerning the use of authority in the group and the 'legitimacy' of challenging that authority. As an observer, it can be useful to note critical incidents and their consequences.

The complete meeting

So far we have looked analytically at a variety of specific issues which can be observed when studying meetings. It is useful to focus on these in order to study and improve what is happening in a meeting. However, it is difficult to carry out more than one or two of the types of observation for any one meeting unless this is done by several observers. A more global observation

General comments about the success or otherwise of the meeting	tick appropriate column for each item	strongly agree	mildly agree	mildly disagree	strongly disagree
1. The purpose of the meeting was clear to all					
2. There was agreement amongst members about their objectives					
3. There was commitment by all to the objectives of the meeting					
4. There was pertinent participation by all					
5. Mutual interest was shown in all members' points of view					
6. Individuals or sub-groups did not dominate the proceedings					
7. Disagreements were expressed and explained in order to try to resolve them					
8. Any criticism was frank and constructive and perceived as such					
9. The atmosphere was supportive and helpful					
10. Group members were interested in the meeting					
11. Decisions were taken when necessary					
12. Everyone contributed fully to the making of decisions					
13. The decisions taken were fully understood and supported					
14. Problems were tackled in an appropriate manner including a full diagnosis					
15. The resources of the group were fully used					
16. Members were able to be creative where this was appropriate					
17. The meeting was able to function in a flexible manner when necessary					
18. The meeting did not stray off course					
19. Time was used optimally and not wasted					

20. The performance of the leader was appropriate to the task and the group			
21. Both task and maintenance functions were fulfilled as necessary			
22. Feelings were expressed freely and accepted			
23. No dysfunctional norms evolved or were present			
24. The group was cohesive			
25. Cohesiveness was channelled towards performance			
Additional comments			

Figure 9 Meetings rating form

and rating of the meeting can be carried out using the meetings rating form in Figure 9. Being familiar with the issues above helps in completing the form. Using this form can be helpful in identifying which area to concentrate your observations on for future meetings of the same group.

One reason for studying meetings is for research purposes and to understand the behaviour that occurs in these settings. Other reasons for studying meetings are to bring about improvements in your own performance in future meetings and/or to help the group being observed to improve. Here we have just dealt with the observation and recording of meetings. The ways of improving meetings leading on from this approach are dealt with in Williams (1984). Where we want to improve the effectiveness of meetings it is important that the results of observations are shared in an appropriate manner with the members of the meeting.

References

Bales, R.F. (1950) *Interaction Process Analysis: A Method for the Study of Small Groups.* Addison-Wesley.

Benne, K. and Sheats, P. (1948) Functional roles of group members, *J. Social Issues*, Vol. 4, pp. 41–9.

Mehrabian, A. (1972) *Non-verbal Communication.* Aldine Atherton.

Williams, G.L. (1984) *Making Your Meetings More Interesting and Effective*. Pavic Publications, Sheffield City Polytechnic.

Graham L. Williams (commissioned for this volume)
Graham L. Williams is Senior Lecturer in Education Management at Sheffield City Polytechnic.

CHAPTER 14

ANALYSIS AND PRESENTATION OF INFORMATION

Sandy Goulding

Data collected by means of questionnaires, interviews, diaries, or any other method mean very little until the data are analysed and assessed. Earlier chapters have stressed the need to consider how responses will be analysed at the planning and design stage. Gathering large quantities of data in the hope that something will emerge from the pile is not to be recommended, as a good many researchers have discovered to their cost. Non-statisticians cannot hope to carry out highly complex surveys involving advanced statistical techniques, but that does not mean that they are unable to conduct worthwhile investigations. However, lack of statistical know-how can be intimidating. In this chapter, Sandy Goulding explains some of the descriptive methods which are useful in analysing and presenting data derived from small-scale surveys. She provides a starting point for researchers who feel they are incapable of carrying out any sort of educational enquiry because they know nothing of statistics and describes 'the minimum tools that the small-scale quantitative researcher needs'.

In undertaking any small-scale investigation or large-scale study, the researcher must be able to understand the methods by which the inform-ation or data collected may be analysed and presented; the same methods may be used to present data culled from official sources. It is, however, likely that the size of small-scale studies will be such that the results produced will be illuminative rather than generalizable.

There are two broad categories into which statistical methods fall: descriptive and inferential. Descriptive statistical methods provide 'pic-tures' of the group under investigation: these 'pictures' may be in the form of charts, tables, percentages, averages, and so on. Inferential statistical methods have a quite different purpose; they may involve the use of descriptive statistics but their prime aim is to draw implications from the data with regard to a theory, model or body of knowledge.

The methods most likely to be useful in analysing information gained from investigations of a limited nature are those of descriptive statistics. Whether the information arises from questionnaires which respondents themselves complete, or whether it arises from a structured interview situation where the interviewer completes a schedule, makes no difference to the way that the data can be handled. The purpose, therefore, of this chapter is to explain some of the descriptive methods which are useful in analysing and presenting data derived from small-scale surveys using questionnaires or structured interview schedules.

No special statistical knowledge is required to understand and to make use of these methods. One straightforward way of recording data is described; the use of different kinds of charts to present information diagrammatically is discussed and simple methods of summarizing data are examined. These are the minimum tools that the small-scale quantitative researcher needs. There are many other statistical methods that might be useful but a description of these is beyond the scope of this article. The use of computers and computer packages is unlikely to be cost effective in small-scale investigations and so the computer analysis of results is not discussed.

The nature of data

In designing a questionnaire or interview schedule, the investigator must plan for the analysis stage in case the point is reached where the data collected are unsuitable for the method of analysis required. It is important to know that there are different types of data. There are different scales of measurement:

Nominal scales are the simplest and arise where simple categories with no numerical significance are used. For example, an item on a questionnaire may require a 'yes' or 'no' response. For the purpose of coding, we may attach numbers to these:

response	yes	no
code	1	2

this is known as the coding frame for the question.

The important point about nominal scales is that these numbers (the codes) are completely arbitrary and are merely labelling devices. Classification-type questions such as 'main subject taught' will also lead to a coding frame consisting of categories to which numbers may be ascribed: these numbers will constitute a nominal scale of measurement.

Ordinal scales arise where items are rated or ranked. A coding frame for questions of opinion might be:

strongly disagree	disagree	neutral	agree	strongly agree
1	2	3	4	5

The implication here is that the higher the category chosen the greater the strength of agreement. A classification question regarding the grade of teacher or lecturer would also involve an ordinal scale: a scale 3 post has a higher status than a scale 1 or 2, but not such a high status as a scale 4. Ordinal scales distinguish order but nothing can be said about how much larger one item is than another, simply that it is larger.

Interval scales are more sophisticated than ordinal scales. Examination marks, IQ and other measures of performance are usually regarded as following an interval scale of measurement. If pupil A achieves a mark of 60 percent, pupil B 45 percent and pupil C 30 percent in a particular examination, then the implication of an interval scale is first, that A is more proficient than B who is more proficient than C in the subject being examined; second, A's greater proficiency than B's (60 percent – 45 percent) is equal to B's greater proficiency than C's (45 percent – 30 percent).

Note, however, that it cannot be said that A is twice as proficient as C even though numerically 60 is twice 30. This is because the range of examination marks, 0–100, does not represent the full range of ability. A pupil who receives full marks is not deemed to know all there is to know about the particular subject; further, he or she may know far more than the examination tests. At best it can be assumed that A knows as much more than B as B does than C. Equal intervals, therefore, represent equal amounts.

Ratio scales are the highest order of measurement. Measurements such as age, salary, etc. follow ratio scales. As with interval scales, equal differences represent equal amounts. However, in ratio scales, absolute measurements are valid. For example, a person who is 50 years old has lived twice as long as someone who is 25 years old. This property applies only to ratio scales.

As well as there being different scales of measurement, variables (characteristics which are measured on any of the above scales) may also be classified as discrete or continuous. A variable is said to be *discrete* if it can only take whole number values, for example the size of each section of the library: only whole numbers of books are counted. A variable which can take any value is *continuous*, for example the age of a person: a member of staff may be 28 years of age or 35½ years.

Distinctions are sometimes drawn between qualitative variables and quantitative variables; the former usually refer to characteristics measured on nominal or ordinal scales (e.g. responses to questions of opinion), whereas the latter refer to data measured on interval or ratio scales (e.g. age, income).

What's all the fuss about?

As we start to look at how data may be summarized, it should become clearer as to the importance of understanding the different types of data. There are methods which can only be applied to data conforming to ratio and interval scales: it is not normally regarded as appropriate, for instance, to use averages with ordinal scales.

Four questions (Figure 1) based on those used by Bradley and Silverleaf (1979) in their study of careers in further education teaching are used to illustrate the various methods available. Bradley and Silverleaf's was a large-scale investigation but the questions selected are ones that could be employed in a study of staff development in a school or college. The data used are fictitious and for the purpose of the illustrations are taken to be derived from staff of a single department in a college of further education.

Recording the information

The importance of planning the analysis of the questionnaire responses in advance cannot be overemphasized. The preparation of summary sheets, onto which all questionnaire responses can be transferred, does in itself

For each question, please circle the number which corresponds with your answer:

Are there sufficient opportunities in your present position to improve your qualifications?

	Yes	No
	1	2

I consider my promotion prospects within the college to be good:

strongly disagree	disagree	neutral	agree	strongly agree
1	2	3	4	5

Since the age of 18, how many years did you spend in employment in the following fields before entering further education teaching?
(please exclude vacation, casual and part-time work)

	None	1–5	6–10	over 10	(No. of years)
School teaching	1	2	3	4	
Industry, commerce	1	2	3	4	
Civil service, local government	1	2	3	4	
Research	1	2	3	4	
Other	1	2	3	4	

Age last birthday

25–29	30–34	35–39	40–44	45–49	50–54	55–59
1	2	3	4	5	6	7

Figure 1 Extract of questionnaire

Respondent	Question 1		Question 2					Question 3			
	1	2	1	2	3	4	5	1	2	3	4

Figure 2 Example of a summary sheet

highlight ways in which the questionnaire might be simplified. The summary sheets should, therefore, be prepared at the same time as the questionnaire. One way of drafting the summary sheets would be as shown in Figure 2.

The first column of the summary sheet is for the respondent's name, or better still his or her 'number' (see below). The responses to each section are coded such that, for example, question 1 requires a response of 'yes' (coded 1) or 'no' (coded 2); question 2 may be an opinion question requiring the respondent to indicate strong disagreement (coded 1), disagreement (coded 2), or strong agreement (coded 5).

When the completed questionnaires are returned they can be numbered for identification purposes. If the subsequent analysis is to involve comparisons between different groups of staff (e.g. with respect to grade or sex or age) then the numbering should, as far as simplicity permits, identify each respondent as such. For example: 01/HOD/F might be the 'number' for the completed questionnaire from the respondent 01, who is the female head of department. 02/PL/M would then be the label for the questionnaire from respondent 02 who is a male principal lecturer.

The questionnaires must be checked for completeness: it may be possible to return to the respondent if there have been omissions. The responses to the questions can then be coded (i.e. the appropriate code allocated to the responses), or if the questions have all been pre-coded, responses can be transferred to the summary sheet.

Open-ended questions need careful handling; it is possible that the responses to these can be classified after all the questionnaires have been returned, in which case a coding frame can be drawn up and the responses coded. It is more likely perhaps that investigators will wish to report word-for-word responses to open-ended questions of opinion; in this case, responses should be written out on separate sheets for each question and included selectively in the report. The basis for inclusion in the report should be the same as for any data collected: to provide a representative view of the responses obtained.

Once the completed questionnaires have been coded, then the responses can be transferred from the questionnaires to the summary sheets using ticks (see Figure 3).

Respondent	Question 1		Question 2					Question 3			
	1	2	1	2	3	4	5	1	2	3	4
01/HOD/F	√			√							
02/PL/M	√					√					
03/SL/M		√				√					

Figure 3 Completing the summary sheet

The process of transferring responses to summary sheets is tedious, but the alternatives are either more tedious or prone to error or both. Once the information from the questionnaires is recorded on the summary sheets in a systematic way such as has been described then it should be unnecessary to consult the questionnaires again, but they should not be discarded until the report is finalized just in case checking is needed.

After recording . . .

The following examples illustrate the different ways in which the information collected may be analysed and presented.

Example 1

> Are there sufficient opportunities in your present position to improve your qualifications?
>
>   Yes   1
>   No   2

For this question, the analysis of the nominal data collected is a simple matter of totalling on the summary sheet the 'yes' responses (coded 1) and the 'no' responses (coded 2). If out of the 40 staff in the department who responded, 10 had responded 'yes' and 30 had responded 'no' then these frequencies, as they are called, can be converted to percentages of the total number.

For the 'yes' responses $\frac{10}{40} \times 100 = 25\%$

For the 'no' responses $\frac{30}{40} \times 100 = 75\%$

So 25 percent of the department's staff feel that there are sufficient opportunities to improve their qualifications, whilst 75 percent think that there are not.

If it is relevant to the study, it is possible to examine the variation in the response to this question according to the grade of the respondent or the gender. With small groups it is important not to carry these comparisons too far. If senior departmental staff are regarded as senior lecturers and above, and their responses to the given question are separated from those of lecturers grade II and from those of lecturers grade I, then the cross-tabulation shown in Table 1 might result.

The table shows actual frequencies rather than percentages. Where there are small total numbers, beware of using percentages. A statement such as '80 percent of the senior staff feel that there are sufficient opportunities to improve their qualifications' is factually accurate, but it is *misleading* as the reader will assume a much larger total number of senior staff than five. It

Table 1   Teachers' perceptions of the sufficiency of opportunities to improve their own qualifications

	Sufficient	Insufficient	Total
Senior staff*	4	1	5
Lecturers grade II	3	12	15
Lecturers grade I	3	17	20
	10	30	40

* Senior lecturers and above

would be better to include the tabulation in the report and to draw out differences of opinions using the actual frequencies. The following statement would be appropriate: 'Whereas four out of the five senior staff in the department feel that there are sufficient opportunities to improve their qualifications, only three out of 15 lecturers grade II and three out of 20 lecturers grade I feel that the opportunities are sufficient.'

Example 2

I consider my promotion prospects within the college to be good:

strongly disagree	disagree	neutral	agree	strongly agree
1	2	3	4	5

The variable here, attitude towards promotion prospects, is being measured on an ordinal scale. It is a simple task to determine the frequencies of each value: the numbers or respondents giving each answer are totalled on the summary sheet. The results might be as follows:

Table 2   Levels of agreement amongst staff that promotion prospects within the college are good

Strongly disagree	Disagree	Neutral	Agree	Strongly agree	Total
10	20	6	2	2	40

These frequencies may be converted to percentages to illustrate the relative levels of agreement and the following statement might be used, accompanied by the table, in the report: 'Only 10 percent (four out of 40) of the department's staff felt any measure of agreement with the statement that "I consider promotion prospects within the college to be good", whereas 50 percent (20 out of 40) disagreed and a further 25 percent (10 out of 40) strongly disagreed.'

A bar chart could be used as an alternative method of presentation in the report (see Figure 4). The researcher has to make a judgement as to which presentation is the clearest.

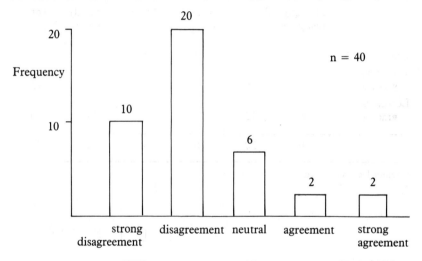

Figure 4   Levels of agreement amongst staff that promotion prospects within the college are good

For vertical bar charts such as the one shown in Figure 4, the variable is placed on the horizontal axis and the frequency on the upright axis; horizontal bar charts are presented the other way round (see Figure 6). For precision the actual frequencies are included at the tops of the bars and the total frequency of 40 is stated in the conventional form 'n = 40' (n stands for number). The important point to note, and this is a principle which should guide the construction of all bar charts, is that the area of the bars on the chart should be proportional to the frequencies they represent, so the height of the bar representing the number who strongly disagree (10) is half the height of the bar representing the number who disagree (20), the width of the bars being the same. It follows from this that the frequency axis of bar charts should always start from zero, in order that the presentation does not give the wrong impression.

As in the previous example, the investigator may wish to compare the responses to this question according to the grade of the member of staff. The resulting cross-tabulation might be as in Table 3.

Table 3   Levels of agreement amongst staff, by grade, that promotion prospects within the college are good

	Strongly disagree	Disagree	Neutral	Agree	Strongly agree	Total
Senior staff*	0	2	2	0	1	5
Lecturers grade II	4	6	3	1	1	15
Lecturers grade I	6	12	1	1	0	20
	10	20	6	2	2	40

* Senior lecturer or over.

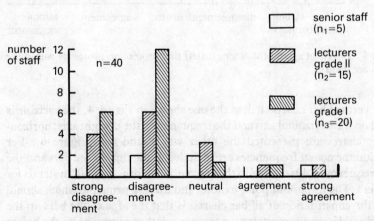

Figure 5   Levels of agreement amongst staff, by grade, that promotion prospects within the college are good

Figure 5 is an alternative representation to the tabulation; it is generally regarded as unnecessary to include both a tabulation and chart of the same data. Figure 5 is an example of a compound bar chart: it compares the frequencies, by grade, of attitudes towards promotion prospects. For each category of agreement/disagreement, the frequencies of the different staff groups are shown side by side. The order of these groups is maintained throughout the diagram: in this case, senior staff, lecturers grade II, lecturers grade I. A further alternative method of presentation is a component bar chart (Figure 6).

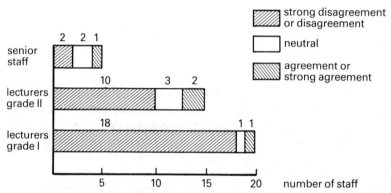

Figure 6   Staff attitudes towards the statement that promotion prospects within the college are good

This is presented as a horizontal bar chart. Notice that the total lengths of the bars represent the number of staff in each grade. For the sake of simplicity the categories have been collapsed into three: disagreement (strong or otherwise); neutral; agreement (strong or otherwise).

The method of presentation chosen (tabulation, compound bar chart or component bar chart) depends on the point that is being made in the report: the table or chart should illustrate that point. If the object is to show the overall view about promotion prospects then Figure 4 would be appropriate. If, however, the object is to show how the different groups of staff vary in their views about promotion prospects then Figures 5 or 6 would be preferred.

In Example 3 respondents are being asked to circle the code against the different employment sectors to indicate the number of years' experience they have had in each. In effect, there are five questions here: respondents are being asked to state the number of years' experience they have had

Example 3

	None	1–5	6–10	Over 10 (No. of years)
Since the age of 18, how many years did you spend in employment in the following fields before entering further education teaching? (please exclude vacation, casual and part-time work)				
School teaching	1	2	3	4
Industry, commerce	1	2	3	4
Civil service, local government	1	2	3	4
Research	1	2	3	4
Other	1	2	3	4

school teaching, the number of years' experience in industry/commerce, etc. The responses would be transferred to the summary sheet as if the question were delivered five times: once for each employment sector. As before, the responses can be totalled and presented in the report in the form of a table (Table 4). In this case, those respondents not having work experience in a particular employment sector are excluded.

Table 4   Number of staff having prior work experience, by employment sector

Years' experience	1–5	6–10	10+
School teaching	10	2	1
Industry, commerce	25	7	1
Civil service, local government	10	3	0
Other	8	0	0

Note that if a member of staff has had experience as a school teacher, then he or she may also have worked in industry or local government; note also that some staff may not have had any work experience prior to entering FE teaching. The totals, therefore, have a different meaning from in the earlier examples. In all, 13 staff have worked as school teachers prior to entering the further education teaching profession, whereas 33 out of the 40 staff have worked in industry or commerce and 13 have experience of civil service or local government.

If a chart is preferred to a tabulation in the project report, then a compound bar chart such as in Figure 7 might be used:

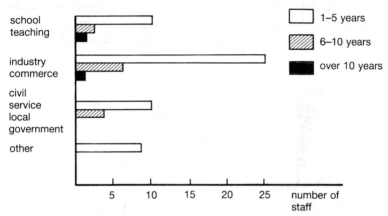

Figure 7   Work experience of staff

If the investigator wishes to illustrate the relative numbers of staff having experience in the employment sectors and wishes to show the length of service too, then a percentage component bar chart (see Figure 8) might be used. The frequencies have been converted to percentages of the total staff (40). This representation, by implication, also shows the percentage of staff not having experience in each sector. Note, however, that none of these representations reveals the number of staff who have had no work experience prior to entering further education teaching.

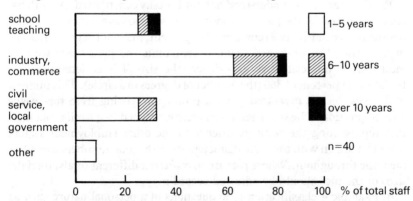

Figure 8   Percentage of staff having work experience, by sector

It might be of interest to compare the work experience of the different categories of staff, that is according to their grade or gender. This might be considered overelaborate in the context of a small-scale survey but it really does depend on what the investigator is seeking to show in the report.

A method of presentation in wide usage is the pie chart (see Figure 9).

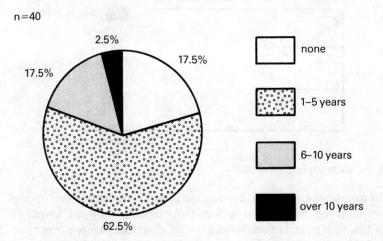

Figure 9   Percentage of staff having work experience in industry/commerce

Separate pies might be drawn to show the work experience in the different sectors.

Pie charts are easily understood but not so easily constructed. As with bar charts, the areas of the pie are proportional to the amounts they represent. The whole pie in Figure 9 represents 100 percent, that is all of the staff in the department. The unshaded segment represents the percentage with no industrial/commercial work experience: the size of it is determined by finding 17.5 percent of 360 (the number of degrees in a circle). This number of degrees (63°) is measured using a protractor starting from the twelve o'clock position. The other segments are constructed in a similar manner. Pies representing the work experience in the other employment sectors would be drawn with the same diameters since the total number (n = 40) is the same throughout. Where pies are to represent different totals, then the sizes of the pies should be adjusted accordingly.

In Example 4 classification-type questions of a personal nature such as age, produce a higher response rate where categories are used rather than

Example 4

Age last birthday						
25–29	30–34	35–39	40–44	45–49	50–54	55–59
1	2	3	4	5	6	7

the respondent's being asked, 'How old are you?' In any case, data have to be grouped to enable a pattern to be seen. The classes chosen (25–29, 30–34, 35–39, etc.) must, as in any coding frame, cover the full range of ages of the department's staff and they must be unambiguous so it is clear to respondents into which categories their ages fall. Note that the categories are such that they each span five years: 25–29 includes the ages of all staff who are just 25 years old up to those who are very nearly 30 years; this span is known as the class interval. In this example all the class intervals are five years; if it is possible, then equal intervals throughout are desirable.

The frequencies of each class are determined from the summary sheet and form what is known as a frequency distribution (Table 5).

Table 5   Age distribution of staff

Years	Frequency
25–29	2
30–34	9
35–39	10
40–44	7
45–49	5
50–54	4
55–59	3
	40

It may be represented by means of a frequency histogram (Figure 10): this term is used for a simple vertical bar chart, depicting the class frequencies of a quantitative variable.

Note that the variable (age) is continuous; it does not just take whole number values: it is merely a matter of convenience that age is often recorded to the nearest year. Hence, the labelling of the horizontal axis: the

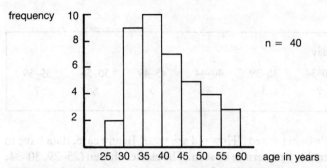

Figure 10   Age distribution of staff

variable is continuous so there are no gaps between the bars. For the sake of simplicity, the precise limits between classes are merged on the histogram.

The frequency distribution and its representation by means of a histogram provide a picture of the age structure of the department, and either or both might be included in the project report. The diagram helps to identify important aspects of the data. A comment on the features of the age structure represented in Figure 10 might be as follows: 'The ages of the department's staff vary from under 30 to over 55 with 65 percent of the staff being aged between 30 and 45.'

What about averages?

Since the variable, age, is measured on a ratio scale, more sophisticated statistical methods are available. An average age of the department's staff may be determined.

There are different types of average (more properly known as measures of location or central tendency) and circumstances determine which is the most appropriate. Three measures of location are considered here: the mode, the median, and the mean; the criteria for deciding which should be used when are discussed later.

The mode is the most frequently occurring value, or in the case of grouped data, the modal class is the one which has the highest frequency. By reference to Table 5, it can be seen that the modal age group is 35–39, that is the age group 35–39 contains the largest number of staff. The mode is a very simple measure which can be used even where a variable is measured on a nominal scale; for example eye colouring: if more people have green eyes than any other colour then the modal eye colour is green.

The median is a different type of average: it is the value below which half the data lie and above which the other half lie. Put another way, the median is the middle value when the data are listed in order.

The easiest way to calculate the median from a set of grouped data is first, to calculate the cumulative class frequencies and second, to plot these by means of a cumulative frequency polygon (otherwise known as an ogive), from which the median can be determined. What follows illustrates this procedure.

Table 6 Cumulative frequency distribution of ages of staff

Upper class limit	Cumulative frequency
30	2
35	11
40	21
45	28
50	33
55	37
60	40

Table 6 shows the results of accumulating the frequencies taken from Table 5. The number of staff who are less than 30 years of age (the upper limit of the 20–29 class) is two; the number of staff who are less than 35 years (the upper limit of the next class) is equal to the sum of the frequencies of the first two classes (2+9); the number of staff who are less than 40 years is equal to the frequencies of the first three classes and so on. The cumulative frequency of the upper limit of the last class is 40, that is all the staff are under 60 years of age.

The cumulative frequency polygon (Figure 11) is constructed from the cumulative frequency distribution (Table 6). The vertical axis represents cumulative frequency and the horizontal axis, the variable (in this case, age). The cumulative frequencies are then plotted against the upper class limits.

Note that a zero cumulative frequency is plotted against the lower limit of the first class. It is now a simple matter to determine the median. The median is the middle value, so since there are 40 staff, the median age is the age of the twentieth member of staff when the ages are listed in order. The cumulative frequency distribution and polygon have put the data in order, so to find the age of the twentieth member of staff, a line is drawn

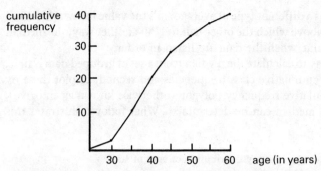

Figure 11   Cumulative frequency polygon of the age distribution of staff

horizontally from the cumulative frequency of 20 as far as the polygon (see Figure 12); a vertical line is dropped from this point on the polygon to the horizontal axis. The position at which this vertical line intersects the horizontal axis is the value of the median. From Figure 12 it can be seen that the median is 39 years, that is the average age, as measured by the median, is 39 years; half the staff are younger than 39, half are older.

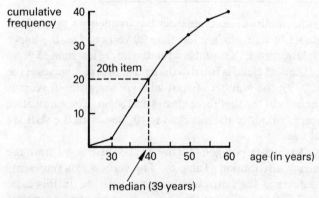

Figure 12   Cumulative frequency polygon of the age distribution of staff, showing the median

By definition, a median can only exist for data which can be placed in order; hence the median can only be used for variables which follow ordinal, interval and ratio scales.

The arithmetic mean, or simply the mean, is a third measure of location.

Where data are ungrouped then the mean is the sum of these individual items divided by the number of items. For example, if the IQs of five children are: 108, 95, 118, 99, 110, and if

$$\text{the arithmetic mean} = \frac{\text{sum of values}}{\text{number of subjects}}, \text{ and}$$

the sum of the IQs is 530 (108+95+118+99+110) and the number of subjects is five, then

$$\text{the arithmetic mean} = \frac{530}{5} = 106$$

i.e. the mean IQ of these five children is 106.

Statistical notation allows us to write down a formula for the arithmetic mean. If x represents the variable, which takes the values $x_1, x_2, x_3, x_4 \ldots$ and n is the number of items, the arithmetic mean is denoted by $\bar{x}$ (x-bar) and the formula is:

$$\bar{x} = \frac{\Sigma x}{n} \text{ where } \Sigma x \text{ is the notation}^\star \text{ for the sum of the values of x.}$$

$$\text{i.e. the mean} \quad (\bar{x}) = \frac{\text{sum of the values}}{\text{no. of items}} = \frac{\Sigma x}{n}$$

When the data are grouped as in Table 5, there is a need to take into account the frequency of the classes (f). Table 7 shows the steps involved in calculating the mean from grouped data. The first class 25–29 has a frequency, f, of 2; for the purpose of calculating the mean, it is assumed that both of these items of data are at the mid-point of the class (i.e. 27.5 – remember the upper limit of the class is 30). The second class has a frequency of 9 and the mid-point is 32.5 and so on. The mean for these grouped data is calculated, first by multiplying the frequency, f, of each class by its mid-point, x; second, these products are totalled, and third this total is divided by the total frequency. So for grouped data

$$\bar{x} = \frac{\Sigma fx}{\Sigma f}$$

i.e. the mean $(\bar{x}) =$

$$\frac{\text{the sum of the products of the class frequencies (f) and the mid-points (x)}}{\text{the total frequency } (\Sigma f)}$$

$^\star \Sigma$ is the Greek capital letter sigma, s, standing for summation.

Table 7   Calculation of the mean from a set of grouped data

Classes	Mid-points x	Frequency f	Frequency × mid-point f × x
25–29	27.5	2	55
30–34	32.5	9	295.5
35–39	37.5	10	375
40–44	42.5	7	297.5
45–49	47.5	5	237.5
50–54	52.5	4	210
54–59	57.5	3	172.5
		$\Sigma f = 40$	$\Sigma fx = 1640$

Mean, $\bar{x} = \dfrac{\Sigma fx}{\Sigma f} = \dfrac{1640}{40} = 41$

The mean age of the department's staff is 41 years.

Which average?

For the purpose of illustration, the mode, median and mean have all been calculated from the age distribution in Table 5. In practice only one of these would be used. The question of which average to use depends on the shape of the distribution. The shape of the frequency distribution in Figure 10 is somewhat lop-sided or skewed; other distributions are more symmetrical. A general guideline is that data on ratio or interval scales which are distributed in a symmetrical or near symmetrical way should be summarized using the arithmetic mean. The reason for this is that the mean is a very powerful measure which takes into account all items of data but which is distorted if there are odd extreme values; a symmetrical distribution does not, however, distort the mean.

Data on ratio, interval or ordinal scales which follow an asymmetrical (or skewed) distribution should be summarized using the median; the median is not affected by extreme values and for nonsymmetrical distributions provides an average that is more typical of the data. The mode may be useful for nominal and discrete data.

Measures of dispersion

Measures of dispersion quantify the variability within a set of data. It was seen earlier that the mean age of staff in the fictitious department was 41 years; without reference to the frequency distribution (Table 5), it is not possible to tell whether staff are mostly aged between, say, 35 and 45 or whether their ages vary more widely. Measures of dispersion, therefore, are used in addition to measures of location (types of average) to summarize a set of data. Just as comparisons may be made between two groups by examining, say, the average age of each, then so may they be compared in terms of the variability of the ages in each using measures of dispersion.

There are many statistical books which explain how measures of dispersion such as the range, the interquartile range and the standard deviation may be determined and it is not intended to explain here their calculation. Suffice to say that if the median is used as the most appropriate measure of location to summarize a set of data, then the interquartile range may be used as well to measure the variation in the data. Similarly where the mean is used, then the standard deviation is the appropriate measure of dispersion. The range is a very simple measure of dispersion: it is the difference between the lowest and the highest item of data: it is a rather crude measure but may be useful where data are evenly spread and there are no extreme values.

Conclusion

Descriptive statistical methods are wide-ranging. This article has attempted to show some of the simple ways in which information can be collated, analysed and presented. There are many more sophisticated techniques. The methods suggested are not meant to be exhaustive: the researcher may well be able to present results in a novel manner. Where a single measure (or measures) or a diagram can be used to present in a simple and straightforward way a concept, a pattern or a set of data, then it is usually preferable to pages of written description.

Reference

Bradley, J. and Silverleaf, J. (1979) *Making the Grade*. Windsor, NFER.

Sandy Goulding, The Open University (commissioned for this volume). Copyright © Sandy Goulding.
Sandy Goulding is a Senior Lecturer in Quantitative Methods at Luton College of Higher Education, having been seconded during 1983/4 to the Open University as a lecturer in Educational Management.

CHAPTER 15

WRITING THE REPORT

J. D. Nisbet & N. J. Entwistle

In Chapter 1 of this book, Daphne Johnson made the point that an investigation is not finished until it is written up and that preparation for the final report should begin at the planning stage. Other authors have made similar observations. The authors of this chapter write that 'by the end of the planning stage, the opening sections of the report should be already in first draft and the description of relevant previous work may be virtually complete'. It takes time and experience to be able to write a good report and, as with so much in this book, reading about 'how to do it' cannot take the place of actually doing it. However, the commonsense advice contained in this chapter and the suggested structure for a report provide good starting points.

Writing the report of a research project always takes longer than one hopes. Often it seems a tedious chore. Yet if the results are not communicated effectively, they will be overlooked. Effective communication is the researcher's responsibility and no one else's: he alone is to blame if no one can understand what he has done or judge its value appropriately. [. . .] The three parts of a project, which deserve approximately equal shares of the time available are the planning, the work itself and the writing up. But the writing should not all be left to the end. Much of the burden can be removed if the work is written up as the investigation proceeds. By the end of the planning stage, the opening sections of the report should be already in first draft, and the description of relevant previous work may be virtually complete. Few research workers do what they ought to do and keep systematic records of work done on a uniform size of paper for convenient reference; but all subsequently regret the deplorable tendency to make notes on the back of envelopes and on scraps of paper, which is such a handicap when the report comes to be written.

Research reports

The aim of a research report is to convey information in a form which is readily accessible to other scholars. Consequently, there is a conventional form of reporting an experimental investigation. Not every report fits this pattern exactly, but unnecessary departures from it are an obstacle to communication. Originality finds expression in the ideas, not in the form of report. The framework is:

1. An outline of the research.
2. A review of previous work.
3. A precise statement of the scope and aims of the investigation.
4. Description of the procedure, the sample and the tests or measurements used.
5. Statement of results.
6. Discussion.
7. Summary and conclusions.
8. List of references.

The general style of the report is impersonal, but this does not mean that it must all be in the passive voice. It does mean excluding the word 'I', and, even more important, such phrases as 'in my opinion'. 'In the opinion of the writer' is no better. The reader is interested in your evidence and not your opinion. Clarity, simplicity of style and brevity are the cardinal virtues. As with other virtues, they are sometimes incompatible: a phrase like 'verbal reasoning test score' may have to be repeated even if 'intelligence' is both simple and brief. Abbreviations are inexcusable except for the most widely known, like 'GCE', and even these should be given in full on the first occasion they occur, since the report may be read by someone who is unfamiliar with them. Technical terms should be avoided in sections 1, 3, and 7 in the framework listed above. In the other sections the use of technical terms may be inevitable, but not jargon, in the sense of unnecessary technical language which can be expressed simply.

Section 1, the outline of research, is a fairly brief general statement of the background to the problem, to give the setting of the investigation and point out its importance. Section 2, the review of previous work, follows on from this. Ideally it should be a reasoned and readable sequence of arguments and evidence, leading into section 3 which sets out the specific purpose and scope of the investigation to be reported. The review of previous work should not be just a series of abstracts of papers: the studies quoted should be grouped to bring out the main themes or principles in the work reviewed. References are conventionally given by adding the date in brackets after the author's name, or by giving author and date in brackets. This is easier than the use of footnotes, which add to the typist's problems.

Section 3, the statement of the scope and aims of the investigation, should be straightforward and brief. Details and arguments are out of place here: the intention is to enable a reader to find out precisely what the inquiry involved. By contrast, section 4 contains the details of procedure, the full description of the sample, and information about the tests or measurements used. Standard tests and procedures which are generally well known need not be described; but when ratings or teachers' estimates have been used, a full account of how these were obtained is necessary to allow the reader to judge their value. A scale or technique specially devised for the investigation should be described in full in an appendix at the end.

The structure of section 5, the statement of results, is determined by the tables in which results are presented. Each table is numbered and has a title which is intelligible without reference to the text. The text itself in this section is little more than a linking commentary to the tables. Inferences from the results should not be included here: this is a factual section about which there should be no dispute. The commentary may appropriately call attention to aspects of the results which are to be discussed in the next section.

Section 6 is the discussion of results, in which interpretations and judgements are made. A special effort should be made to keep this section under control, and to limit the conclusions to what can reasonably be justified by the evidence. These conclusions are brought together in a brief section 7. This section is sometimes written as a summary of the investigation, listing in three short paragraphs the aim, scope and findings.

The list of references should be set out alphabetically by author's name. Only titles referred to in the text should be included here: the list is not intended as a bibliography on the subject. To a reader who is himself planning research in this field, this may be the most important part of the report. Again, there is a conventional form for references which must be observed. A journal article is described by author, initials, date, title of article, title of journal, volume number, page numbers. A book is described by author, initials, date, title, place of publication, publisher. Details of accepted abbreviations and other conventions are given in the British Psychological Society's pamphlet, *Suggestions to Authors* (1967) (BPS, 18–19 Albemarle Street, London W1X LDN).

An additional section which has not so far been mentioned is a simple statement of acknowledgement to those who have assisted in the investigation. This is often inserted at the beginning of a report, immediately after the list of contents. Especially when teachers and headmasters have helped with an investigation, a personal expression of thanks – and, perhaps more important, a brief summary of results sent to each personally – is a necessary recognition of the extent to which research is dependent on their help and tolerance. [. . .]

This description of the structure of a research report has touched on only a few important points. The student who is writing a report for the first time – and others, too, who consider themselves experienced – would be well advised to consult Wiseman's short booklet, *Reporting Research in Education* (1952). This can be read in less than one hour, but will save many hours of labour in writing. Guiding principles, specific examples and useful suggestions are set out simply and lucidly. The pamphlet itself is a model of the style it recommends.

Why should this pattern of reporting be prescribed so rigidly? The answer will be found in the first paragraph of this chapter. The purpose of a research report is to communicate results, and the volume of research publications is now so overwhelming that no active research worker has time to read reports through from cover to cover. He must be selective, reading certain sections at very high speed because they deal with familiar previous research or give details to which he will refer back only if he wishes to check some finding. A research report is not a story: it is an arrangement of information. Because the information is laid out in a standard form, a reader can discover quickly what he wants to know about a piece of research.

Few readers start at the beginning of a research report and read through to the end. Similarly, the way to write a report is not necessarily to start with Chapter 1. Each person must find the pattern of writing which suits him best. But often, section 2, the review of previous work can be written first; and section 4, the details of procedure, sample and measurements, can be sketched out at an early stage. Section 3, the precise statement of the scope and aims of the inquiry, is so brief that it can be put into its final form at a late stage; but a first draft must be prepared at a very early stage in planning. Writing down in a single page an outline of what is planned is a valuable way to test the adequacy of a plan, and a provisional outline like this is a useful touchstone at a later stage in deciding the relevance of this or that aspect.

The heart of a report is section 5, the statement of results. When the analysis of data is complete, and the research worker turns to face the task of writing, his first step should be to design the layout of the tables in section 5. This requires careful thought and frequent revision, to obtain a proper balance between detail and conciseness, and to develop a logical sequence of presentation. Once the tables are ready, the rest of section 5 is easy.

The Discussion section is possibly the hardest section to write, because it is difficult to know how much to include. Most discussions are too long, and too long-winded. Readers appreciate quality and are wearied by quantity. This is the one sure guide in writing this section.

With Results and Discussion complete, Previous Work more or less in final draft, section 4 fairly well sketched out, and a provisional version of the Statement of Research for section 3, sections 1 and 7, the General Outline and the Summary and Conclusions can now be tackled. Section 8, the List of References, should not be left to the end. Inevitably, it turns out that some detail has not been noted – an author's initial, a volume number, a date of publication. Checking the references and filling gaps takes time, but it will be done methodically by the research worker who has experienced the frustration of an incomplete or incorrect reference in some other writer's work.

Summary

Educational research [. . .] is a form of systematic inquiry which progresses through a series of well-defined stages. It should demonstrate the logical structure and hard reasoning to be found in the best scientific research, though the difficulty in measurement precludes the same precision in the results. The findings are rarely definitive and thus require careful interpretation.

The research report should reflect the whole research process. Logical structure and hard reasoning together with clarity, simplicity of style and brevity are cardinal virtues. The aim is to communicate the result effectively; any unnecessary details or clumsy wording distracts from this purpose. The structure of the research report reflects the stages in planning a research study. This scheme of presentation, though formal and artificial, does facilitate communication. It allows readers to anticipate where to search for the particular details they require, where to find a summary or a definition of the sample, for example.

Research in isolation serves no purpose. Effective communication, both to other research workers and to teachers and other educationists, is the essence of good educational research.

References

British Psychological Society (1967) *Suggestions to Authors*. London, British Psychological Society.

Wiseman, S. (1952) *Reporting Research in Education*. Manchester, Manchester University Press.

J.D. Nisbet, N.J. Entwistle (1970) *Educational Research Methods*. University of London Press Ltd., pp. 167–172, 175–176, (References 181, 186). ISBN 0 340 11823 7.

Copyright © 1970 J.D. Nisbet and N.J. Entwistle. Reprinted with permission of Hodder & Stoughton.

John Nisbet is Professor of Education at the University of Aberdeen. Noel Entwistle is Bell Professor of Education at the University of Edinburgh, and Director of the Godfrey Thomson Unit for Educational Research.

CHAPTER 16

EVALUATING A RESEARCH REPORT
R.J. Sapsford & Jeff Evans

Chapter 2 of this book describes three methodological types of research, namely the ethnographic study, the survey and the experiment. This chapter refers back to Chapter 2, discusses the strengths and weaknesses of the three styles and provides a checklist for assessing research reports. There is no one 'right' way or 'best' way of judging research reports, and the checklist provided here is only one of many approaches.

A great deal can be learned about planning investigations and writing reports by reading work done by other people. It helps to establish a systematic approach to such reading, so that comparisons and judgements can be made. If you decide a report is 'good' or 'bad', 'interesting' or 'boring' and can provide answers to the questions *why* is it good, bad, interesting or boring, then you will be well on the way to producing good and interesting reports yourself.

The strengths and weaknesses of research styles

As was suggested in Chapter 2, one may usefully consider research as falling into three methodological types: the ethnographic study, the survey and the experiment. In experiments there is an attempt to control all relevant sources of variance, in so far as the experimenter has correctly identified them, and one or several independent variables of special interest are manipulated with the aim of demonstrating the causal effects on dependent variables of variations in the independent one(s). The survey collects information from a range of respondents, attempting to control extraneous sources of variance by statistical techniques and by the selection of the sample, with the aim of showing the distribution of beliefs, traits, abilities and observed or reported behaviour in a population and the degree to which they intercorrelate. The ethnographic approach attempts to study the totality of a phenomenon in greater depth and in its natural setting, to *understand* it from the point of view of those involved in it; it deals more in 'reasons', 'motives' and 'perspectives' than in statistical associations between aspects of behaviour or causal factors producing them. Where 'causal' hypotheses are tested, it is most likely to be by analytic induction, and the hypotheses themselves are more likely to be based on the actors' own perspectives than would be true of other research styles. [. . .]

If you were asked to appraise the methodology used in a piece of research [. . .] we should expect the words 'validity' and 'reliability' to crop up somewhere in them as useful 'shorthand' expressions for a whole range of related methodological problems. Reliability is the easiest to describe: 'reliability is the consistency of the results obtained when using a measure in research'. It is a word used of measuring instruments, including the human observer functioning as such in ethnographic studies (and elsewhere), and refers to the basic scientific requirement that it should be possible for another worker to duplicate one's results or produce comparable evidence, at least in principle. The problem is equally great for 'descriptive' and 'causal' research. At the simplest level, a tape-measure is unreliable if a distance measured as nine inches on Monday comes out as ten inches on Tuesday. Human observers are notoriously unreliable: even in the physics laboratory it is usual to repeat work or to read meters more than once, to 'average out' errors of observation; and rating-scales or observers' descriptions are also inherently suspect: one may always argue that different raters or observers might have come up with different results. There are two types of error – 'systematic' and 'random'. Random errors, or errors of measurement, are subsumed under the notion of reliability. Systematic errors, or biases, are part of what is meant by validity – and validity is an altogether more complex concept.

Open University course DE304, *Research Methods in Education and the Social Sciences* discusses the concept of validity, starting with a simple definition that 'validity is the extent to which an indicator is a measure of what the researcher wishes to measure', leading to the conclusion that 'if the conclusion is properly deduced from the premises then we have a valid argument' (DE304, Block 8, Part 1, p. 10).

This implies two distinct senses of the term 'validity', one nested within the other.

[. . .] In the second definition, 'validity' is being used as the assessment of the soundness of a logical argument: the exclusion of biases, the disproof of competing hypotheses and the assurance that the data collected are *actually* measures of what they purport to measure are all necessary premises leading to a logical conclusion. The first definition deals specifically with the question of whether the research data are actually what they are supposed to be, and this sense of the term is often sub-divided further, according to the methods used to give us this assurance, into:

(a) *face validity*, which translates as, 'Well, it certainly *looks* as though it ought to measure that' and constitutes a very weak argument;

(b) *predictive validity*, that the test successfully predicts behaviour or results, as when a test of mental instability is validated by the occurrence of nervous breakdowns later or a test of scholastic aptitude is validated against future examination results;

(c) *concurrent validity*, which is assessed by comparison with another test of known or assumed validity: for instance, when a new introversion scale is validated against an existing one, or a test of depression is validated against the ratings of experienced clinical psychologists.

Block 5, Part 2 of DE304, also discusses *construct validity*, a very important concept in the theory of measurement. (Possibly this might more accurately be called '*construct validation*' – a part of the *process* of assuring oneself and one's readers that the conclusions have some meaning.) Simple predictive validity is the degree to which our test predicts performance on some task whose nature we already know, or think we know. Construct validation tests the degree to which the test fits the full range of theoretical predictions about an intervening variable whose very existence or usefulness may be merely a hypothesis of the tester. (Thus in some ways the other uses of the term only name aspects of construct validation.) [. . .]

Campbell (1969) drew yet another distinction, namely the difference between 'internal' and 'external' validity.

> Internal validity has to do with whether what is interpreted as the 'cause(s)' actually produce the 'effects' in a given piece of research. External validity is concerned with whether the results of this study can be generalized . . .

[. . .] Bracht and Glass (1968) devised a finer sub-division of external validity into 'population' and 'ecological'.

> Population validity has to do with generalizations to populations of persons (from the research sample) . . . and ecological validity has to do with generalization to other conditions (i.e. settings, causal factors, researchers, measures of effect) . . .

In other words, internal validity refers to the soundness of an explanation, that is, the appropriateness of the measuring instruments and the soundness of the research design; external validity, on the other hand, is to do with the generalizability of the results: that they are not specific to the measure used, the setting in which it is used or the nature of the sample.

A similar question is 'inclusiveness' – whether the term we use to describe what we have measured is one in ordinary use and, if so, whether we have caught its full flavour. Our sense of the term 'intelligence' is a strange and potentially misleading one if, for instance, we call people unintelligent who fail IQ tests but by their behaviour are extremely competent intellectually. Content validity, ensuring that a test samples all the appropriate subject matter, is a related concept. Another related concept is 'naturalism': it is necessary to establish that the phenomenon being studied is one which occurs in 'real' life – that it is not a laboratory artefact – and that the behaviour used as a sign of it is indeed an example of it. In its turn this relates back to ecological validity (see above).

In so far as we acknowledge that any piece of research – from the highly artificial laboratory experiment to the highly naturalistic field study – involves an interaction between researcher, research circumstances and research subject, one can *never* be totally sure that the observed results would be the same as if there were no observer; reactivity can never be totally eliminated. The experiment and the survey attempt to identify every such source of error, or at least to keep the biases constant by standardized procedures, reasoning that the research procedures may indeed have different effects on different subjects, but that if the procedures themselves change from subject to subject then their potential effects are almost unassessable. The ethnographer tries to deal with the problem by working in the 'real', 'natural' setting, and sometimes by remaining anonymous or 'keeping a low profile' and impinging as little and as naturally as possible; reflexive accounts of how the researcher feels he or she interacted with the research environment and cross-checks on validity by means of triangulation are further devices commonly used by ethnographers. Inevitably, however, neither approach is *guaranteed* to succeed.

In a sense validity and reliability are both aspects of the requirement that research conclusions shall 'generalize' beyond the group under immediate consideration or, more precisely, that the extent to which one may generalize from results shall be specifiable. If measuring instruments are not the valid measures they purport to be, the results cannot lead to statements about traits or qualities, but only about the measuring instruments. If competing hypotheses are not eliminated successfully (internal validity), even tentative formulations of possible causal connections cannot be made, and the same is true if important information has been missed out. If the measures are unreliable, there is no guarantee that a different situation (or even the same situation with a different researcher) would not produce different results. Everyone who conducts research is trying to make generalizable statements (descriptive or causal) about the human race or some sub-section of it. Even the ethnographer, constructing a life-history of a single subject, expects to be able to make at least tentative statements about the various classes or categories in which any one actor may be seen as having membership. Some theorists now feel that validity and reliability are words better suited to questions of measurement than to the wider question of validation which is being discussed here, and some have tended to develop this viewpoint under the heading of generalizability. [. . .]

A factor which we might have considered is the extent to which supposed 'observations' are coloured by previous theory and knowledge, but upon reflection we decided that the styles do not differ in this respect. In one sense one could say that the experiment takes most for granted and the ethnographic project least; the former applies crucial tests to a highly articulated and developed hypothesis, while the latter is liable to discover and refine its research hypotheses as it develops. In a sense, however, all research is dominated by theory. Research in all styles is carried out in the context of knowledge which is taken for granted. Observation involves selection – and interpretation – of the relevant while the irrelevant is discarded; even where tape or film is used the recorded material will be selective (the camera or microphone has to be pointed at someone and switched on). In any case, selection and interpretation still occur at the stage of coding and analysis. The selection of the research hypothesis itself involves a decision as to relevance. [. . .]

Each of our three styles is the strongest in some of these respects at the expense of grave weakness in others. The well-designed experiment is very strong on validity (of the internal variety) and on reliability. If the knowledge of the subject matter has progressed to the stage where the nature of the phenomena under study and the irrelevance of all but a small number of other factors may safely be taken for granted, the experiment is undoubtedly the best way to establish causal connections between variables. For these strengths it trades naturalism and representativeness (i.e. ecological validity). Working in a laboratory, or at best in a field setting which the experimenter is manipulating, and with fairly small numbers of subjects as a rule, the experiment's claim to generalizability beyond its own immediate situation has to rest on other factors which are taken for granted or established by reference to research in one of the other styles.

The survey is potentially strong in that it can be made very representative by careful selection of large samples. Its weaknesses are that it is again a relatively artificial situation, it may lack inclusiveness, and thus its claim to generalizability of results depends on establishing that the right and relevant variables were measured – a question not only of validity, but also of inclusiveness (content validity) and degree of prior first-hand experience in the area being studied. Furthermore, as we said above, its inability to control extraneous variation (except by sampling, or after the event by multivariate statistical methods) weakens any causal conclusions at which it might arrive [. . .].

The experimental and survey styles of research place great emphasis on reliability of measurement – hence their great concern with measurable behaviour and standardized measuring instruments. [. . .] The ethnographic style has great problems in ensuring reliability. These may be overcome to some extent by using several observers or by comparing the researcher's interpretations (as to degree of alienation, for example) with data which are more directly observable (like work-output or job mobility), but such 'anchoring' depends on agreement about the relevance of the 'hard' data to the problem under discussion. [. . .]

Both experiments and surveys produce relatively simple quantitative data, which is a boon to the researcher when he comes to analysis and 'writing up'. The good ethnographic project, on the other hand, produces large amounts of complex, qualitative information which is often very difficult to analyse. It is the most likely of all the styles to include most of the relevant variables. In both experiments and surveys a long process of filtering precedes the collection of data. The researcher selects concepts to study; he operationalizes them; he selects or designs measuring instruments; he selects a sample or, in the case of an experiment, he designs experimental procedure. At each stage he throws away information. The ethnographer, on the other hand, goes into a real existing situation and tries to describe it *as a whole*. There is still a filtering process – no one can record every aspect of a situation, and the observer has to select those aspects which he considers relevant – but the ethnographer is more likely than other researchers to become aware of important factors which did not form part of his preconceived notion of the situation, through progressive focusing in which the researcher's theoretical perspectives change or develop as the research progresses. Moreover, the ethnographer is perhaps the most likely to avoid reactivity. (This is why large-scale surveys often include an exploratory 'pilot' stage of unstructured depth interviews and tests of the data-collection procedures.) These advantages are acquired at the cost of low internal validity, and in all probability a low claim to be reliably representative of more than a small class of phenomena. [. . .] The strengths and weaknesses of the three styles may be summed up as shown in Table 1.

Table 1   A comparison of the three 'research styles' [. . .]

	Experiments	Surveys	Ethnography
Emphasis on reliability	A great deal	Generally a great deal	Generally little since observations are acknowledged to differ across observers and to be situation-specific; however, attempts to assess differences of the former type via reflexivity and triangulation
Commitment to generalization	Generally great	Generally great	Generally less
Emphasis on control of extraneous factors	Generally great	If purely descriptive, none, otherwise generally great	Depends on the stage of the research and progressive focusing
Emphasis on setting	Generally little	Generally little	A great deal
Emphasis on description of 'explanatory variables'	Generally little	Often questionnaire presented in reports but little attention to unwritten and nonverbal elements of interaction	Generally a great deal
Data yield	Numerical, easily analysed	Often numerical and easily analysed	Qualitative, often difficult to analyse
Particular strengths leading to generalizability (in the best examples) (*indicates strongest points)	High internal validity* High construct validity High reliability	High construct validity High reliability High population validity*	High ecological validity* High inclusiveness*
Potential weaknesses detracting from generalizability († indicates greatest weaknesses)	Low ecological validity† Usually low population validity Low inclusiveness† (content validity)	Low ecological validity† Often low inclusiveness† (content validity)	Low internal validity† Low reliability† Low population validity

Table 1 *(continued)*

	Experiments	Surveys	Ethnography
Types of research for which most appropriate	(1) Testing causal hypotheses	(1) Large-scale	(1) Initial, small-scale exploratory work to discover areas worth investigating by other methods
	(2) Establishing statistical association between variables	(2) Establishing statistical association between variables	(2) Cross-validating, in a natural setting, results obtained by other methods
		(3) Cross-validating, on large representative samples, results obtained by other methods	(3) Investigation of relatively unknown social phenomena in detail and in their natural setting to develop theories which might be further validated by other methods

Research evaluation

Methodological considerations

We are now in a position to draw up a list of questions that should be asked of *any* piece of research. The aim here is not destructive criticism (the only researchers we should be anxious to prove foolish are ourselves) but the constructive purpose of getting the most out of someone else's work. We have therefore to consider not only faults in research design but whether these are sufficient to invalidate the author's conclusions, and not only whether the author's conclusions stand up to criticism but whether there is anything to be learned from the paper which the author has overlooked or has not had the space or interest to consider.

Clearly a first question is 'What is the research about?' What did the researchers try to show? What were their hypotheses? Are these well-formulated and well-grounded in theory? Is the area an interesting one? Would the results have practical implications? In a sense, however, these are questions not about *method* but about the *value* of the research – whether it was worth doing in the first place and well-conceived when it was undertaken.

Assuming for the moment that there is some potential value to the research, in our opinion the first methodological questions which have to be asked of any piece of research, before any detailed study of data or conclusions, are:

(a) What are the 'units' being investigated ('subjects', 'actors', 'settings', etc.); and
(b) To what larger populations should the results be generalizable?

[. . .] If the selection of subjects is such that generalizability is not guaranteed by it (i.e. if population validity is low) we take note of this fact but we do not necessarily reject reports as invalid. Given a patently unrepresentative group, research may still provide interesting data. This is particularly true of the ethnographic approach, where in general the loss of population validity is well compensated by the gain in detailed information, allowing us to examine the comparability of different samples more precisely than is possible in other approaches.

The next step is to examine how the data were collected, and how reliable they are, again with the aim of establishing how far we may go in generalizing from one sample's results to the population. Here we have to bear in mind that the ethnographic approach is inherently less reliable than others. In experimental studies or surveys there is a range of standard checks on reliability, at least some of which ought to be built into any project. If standardized measuring instruments are used, tests of their reliability should have been carried out, and these should be reported for all except the most commonly used of instruments. If the study replicates earlier work, the details of method should be as similar as possible, or every departure from the earlier method should be defendable. The method should be described in sufficient detail that one can see where it might have 'gone wrong'. (Some would argue that one should describe not just the 'idealized' method but the actual course of the research as the ethnographer is supposed to do routinely.) In the case of surveys using hired interviewers there should be an indication of what precautions were taken to check the accuracy of their recording and the consistency of the way they interpreted instructions and definitions. Where the 'measuring instrument' is a human rater or observer, there should be some indication of whether reliability was checked, by using more than one rater, or by some other method. (Seldom will research reports give this kind of information in detail, which means that conclusions based on them must often be at best tentative.)

Similar points can be made about operationalized concepts (question 4 on our list: see below). The vast majority of research reports contain analysis in terms of variables which are not directly observable, such as social class, alienation, intelligence, depression, introversion, motivation, need, but are 'indicated' by something which is observable. These are most evident in experimental studies and the more complex kinds of survey, but they exist in simple descriptive surveys, for instance where there is talk of attitudes to political parties or of voting intention, when the evidence presented is actually answers to finite numbers of specific questions, and in ethnographic reports, where the author may discuss the degree of alienation in the group under study on the evidence of observable behaviours, or what the subjects said, or even his own general impression of their experience. (Social class, for example, is not a directly observable phenomenon; we place subjects in a social class on a basis of income or employment or expressed attitudes or observed behaviours, or some combination of these.) A researcher is free to use any name for his operationalized concept by defining it as a 'technical term'. However, all the terms cited have commonly understood meanings (or fuzzy ranges of meaning) and one has to approach them with caution, working out exactly what is meant by the concept *as operationalized* and how close it comes to the 'common language' term, or else run the risk of thinking that two papers describe the same phenomenon merely because they use the same word to name it.

Now, having found out who the subjects are and what is being measured or observed, and having formed our conclusions as to the generalizability of the results, we are in a position to examine the results themselves and the conclusions which are drawn from them – a relatively easy process once the preliminary 'spade-work' has been done.

(a) What conclusions does the author present?
(b) Do these stand up to examination?

(Naturally, these questions presuppose that we have identified the author's research question or hypothesis and seen what body of formal or informal theory [. . .] leads up to it.) If there are lacunae in the argument, or the data presented do not support the conclusions:

(c) Does he or she present other material which does support them?
(d) Can I, the reader, supply material from my own knowledge which will plug the gaps in the analysis?

(e) Do I know of anything which has been overlooked in the research which would invalidate the results (another aspect of the 'inclusiveness' criterion)?

All this leads up to the two major questions:

(f) Is what the author says probably true, probably false, or undecidable on the available evidence?

(g) What else can I learn from the material presented in the paper? Remember that the aim is not to criticize an author's paper in the way that a critic deals with a new novel, but to learn something about the social world.

Now you have done what is necessary in order to assess the contents of a paper. Your final (perhaps written) assessment is a summary of this process and should cover the ten issues listed in question 6 on our list. You should say what descriptive or causal conclusions are presented by the authors, whether they are valid, and what further interesting conclusions may be drawn. You should assess the extent to which all of these are generalizable, and here you will be particularly interested in studies which partly or wholly replicate earlier ones, thereby vastly increasing the reliability of the results. Given that the results are valid and reliable, you will want to relate them to the 'real' world and look at their practical implications. If there are any obvious gaps in inclusiveness or in the logic of the arguments, you should suggest how these are to be filled, and if any of the researcher's mistakes, miscalculations or misfortunes teach lessons of relevance to other researchers, these should be noted.

Two final points:

(a) Beware of *post hoc* reasoning. Faced with a miscellany of results, it is always tempting to look for a common theme and make sense of them, to speculate on what they mean when taken together. Indeed, this is not only a tempting activity, but a salutary one and an important part of the art of research interpretation. It is only speculation, however; the outcome may be plausable, but it must never be treated as compelling. (The problem is that any competent writer should be able to construct an interpretation both of a set of results and of their exact opposite, given sufficient ingenuity.) Thus it is important to sort out what the author set out to prove, even though one may legitimately go further.

(b) Very few research reports actually contain enough detail about the methods which have been used for all of our questions to be answered. Your appraisal of a report should contain a note of the conclusions which *may* be true, given certain assumptions about the methods used, but which are not fully established by the evidence presented.

A checklist for assessing research reports

1. Who are the research subjects (or 'actors', or 'settings')?
2. To what larger universe should the results be generalizable?
   (a) Are there aspects of the selection of subjects which may prevent generalizability to certain populations or contexts?
   (b) Is the nature of the subject matter such that atypical subjects or settings would not lead to loss of generality?
   (c) To what extent can we generalize tentatively despite the atypicality of the subjects or settings?
3. How were the data collected?
   (a) What steps were taken to ensure that the data are reliable, that is repeatable?
   (b) What steps were taken to eliminate the effects of the researcher or the research procedure on the responses of the subjects?
   (c) Where such steps were not taken or were probably ineffectual, to what extent does this failure invalidate the results, that is how *certain* can we be that the data are produced by researcher bias or researcher-subject interaction and do not reflect what would be found under more 'natural' conditions?
4. What operationalized concepts are used in the data collection or analysis?
   (a) What evidence is offered for the construct validity of the operationalization?
   (b) What evidence is offered that the concept is ecologically valid?
   (c) What evidence is offered for the inclusiveness of the operationalization?
5. What claims does the author make for his or her results?
   (a) Do the analyses which he presents in support bear out his claims?
   (b) Where it is argued that competing hypotheses are eliminated, is the argument valid?
   (c) Are there other plausible competing hypotheses which the author has failed to identify?

    (d) If so, do these invalidate the author's conclusions?

    (e) Can other analyses be performed which would support his claims?

    (f) Are there other conclusions about causality to be drawn which the author has not highlighted?

    (g) Are there further conclusions to be drawn which do not concern causality which he has overlooked?

6. *In summary,* what have I learned from this paper?

    (a) What descriptive information is to be gleaned from it?

    (b) To whom does this information apply?

    (c) What causal conclusions may be drawn from it?

    (d) How general are these conclusions?

    (e) What previous studies does this one replicate?

    (f) Are its results replicable?

    (g) To what extent does it describe or bear on the 'real world'?

    (h) What major gaps remain in my knowledge?

    (i) How can I fill them?

    (j) What leads (or warnings) for future researchers does the paper give?

The ethics, politics and value of research

This chapter does not propose to offer detailed guidance on ethical questions; these are for the individual researcher to sort out with his colleagues, his employers and his conscience. (Virtually every learned or professional society in this country subscribes to some form of ethical code, ranging from the vague statement of principle adopted in 1978 by the British Psychological Society to the code of the Market Research Society which covers in detail such specific matters as whether respondents' names and addresses may be given to a client.) The authors consider it important, however, that potential researchers and their potential employers should at least be aware of the ethical issues which may be raised by research projects.

One basic ethical question is: 'Who might be harmed by my research?' Where people are made the subjects of research without their knowledge, and thus have no chance to safeguard their own interests, it should be the special concern of the researcher to look after these interests. The same applies where subjects volunteer for or cooperate with the research but are deceived as to its purpose. The researcher should, ideally, anticipate every possible side-effect of his procedures and guard against them.

One cannot stress too highly the importance of thorough acquaintance with the field of research, thorough perusal of the literature connected with it, extensive periods of observation and discussion with potential subjects and with others whose interests might be affected. This period of intensive work, which is often dismissed as 'preliminary', not only helps one in formulating hypotheses which are practical and researchable but also in sensitizing one to the ethical dilemmas which have to be faced. [. . .]

The final point to be made in this section concerns the 'value' of a piece of research. [. . .] Tedious and imprecise research hypotheses lead almost inevitably to tedious and imprecise research reports: one is reminded of the acronym 'GIGO', once a commonplace of the computer world, which translates as 'garbage in – garbage out'. Determining value is always difficult. We need to consider how much of a contribution the research has made to the knowledge and understanding of the process under investigation (and, to an extent, the originality of the theoretical perspective used). Decisions based on these criteria are mainly matters of personal judgement. So too is the specification of the criteria themselves. Some research contributes to the solution of practical problems. Some expands theoretical perspectives – and sometimes one needs a detailed knowledge of the relevant theory to understand why the questions were interesting. Sometimes the research topic may be tedious but used as an example of an original development of methodology. However, the reader is entitled to demand that a report has *something* to contribute.

The final step in assessing a piece of research is to determine how far it has contributed to our knowledge and understanding, and here there has to be a 'trade-off' between soundness and value. Would we decide a piece of research was 'good' if we could place great confidence in the findings reported but felt that they were of little value in answering any of the types of problem discussed above? Would we decide a piece of research was 'poor' if it had many technical faults but investigated an important hypothesis? Do we call a piece of research 'good' or 'poor' which fails entirely to answer the questions it sets itself but provides the solution to a practical problem of some importance or amasses descriptive data invaluable for answering other researchers' questions? We do not propose to offer guidelines for judging the value, as opposed to the methodological soundness, of research papers: such decisions have to be made by the individual, in the light of his own interest. Our own inclination, as you will have gathered already, is to ignore the question of whether a report is 'good' or 'poor' and concentrate rather on what we can learn from it.

Questions of ethics, politics and value are best anticipated at the planning stage or dealt with in the course of the research; by the time the research has been carried out and the report written it is a little late to undo any damage that has been caused or to ensure that the original idea was an interesting one. However, we could fruitfully add some questions to our checklist of points to look out for when evaluating a report:

7. (a) What precautions were taken to ensure that the research subjects came to no harm?
   (b) Did the research subjects come to any harm?
   (c) Is anyone else harmed by the research?
   (d) Did the selection of the research topic or method prejudge a disputed issue in favour of one party?
   (e) Has something important been ignored which would cast a completely different light on the result?
   (f) If so, do I wish to comment on the ethical shortcomings of the project? Alternatively, are the researcher's solutions to ethical problems so good as to merit comment?

8. (a) Where the researcher identifies groups who might feel harmed by his research and offers reassurance to them, are the arguments sound or spurious?
   (b) Are there groups not identified by the researcher who might feel threatened by the research?
   (c) Do I want (and am I able) to reassure them?
   (d) Has my appraisal of the research results been influenced by the fact I myself feel threatened by them?

9. Of what interest is this research? Does it:
   (a) offer a practical solution to a social problem?
   (b) extend our knowledge in a theoretical discipline or a practical area?
   (c) show us how awkward facts or theories can be reconciled with our existing picture of the world?
   (d) show us how our picture of the world must be changed to accommodate awkward facts or theories?
   (e) challenge our picture of the world by presenting awkward facts or theories?

These are questions which should always be asked. Whether in practice the answers appear in a written evaluation will depend on the audience to whom the evaluation is addressed.

References

Bracht, G.H. and Glass, G.V. (1968) The external validity of experiments, *American Educational Research Journal*, Vol. 5, pp. 437–474.

Campbell, D.T. (1969) Reforms as experiments, *American Psychologist*, Vol. 24, pp. 409–429. Reprinted in Bynner, J. and Stribley, K.M. (eds.) (1979) *Social Research: Principles and Procedures*. London, Longman/The Open University Press. Ch. 9.

R.J. Sapsford and Jeff Evans for the course team. Open University course DE304, *Research Methods in Education and the Social Sciences*, Block 8, Part 1, pp. 9–22. Copyright © 1979 The Open University.

Roger Sapsford is a lecturer in social sciences with special responsibility for research methods, and sub-dean (research) at the Open University

Jeff Evans is a Senior Lecturer in Social Statistics at Middlesex Polytechnic.

INDEX OF NAMES

INDEX OF SUBJECTS